THE ULTIMATE ULTRA RUNNING HANDBOOK

THE ULTIMATE ULTRA RUNNING HANDBOOK

FOR RUNNERS LOOKING FOR THEIR NEXT CHALLENGE

CLAIRE MAXTED

BLOOMSBURY SPORT
LONDON · OXFORD · NEW YORK · NEW DELHI · SYDNEY

BLOOMSBURY SPORT
Bloomsbury Publishing Plc
50 Bedford Square, London, WC1B 3DP, UK
29 Earlsfort Terrace, Dublin 2, Ireland

BLOOMSBURY, BLOOMSBURY SPORT and the Diana logo are
trademarks of Bloomsbury Publishing Plc

First published in Great Britain, 2024

Copyright © Claire Maxted, 2024
For photo credits see page 219

Claire Maxted has asserted her right under the Copyright, Designs
and Patents Act, 1988, to be identified as Author of this work

For legal purposes the Acknowledgements on p.219
constitute an extension of this copyright page

All rights reserved. No part of this publication may be reproduced or transmitted in
any form or by any means, electronic or mechanical, including photocopying, recording,
or any information storage or retrieval system, without prior permission in writing
from the publishers

Bloomsbury Publishing Plc does not have any control over, or responsibility for,
any third-party websites referred to or in this book. All internet addresses given in
this book were correct at the time of going to press. The author and publisher regret
any inconvenience caused if addresses have changed or sites have ceased to exist,
but can accept no responsibility for any such changes

The information contained in this book is provided by way of general guidance
in relation to the specific subject matters addressed herein, but it is not a substitute
for specialist advice. It should not be relied on for medical, health-care, pharmaceutical
or other professional advice on specific dietary or health needs. This book is sold with
the understanding that the author and publisher are not engaged in rendering medical,
health or any other kind of personal or professional services. The reader should consult a
competent medical or health professional before adopting any of the suggestions in this
book or drawing inferences from it. The author and publisher specifically disclaim, as
far as the law allows, any responsibility from any liability, loss or risk (personal or
otherwise) that is incurred as a consequence, directly or indirectly, of the use
and applications of any of the contents of this book.

A catalogue record for this book is available from the British Library

Library of Congress Cataloguing-in-Publication data has been applied for

ISBN: PB: 978-1-3994-1130-1; ePUB: 978-1-3994-1131-8;
EPDF: 978-1-3994-1132-5

2 4 6 8 10 9 7 5 3 1

Typeset in Nunito
Designed by Austin Taylor
Printed and bound in China by C&C Offset Printing Co., Ltd.

To find out more about our authors and books visit www.bloomsbury.com
and sign up for our newsletters

PERSEVERANCE

*You may see me struggle
But you won't see me quit
When life gets difficult
I'll continue with extra grit.*

*I'll always wear a smile
Even though I may cry
I'll carry on regardless
And bid my fears goodbye.*

*You may see me struggle
But you will never see me quit.*

LYNI SARGENT, ULTRA RUNNER WITH SCOLIOSIS OF THE SPINE

CONTENTS

FOREWORDS 8 | WELCOME 11

1
QUICK START 12
What is Ultra Running? 14
Why Ultra Running? 21
Ultra Running Myths – Busted! 24
Pick the Right Ultra 26
Essential Gear 28
Key Ultra Skills 32
Fitting it In 34
Being Eco-friendlier 37

2
PREPARATION AND SKILLS 40
Train Smart – Prepare First 42
Pace it Right 50
Using Running Poles 52
Dealing with Race Low Points 54
Night Running 58
Sleep Deprivation 61
Toileting Outdoors 63
Multi-dayers 65
Navigation and GPS 68
Train Right for Your Age 72
Women's Running 75

3
PHYSICAL TRAINING 84
Strength Training is Essential 86
20–30-minute Strength Routine to Beat Injury 90
10–30-minute Strength Routine for Speed 93
Warm Up and Cool Down 96
Strength Yoga and Pilates 98
Ultra Stretching Routine 101
Training Plans 108

4
NUTRITION AND HYDRATION 120
Food Made Simple 122
Nutrition Myths Busted 126
Hydration 131
Recipes 139
Fuel Timeline 146

5
BEAT INJURY 148
Prevent Injury 150
Treating Common Injuries 154
Blisters and Chafing 158
Cross-training 164

6
ULTRA GEAR 167
Ultra Running Shoes 168
Ultra Clothing 171
Ultra Running Jackets 176
Ultra Running Packs 181
Ultra Running Watches 183
Running Poles 186
Mandatory Race Kit 188
Drop Bags and Support Crew Kit 194
Head torch 197
Cold-weather Running 200
Hot-weather Running 204

7
EVENTS 206
Your First Ultra? 208
My Fave 50 Milers 210
Your First 100 Miler 211
Your First Multi-dayer 213
Dream Races 214

FURTHER READING 218 | ACKNOWLEDGEMENTS 219 | INDEX 221

FOREWORD BY JASMIN PARIS

I have known Claire for many years – I think we first chatted after my Bob Graham Round in 2016 – and I love her enthusiasm for running, runners and the natural world. Combining that passion with personal experience of running and reporting on ultra-distance races, she is perfectly placed to talk you through the sport of ultra running, and to inspire your next running challenge.

My own ultra running journey started in 2009, with the Howarth Hobble, a 51km loop over the Yorkshire moors with 1341m of ascent/descent. I'd only been running for 7 months and I had no idea what I was signing up for when my clubmates from Glossopdale Harriers persuaded me to give it a go. I remember feeling woefully unprepared on the start line (the longest I'd run in training was 17 miles, after which both me and the dog were pretty tired!), but also really excited by the atmosphere and the challenge ahead. That day turned out to be a tour of the very best aspects of ultra running. I made so many new friends, laughed with fellow runners as we traversed the bogs and sampled the checkpoint buffets with abandon – jam doughnuts, hot dogs, there were even some marshals offering a dram of whisky before the biggest climb! I remember feeling so lucky, to be crossing those beautiful moors with splendid views on all sides and sharing the joy of that challenge with other runners I met.

Since then, I've enjoyed many more ultra running challenges and races, from the Charlie Ramsay Round in the Scottish Highlands to the Barkley Marathons in the forests of Tennessee. Every time I have felt lucky and proud to be part of this sport, and the community that comes with it. I hope that you will read Claire's book and see that ultra running really is a sport for everyone and most importantly is tremendous fun.

Jasmin Paris, national fell running champion and the first woman to successfully complete the Barkley Marathons

FOREWORD BY SABRINA PACE-HUMPHREYS

There's not much that I don't love about trail running and ultra running. Put them together and, for me and many others that I have come to know, it's the perfect mix. Trail running and ultra running have enabled me to live a life beyond my wildest dreams while using all I have learned to open up the outdoors for people who want to explore the world via this form of joyful movement. To me, there is nothing better than a long day spent on the trails with good company, cheese and pickle rolls and fat coke!

But, for so many years of my life, this ultra running world – the sport – wasn't somewhere I felt a sense of belonging. For so many years spent training alone I had to find my own way, make friends with (I won't call it stalking) people who had 'been there and done that'. I had to loan kit I couldn't afford to buy and, by sheer will and determination, I had to build my own confidence to navigate my body around spaces and places that didn't feel welcoming.

I know I was and am not alone in experiencing this.

A life-threatening situation that I found myself in during an ultra marathon in 2019 changed my life and, from then on, I have worked tirelessly alongside others to address the lack of diversity in trail and ultra running. Hard and soft barriers exist for diverse, marginalised populations and as a passionate advocate for the sport, I believe we must all come together to eradicate them.

Ask yourself, how can someone feel confident reading a map when that skill hasn't been handed down or taught? How do they know what distance constitutes an ultra marathon or what kit is needed when nobody in their community 'does that'? What is mandatory kit and what food should you consume to keep you moving forwards when going long? Also – and this is important – where do these people go to ask questions and find others who won't make them feel silly for asking, people who gladly share their lived experience in this sport to ensure the safety of others?

This book goes some way to answering those questions and so many more. It's that companion who many of those starting out and even those with years in the game will benefit from reading cover to cover and using as a reference tool. Claire draws on both her professional and personal experiences and those of other runners to share tips, tricks, hacks and stories that bring this ultra running world to life in a way that is digestible and fun.

Running in whatever form it takes *should* be for everyone but, believe me, it takes more than a pair of shoes. This book is a great companion for those people who want to immerse themselves in all that is beautiful and brutal about this amazing activity.

Sabrina Pace-Humphreys, co-founder of Black Trail Runners, motivational public speaker and author of *Black Sheep: A Story of Rural Racism, Identity & Hope*

WELCOME

FANTASTIC TO SEE YOU HERE. Just by picking up this book and expressing interest in the awesome sport of long-distance running, you can consider yourself part of the ultra running community. Are you ready to build up your endurance and start your adventures? Read on!

I was a run-a-phobe!
Unfortunately running at school isn't my most treasured memory – can you relate to that? The perpetual fear of the annual bleep test, endless loops of the track in boiling summer sun and dodging dog poo on cross-country runs in the local park. Running seemed to be all about times, competition and pushing yourself to go as fast as you could until you got that blood taste in your mouth. Not to mention the enforced communal showers afterwards. (Are they still allowed to do that?) Hopefully schools take a different approach to running and sport these days, because this introduction could have put me off for life if I hadn't found trail running in my early twenties, while working for *Trail*, the hiking magazine. With trail running, you jog along steadily, hike up the hills, explore exciting new places with stunning views; there's a good amount of cake and chatting involved; and running to complete rather than compete is just as valid. Up the distance to ultra running and there's even more hiking involved, and much more food too! I'm not saying that trail and ultra running aren't challenges – if you want, they can beat you up, give your body a beasting and rub bits of flesh you never knew you had until they're raw. But for the most part, the training and racing experience is a joyous and wonderful one filled with friends and adventure. After co-founding *Trail Running* magazine in 2010, I've been lucky enough to run ultras all over the world, sometimes successfully and sometimes not, which very much is part and parcel of this incredible yet humbling sport. From the Dodo Trail Xtreme 50k in Mauritius to the Montane Lakeland 50-miler in the Lake District, ultra running has given me so many incredible memories to look back on in my dotage. I hope this book will help you do the same.

Happy ultra trails,
Claire Maxted

1. QUICK START

The rest of the book will cover these important topics in more depth, but if you can't wait to get started with ultra running, this section will give you all the info you need to get going pronto.

WHAT IS ULTRA RUNNING?

VERY SIMPLY, ULTRA RUNNING is anything over the magic marathon distance of 26.2 miles (42.2km), on any surface – road, track and trails. Popular ultra distances include 50km or 31 miles, 50 miles (80km), 100km (62 miles) and 100 miles (160km), but ultras really can be any distance over the marathon. However, it isn't just the length that makes an ultra tough – aspects like ascent, terrain, navigation, altitude, climate, weather and level of support en route are all big factors in determining their difficulty.

> *Ultramarathons are great for building resilience. You will have highs and lows. They're all life lessons for when tough times come outside of running.*
>
> JEN SCOTNEY, ULTRAMARATHONER AND HOST OF *RESILIENCE RISING PODCAST*

Is it always running?

Don't be fooled by the term ultra *running* – you're very much expected to do some walking. I sometimes think it would be more accurate to call this sport ultra *jog-hiking*. Jogging steadily and walking briskly are encouraged and the latter is often known by the much sexier term of 'power hiking' to make it sound more impressive and less like the good, old-fashioned walking that many of us can do. The longer and hillier the race, the more walking is required, especially uphill where even the elite athletes will whip out lightweight poles to help them hike (powerfully) upwards. On the very long ultras (like the 100-milers) there may also be some napping involved as you push into night number two. However, it's very possible to run through one night and finish in the morning without having a sleep if you're a fast 100-miler or a steady 70-miler, and if you're doing 30–50 miles you might finish late at night in the dark, but most people won't need to nap.

Ultramarathons

Ultras are also known as ultramarathons, because 'ultra' just means 'beyond' in Latin, so they go beyond the traditional marathon distance of 26.2 miles (42.2km). So strictly speaking, 26.3 miles (42.3km) is an ultra, but the most common 'short' ultra is 50km (31 miles) and they can go up to, well, how long is a piece of string? Mainly these long races are just abbreviated to 'ultra' because it's quicker to say, shorter to type and sounds coolly elusive… 'Yeah, so I'm doing an ultra,' 'An ultra what?' 'You know, just an ultra.' 'Wowwwww.'

Terrain

An ultra road race would require a lot of road crossings and dicing with traffic, pedestrians, bins, lampposts, dog poop, etc., so while there are some road and track ultras, many are run on trails. So that's mainly on tracks, paths, bridleways, canal towpaths, but also on sections of pavement through villages and towns depending on how remote the route is. Many ultras follow established National Trails like the Pennine Way, with regular signage, which makes them easier to follow. Others do not and require basic to excellent navigation skills (see p. 68 for more).

Accuracy

Unlike road races, ultras are much more like trail (off-road) races in that they tend to publicise an approximate mileage figure, often rounded down to the nearest five or ten. So a race called the Trickybogs Ultra 80 may actually be 83.4 miles (134km, or more if you get lost!). In the ultra running community this is all considered free, bonus mileage.

Point to point

Point to point is a popular format for ultras with a real sense of a journey and an adventure from one start point to a different finish point. This could be a National Trail along the coastline, through an entire mountain range or country, coast to coast or city to city via a canal towpath – for example the 145-mile (233km) Grand Union Canal Race in the UK, which goes from Birmingham to London.

Circular

Looped races are also popular, perhaps circling a national park, city, country, island, lake or whole mountains. It's a great way to see a huge chunk of an area in one fell swoop, like the 106-mile (171km) Ultra Trail du Mont Blanc (UTMB) around Mont Blanc through France, Italy and Switzerland.

Out and back

Just as it says on the tin, you run to a certain point, then turn around and go back the same way. This style of race is great for getting to see the race leaders fly past on their return, and then saying, 'Hi!' to all other runners coming in the other direction, in front of or after you.

Lapped

With ultra distances being so long, there is a big trend for lapped races. The most extreme of these being around a block in New York, USA (the Self-Transcendence 3100-Mile Race) or a running track (like the IAU 24 Hour World Championships). More usually there are 5–10-mile (8–16km) loops to make a 50–100-mile (80–160km) event, and these are fantastic for runners unsure of completing the entire distance. There's no chance of getting stuck in the middle of nowhere, and it's also much easier for a support crew to stay in one place and keep topping you up and cheering you on.

Sleep

The longer the race, the more likely you are to need a sleep en route, which might be allowed at certain aid stations, or runners might have to grab a few minutes' or hours' kip at the side of the trail as in the non-stop 268-mile (431km) Spine Race along the Pennine Way, UK. If sleep is built into the route with certain amounts of daily mileage and definite overnight locations, the event is known as a multi-day stage race (see below).

Multi-day stage race

Each day there's a certain distance competitors need to run and a designated place where everyone spends the night. Some or all of the days may be ultra distances in themselves, and these events can be anything from a couple of days to a whole week long or more. Multi-day ultras are fantastic as holidays exploring exciting places with likeminded people, within the safety of a well-managed race setting, like the 250-mile (400km) Cape Wrath Ultra in Scotland.

Multi-day non-stop race

Everyone starts at the same time and decides when and where they will sleep along the route, with the aim being to sleep as little as possible to lessen the impact on your overall race time. There may be dedicated aid stations with sleeping areas or even beds available, and/or trailside power-napping when you can't keep your eyes open anymore, like on the 205-mile (330km) Tor des Geants in Italy.

Aid stations

Ultras vary massively in their provision of aid stations, with smaller or more remote events offering no food and drink at all as you pass through manned or unmanned checkpoints, while bigger races might provide all manner of cheeses, meats, soup and beer, with energetic music, a 20-piece live band and smiling marshals in fancy dress ready to welcome you to the party. The checkpoints at the Montane Lakeland 50 and 100 races have a carnival atmosphere like this, designed to pick you up and motivate you onwards. If you can find out what nutrition will be available at the aid stations before the race, this gives you a chance to try it out in training to make sure you can stomach it during the race.

Black toenails

Never before have your feet been so precious, but it can take a fair few events and training runs to get your footcare routine right. And even with a lot of experience, weather conditions, uneven terrain and trials of different socks and shoes can lead to all sorts of horrendous foot-based torture like blisters, callouses, chafing and black toenails that eventually fall off. This doesn't have to be you – see p. 158 for the best way to stay blister-free.

Never enough kit

Ultra running does seem to require the purchasing of a great deal of kit these days – several pairs of running shoes (never enough), a running pack, GPS watch, waterproof jacket, running poles and sports nutrition that doesn't make you hurl at mile 50. There is a certain amount of mandatory kit, especially for more remote or extreme races, but if you ease yourself in gradually, buy good quality gear and look after it well, you can spread the cost over a good few years. Find out exactly what you need, where you can and can't scrimp, and how to make it last on p. 188.

Navigation

Most ultras don't require you to be a navigation genius, but unlike shorter races that can hold your hand the entire way with clear signage and marshals at every turn, many long-distance events need you to look up from your feet to spot National Trail signage or more subtle, spaced-out flags and markings. Often if the ultra is more remote, along with having the skills to keep yourself alive in the wilderness, you will need to follow a GPS track (if allowed) or navigate using a map and compass (see the navigation and GPS section on p. 68).

Safety

In more remote, mountainous areas and places with extreme weather conditions and climates, ultra runners do have to switch up a gear and acquire some extra skills, like mountain sense, navigation and what gear to wear when in certain weather. You might also have to carry a tracker, not only for your own safety but also for the entertainment of those 'dot-watching' at home (see below).

Dot-watching

This is basically armchair ultra running for those back home watching either incredulously or incredibly jealously online. If you're carrying a race tracker, you will be assigned a dot that will move painstakingly slowly across a map, then possibly stop for a while, causing those at home to become frantic with worry before it suddenly leaps to the other side of the screen as your tracker comes back into range.

Sustainability

There are loads of choices we can make as ultra runners to help protect the natural environment that we love to run in. We can fly less, drive less, buy less, invest in good-quality gear and look after it to get more wear out of it. We can also join together powerfully to demand action from big companies. For more easy eco ideas, turn to p. 37.

Madness

You possibly do have to be slightly on the mad side to be an ultra runner. The sport does have a reputation for attracting slightly crazy people (myself included: I consider this term a compliment) and as time passes on the longer events, you may find yourself experiencing hallucinations, extreme joy, tears, tantrums and hysterical laughter. All this is to be embraced and celebrated as part of the ultra running experience. And remember, whatever caused it usually makes for a heck of a good story afterwards.

WHAT'S IT LIKE?
DAY IN THE LIFE OF AN ULTRA RACER

All ultras vary, but here's the timeline of the Lake District's Montane Lakeland 50, a very popular first ultra with a generous cut-off of 24 hours to complete the mileage from Dalemain to Coniston with almost 3,000m of total ascent.

SATURDAY

06:30-08:00
EMERGENCY REGISTRATION
This is for anyone who wasn't able to come down the day before and register on the Friday.

08:30
RACE BRIEFING
If you weren't able to attend the Friday evening briefing you can catch up.

09:30
TRANSPORT
I board a coach to the start at Dalemain Estate.

11:30
RACE START!
In waves from Dalemain, a 4-mile warm-up loop of the estate then out into the mountainside.

14:00
FIRST CHECKPOINT (CP1) HOWTOWN (11.2 MILES/17.8KM)
Grab more sweeties and flapjack bites to take with me and refill a couple of empty soft bottles with water and electrolytes.

16:55
CP2 MARDALE (20.6 MILES/33KM)
Choose savoury ham and cheese sarnies, flapjack, a marshal refills my water while I queue for the portaloos and drink the hot soup while walking out of the CP up the next hill.

19:15
CP3 KENTMERE (27.1 MILES/43.4KM)
Bites of watermelon moving through the village hall, pasta and sauce in my cup to slurp on the go, take sweets and flapjack with me too.

19:30
FIRST ANTICIPATED LAKELAND 50 FINISHER
This is very much not me ever! The final cut off is 11:30 Sunday.

21:25
CP4 AMBLESIDE (34.4MILES/55.2KM)
Time to put on the headtorch, take a packet of salty crisps and eat two ham sarnies walking away from the CP, plus more sweeties and water refills.

23:00
CP5 CHAPEL STILE (40 MILES/64.2KM)
There is veg stew here but don't fancy it, just more sarnies, a cuppa with sugar, a chocolate biscuit or three, and grab more sweet items. Wait for someone who knows the route and leave with them to make sure I go the right way in the dark.

SUNDAY

01:00
CP6 TILBERTHWAITE (46.4 MILES/74.8KM)
Only about 4 miles from the end now so not hanging around here, just a bit of flapjack and £1 in Jacob's Join, the Cancer Trust charity box for toddler Jacob who died of cancer and a chat with his incredible dad, a regular Lakeland racer, and off up the steep final climb of Jacob's Ladder in his memory. Feel tired but can't give up thinking of the strength of Jacob's family.

02:20
FINISH LINE CONISTON (50 MILES / 80.5KM)
Very happy to reach the finish line of the furthest I have run since having Finny two and a half years ago. Job done. A quick bite to eat and a hot drink from the cafe, then time for a shower and an uninterrupted sleep in my tent at the campsite down the road before the journey back home on Sunday.

WHY ULTRA RUNNING?

IF YOU'VE VERY DILIGENTLY READ the previous section on 'What is ultra running' you might now be thinking (especially after the black toenails paragraph), 'Erm, why?' Well, the very fact that you've picked up this book tells me you're at least a little bit ultra curious, so here I'm going to share my ultra 'whys', and then some more from both unknown and well-known ultra runners.

My ultra 'whys'

1. I love exploring new places, and booking ultras in new places is a great way to see the world, while training for them is the perfect excuse to get the map out and check out new local trails or head further afield.
2. Sometimes you can get into this super-nice zen mode where nothing hurts and the pace is steady – you feel like you're bobbing along nicely with your legs trotting out the miles under you and your mind free to problem-solve or just enjoy the views.
3. It makes the little things – a biscuit, a cup of tea, a hot shower, a nice sit down, a friendly hello from a passer-by – feel even better. You appreciate the small things in life more after running a long way.

'Normal' people who love ultra running:

'I ran my very first ultra this year; after 20 years of running, it was totally a game of confidence! I took up running to manage PTSD when I was 22 and it has been my saviour in many dark moments. My only regret is that I wish I had taken the leap and done it years ago. Here's to many more years of marathon and ultra running and exploring our beautiful Cornish coastlines.'
CHARLOTTE CHAPMAN

'Ultra running is an intimidating term. It's more like a supported running holiday en masse to see some of the world's best running trails in a weekend.'
CHIN CHEAN YONG

'A friend once told me running an ultra was easier than running a marathon and I finally decided the only way to find out if this was true was to just go and run one. She was right! Unless you are at the sharp end of the field, it's just a moving picnic and nobody knows or cares how long it took you, as they have no frame of reference like you would a marathon. And being able to say I ran 50, 70, 100 miles, etc. is just epic and it still blows my mind that I've managed to do that (even if loads of it was walking!).'
ELEANOR GALLON

'I ran Race to the Stones this year because I could. Post multiple back operations and a spinal stimulator implant, I was told I'd never run again. I went to quite a dark place after that, but once I stopped mourning the person I was and started focusing on the person I am now, I found I could do more than I ever dreamed I would.'
SARAH CREWE-READ

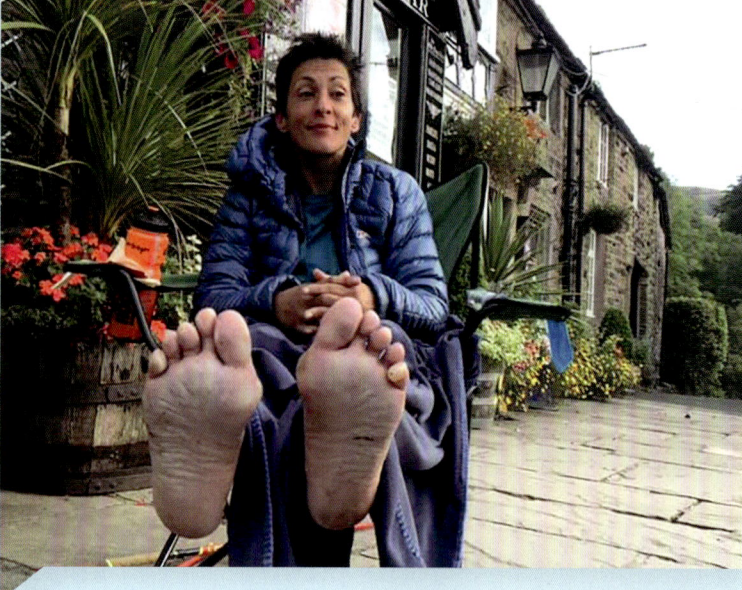

'I mainly aspire to continue to love running and time spent in the mountains, and to share that with friends and family. Races and challenges are less important.'
JASMIN PARIS, NATIONAL FELL RUNNING CHAMPION AND THE FIRST WOMAN TO SUCCESSFULLY COMPLETE THE BARKLEY MARATHONS

'Running in the mountains, whether training or breaking a record like the Wainwrights or the Pennine Way, it's my "playtime" – it's fun. I like to run and race such long distances in one go because I just don't like to stop!'
SABRINA VERJEE, WAINWRIGHTS WOMEN'S RECORD HOLDER

'Trail and ultra running is so good for my mental health and I have been hooked from day one, since training for the Marathon des Sables.'
SABRINA PACE-HUMPHREYS, CO-FOUNDER OF BLACK TRAIL RUNNERS, MOTIVATIONAL PUBLIC SPEAKER AND AUTHOR OF *BLACK SHEEP: A STORY OF RURAL RACISM, IDENTITY AND HOPE*

'It's difficult to explain exactly, but other than when with my kids, I'm happiest with my shorts and daps on, out in some lumps for a big, possibly ouchy, adventure. It's about freedom, exploration, some nut butter sangers [sandwiches] and good quality DOMS [delayed onset muscle soreness].'
DAMIAN HALL, CAPE WRATH ULTRA WINTER RECORD HOLDER

'I think going through the finish line is definitely a time to slow down and savour the moment; that's a big reason why I like ultra running. On the track you don't really get to savour any moment because you're kicking all the way through the line.'
JIM WALMSLEY, UTMB MEN'S WINNER 2023

'It's important to stay in touch with why you love running. It really can be just you out in nature with the sound of your breathing and footsteps, rolling with the terrain at whatever pace feels good that day.'
COURTNEY DAUWALTER, FIRST PERSON TO WIN WESTERN STATES 100, HARDROCK 100 AND UTMB IN THE SAME YEAR, SETTING NEW COURSE RECORDS AT THE FIRST TWO

'The mountains took my heart away and ever since then I have loved skiing, running or climbing in them.'
EMELIE FORSBERG, FORMER ULTRA SKYRUNNING WORLD CHAMPION

WHY ULTRA RUNNING? 23

ULTRA RUNNING MYTHS – BUSTED!

ULTRA RUNNING DOES TEND to get put on a pedestal as a sport. Yes, there are some frighteningly invincible people hacking out incredible mileage in unbelievable times out there, but they are in no way the norm. Here the biggest myths about ultra running are debunked.

You have to run all the way
100 per cent nope. Hiking is definitely part of the ultra running experience even for the elites, especially as the distances get longer, hills spikier, altitude higher, paths boggier or rockier and weather more challenging.

There's LOADS of training
You don't have to run hundreds of miles every week and sink 20 hours doing so, letting your social life, family and job go into free fall (unless you want to of course!). Training for shorter ultras is possible on a 25–35-mile (40–56km) week.

People like me don't run ultras
It's harder to be what you can't see, but there are groups that are breaking down barriers and banding together to make ultra running more diverse. Check out the Black Trail Runners, Into Ultra and SheRaces for more.

Your toenails will go black and fall off
You may have seen revolting photos on social media, but this is no longer a rite of passage for ultra runners as long as you get your shoe size and fit right. Even if this does happen to you, eventually the nail should grow back.

> **MY STORY**
> ### ULTRA RUNNING SAVED MY LIFE
> '**I loved running as a kid,** but I was diagnosed with scoliosis, a disease that causes curvature of the spine, when I was 14 years old. Doctors told me not to do any high-impact sport so as not to speed up the onset of arthritis. I did as they said and took painkillers for 20 years, but still developed arthritis anyway. So I decided to try running again and I got the bug immediately – it does hurt but it's a different kind of hurt. I weaned myself off the painkillers and managed the pain through exercise and rest instead. I'm in pain whether I do or whether I don't run; sitting on the sofa doesn't give me happy hormones, so I may as well do the thing! I'm never going to be a fast runner, so that's why I like ultra running – it helps me to be a happier person. I started with a 50k and now I've run four ultras and climbed Mount Toubkal in Morocco. I'll keep running as long as I can.'
> **LYNI SARGENT**, FROM HINCKLEY, LEICESTERSHIRE

You'll ruin your knees/ankles/hips
It's true, runners do tend to pick up injuries, but it's also true that most of us completely neglect the 20–30 minutes weekly strength exercises that we know we should do to help prevent them happening in the first place.

You need a hipster beard, long hair and a bare chest
Sometimes the start line of an ultra resembles a motley crew of pirates with bandanas round their straggly hair, big beards aplenty and a spattering of bare chests if the sun's up, but rest assured, there are plenty of fully clothed, clean-shaven ultra runners out there, even the women.

You need a lot of expensive kit
Yes, you can empty your wallet on ultra running gear, but it doesn't always need to be top of the range, this season's latest design or even yours – although I do recommend asking your mate if you can borrow it first.

You have to be vegan/paleo/carnivore
There's always some trendy diet making the headlines or being touted by Instagram influencers with no scientific background whatsoever, but all you really need is a healthy, nutritious diet. And the upside of being an ultra runner is that you really do *need* that second slice of cake.

ULTRA RUNNING MYTHS – BUSTED! **25**

PICK THE RIGHT ULTRA

OF COURSE YOU CAN be an ultra runner by simply running distances longer than the marathon and inventing your own challenges (see p. 67), but many people start by picking an exciting/terrifying race. Here's how to choose the right challenge for you; also see my list of dream races starting on p. 214.

> *That feeling of flow you get on a long, long run – stripping yourself down to the bare essentials, and when you put yourself back together afterwards, you'll find it's a slightly better version!*
>
> VASSOS ALEXANDER, ULTRA RUNNER AND SPORTS REPORTER, PRESENTER AND AUTHOR, @VASSOS.ALEXANDER

1 Why?

First, think about your own personal 'why'. What do you want from the training journey and race itself? Do you enjoy pushing your body to its limits or chatting and taking photos of the views? This will determine the difficulty level you might want to aim for – too easy and it might not be enough of a challenge, but too hard and you might be in for an unnecessary sufferfest.

2 Difficulty

With ultra running there are lots of different types of difficulty... the distance is the most obvious at first glance, but shorter, hillier ultras can actually be harder and take longer than longer ones. So look at the total ascent, terrain underfoot, navigation required, altitude and climate. Also look at the number of and level of support at aid stations on the day, cut-off times for the aid stations and time limit for the whole race, the time of year and potential weather conditions.

3 Wow factor

Pick a race that inspires you – it might be in a place you've always wanted to visit or that you can plan an amazing family holiday around, a local event that's been going past your house for years, or an iconic race steeped in tradition, or one known for being quirky, family-friendly, low key, with lots of hype or simply known for having really great home-made flapjacks. See some of my faves on p. 208.

4 Price

Ultras can be as expensive as a holiday, with a big event village, drumming bands, showers, t-shirts and huge bling medals, but there are still low-key events like the Long Distance Walkers Association (LDWA) hikes that you can also run. Often (but not always) the more you pay, the more hand-holding you get during the race, so make sure you have the experience to manage things like less aid station support and more navigation.

MY STORY

I CHOSE THE WRONG FIRST ULTRA!

'**I thought I'd be able to handle** the 75k Perímetral de Benissa in Spain with 4115m (13,500ft) elevation, but even the flatter terrain was brutally technical over jagged rocks. I missed the cut off around 60k. Didn't feel too bad. Just couldn't run at any pace on the terrain without risking breaking an ankle!'

MARTYN THOMPSON

---

26   1. QUICK START

5 Training time
What amount of training can you commit to around family, work and other social commitments this year? Do you like a busy life and will your family support you? Will it be stressful or exciting to train for a big step up right now? The more experienced an ultra runner or endurance hiker you are, the more you can 'get away with' less weekly mileage, but there are still long runs, potential trips away to train on similar terrain, and gear and nutrition choices to consider.

6 Speed
Most ultras have one or more cut-off times for safety and consideration to the marshals and event team, so check what these are and if you are likely to meet them by race day if your training goes to plan. It's a good idea to choose races with generous cut-off times until you're more experienced and have an idea of your likely pace.

ULTRA HACK

EASY TIGER!
A lot of newcomers to ultra running have their heart set on a particular race (often a really hard one!) or a particular distance (often a really long one!), but it really does pay to step up the difficulty level gradually to avoid injury, having a miserable race experience, getting a possible DNF (Did Not Finish) and burn-out. The training plans in this book are designed to help you do just that (see p. 84).

ESSENTIAL GEAR

IF YOU'RE ALREADY A RUNNER, you've probably got everything you need to start training for ultras apart from perhaps a running pack, and maybe a fully waterproof jacket. Running poles aren't essential for everyone on every event, but many (including myself) do consider them a vital part of their ultra running kit so I've included them here. I deep dive into ultra kit on p. 166, but here are the most common items.

Running shoes
Ultra running is often confused with trail running, which takes place off-road on paths and bridleways – see my previous book *The Ultimate Trail Running Handbook*. This is because many of today's most popular and famous ultras tend to be on trails. However, ultras can be on any surface, so you need to get the best-fitting shoes that are suitable for the ground you'll be covering.

Socks
Often overlooked, socks are super important in helping you avoid blisters, chafing and hotspots. Splashing a bit of cash on a few pairs of technical, well-cushioned, quick-drying and vented sports socks is well worth it for ultras.

Sports bra
Essential for those with boobs, especially of the larger variety, although using a running pack also helps to beat the bounce with the straps across the chest. Bras with flat, comfy seams are best – try on new bras with your fully loaded running pack to check for pressure points and chafe.

Top and bottoms
There are so many options here depending on the weather and climate, but your normal running gear may well suffice – check for chafing (for example, thigh rub while wearing tiny shorts, chafing of vest tops under running packs) on your long runs and carry or pack clothing accordingly for longer adventures.

Waterproof jacket and trousers
Most ultra events will stipulate 'full body waterproof cover with taped seams and a hood'. This means a good-quality waterproof, hooded jacket and trousers. Superlight, just-in-case emergency jackets are also an option but are very expensive.

Running pack
The biggest sign that you're an ultra runner on a long run is a running pack that is big enough for food, drink, first aid kit and extra layers, with lots of handy pockets at the front so you don't have to stop to take on fuel. They range from 5 litres to 25 litres, but 10 litres is a versatile, catch-all capacity to start off with.

ESSENTIAL GEAR 29

Poles

The longer the distance and steeper the hills, the more likely you are to see ultra runners using poles for extra support, especially uphill. However, they're not useful when scrambling over difficult terrain, when you need to use your hands; it can be more tricky to hold a map, eat or use your phone or GoPro with them, too.

Watch

You don't need a GPS watch, but it does make it super-easy to see your distance, speed, pace, heart rate and time elapsed, plus a whole host of other whizzy training features and, in more advanced models, navigation. Alternatively there are lots of great running apps like Strava, MapMyRun and Runtastic that will track your stats via your smartphone.

Head torch

Some ultras will go through a night (exciting!) or two (exhausting!), so here's where you start looking at longer-lasting batteries, extra batteries, a spare headtorch and brighter lights to navigate through the darkness.

Accessories

A hat, cap, gloves and sunglasses are small but essential items in the ultra runner's gear cupboard – sometimes you might need all four on the same run!

MY STORY
I COULDN'T RUN WITHOUT MY...

'**Being a bald man** – I like to invest in a good hat to keep the cold and the heat at bay! Once, I forgot it, in a summer marathon training long run. I had to use my vest as a sort of head scarf towards the end and shorten the run because I could feel I was burning. Never done it again and always carry a little sunscreen top up, too, now.'

LEON YOUNG

KEY ULTRA SKILLS

FOR AN HOUR OR TWO you can put up with a rubbing little toe, a light knicker chafe, a hood that doesn't fit properly, gels that give you a tummy ache and an irritating running pack strap that slaps you in the face every time the wind blows. However, a few hours in, these tiny things become less tolerable. So a lot of ultra running isn't just about the running but the everything else…

Get the right gear
Nothing new on race day! Test your race gear during long runs to make sure you know how to use it easily and quickly, and that it doesn't slap, tickle or chafe you in any way. Pack your bag with the mandatory race kit to make sure it fits and that you have all the items on the list.

Blisters and chafing
Your long runs are a good place to test for chafe and try out various blister prevention and treatment methods, like taping hot spots (precursors to blisters) and lube. Some runners might even need a pair of half- or one-size-larger shoes available from your crew or in a drop bag half way through the course (as some races offer) to cater for swollen feet. For more on treating blisters see p. 160.

Fuel right
Gastro-intestinal issues and nausea (and in the worst cases, vomiting) are top causes for ultra DNFs, so use your long run to test your fuelling ideas to find out what food and drink you will be able to tolerate on ultra races. If the race organisers have a certain brand of fuel available at checkpoints, try it during training if possible. Take a variety of sweet and salty foods along with you, as you never know what you might feel like eating on the day.

> *Ultra running has definitely changed my life. I've gone from couch to 5k to ultramarathon in two years, losing seven stone along the way. My favourite thing about ultra running is time – the time to escape the pressures of life and enjoy the countryside we are lucky to have. The hours-long picnic doesn't hurt either.*
>
> GRAHAME WOMERSLEY-WESTLAKE

Night running
Some ultra events might deliberately have participants running through the night, or if you're out for longer than anticipated in, say, a winter race, it might get dark, so including some running in the dark to test out your head torch and navigation skills (if needed) is a must.

Sleep
When to sleep or power nap should become part of your race plan for longer ultras that will take you through the whole night or even multiple nights. It's hard to specifically train yourself for sleep deprivation (see p. 61), but you can try going through the night in training or on shorter races to understand how it's likely to affect you, and take steps to mitigate the effects.

Navigation

It's a good idea to check the level of navigation required on an ultra, so you can practise accordingly – there's nothing worse than adding an extra 2 miles (3.2km) to an already long race!

Safety

Some ultras need you to be more experienced with keeping yourself safe in remote wilderness or mountainous locations or certain weather conditions, so consider trips to areas with similar terrain and weather, or recces to the actual area to practise navigation, or take a navigation course. Take a fully charged mobile phone and consider a portable battery and charger.

Women's safety

It seems a no brainer not to make sexist, creepy or lewd comments here in 2024, but a few still spoil it for the majority. And sometimes some male runners don't realise they are making a woman feel unsafe, however unintentionally. Say a friendly, 'Hi, how's it going?', pass with some space, and don't tail or stick next to a lone woman for miles and miles (especially at night), unless you've asked and she's cool with it. If you see any behaviour making a woman uncomfortable, be brave and call it out.

Technique

Walking every uphill is a very sound ultra strategy used even by the pros. The longer the distance or harder the terrain and hills, the more likely you will be to walk every single hill, even the ones you can easily run at the start. Consider training with poles, so you know how they might help or hinder you on uphills, downhills, river crossings and certain types of tricky terrain.

Mindset

Many runners get very caught up in the physical aspects of training, but not giving up when you're tired and hurting starts to become more of a head game the longer you're out. It can help to break the distance down into smaller chunks to tick off, remembering your 'why', visualising the finish and having a plan for what to do if XYZ situation arises.

FITTING IT IN

A LOT OF PEOPLE THINK that ultra runners must run every waking moment; and, yes, if you want to enjoy your race without being broken after it, there will be a certain amount of training to fit in, but it doesn't need to take over your life. Here are some ways you can wangle a few extra hours each week.

1 It doesn't have to be long

Although you're training for an ultra, it might excite you to know that even a 30-minute run is worthwhile training if that's all the time you've got – you don't always have to go long, and every little bit of time on your feet helps. If you want to maximise a short run, you could do a speed, interval or tempo session once or twice a week, too. See the training section on p. 84.

2 Split it up

If you don't have time for the full length of your planned workout, try half an hour before work, 45 minutes at lunch and half an hour after work. You (and your colleagues) might have to get used to you being a bit sweaty if there's no shower at your work – get campaigning! But what's more important, really...? That's surely why flannels, the eco-friendly version of wet wipes, were invented.

3 Use your commute

Can you walk, run or cycle the whole or part of the way to work? It might be a case of just getting off the train earlier or parking further away, but this is an amazing trick if it's possible for you because once you get into a routine, the miles really do fly by and the consistent extra training pays dividends, plus it's good practice for carrying gear in a backpack.

4 Get organised

Lay out your running gear the night before, so it's dead easy to slip into it when you wake up and do a workout before work or post-kid-drop-off run.

ULTRA HACK

ARE YOU FEELING DESPONDENT?

Sometimes staying motivated can be as simple as booking a race that massively inspires or perhaps slightly terrifies you! But if your running mojo has still run out of fizz, try watching an inspiring running film, arrange to meet a running friend for a run or just a coffee even, run with a dog, join a running Facebook group, write down your goals and tell supportive people what you're up to. Use headphones while running to listen to music or inspiring running podcasts and treat yourself after completing training blocks. If you still don't feel like running, maybe it's your body and mind trying to tell you that you're burned out – it's ok to take a break from ultra training for as long as you like. Defer that race, run shorter, try a different sport, rest, spend time with family and/or friends; reconnect with what is important in your life this year.

You could also keep a set of kit in the car in case you have a chance to go out while providing a taxi service for the kids, during a lunch break or while driving somewhere for work.

5 Make running a priority

If you struggle with prioritising your run, arrange to meet a friend, block it out in your diary, join a club, save your favourite podcast for it or go first thing, so the day doesn't run away with you. Think about the excuses you use not to run and see if you can solve them. It might be as simple as giving yourself permission to make running a priority in your day.

6 Do a screen detox

Take a social media or TV detox day one or two evenings per week. Of course, it's good to connect and relax with these technologies, but consider if addictive scrolling could be robbing you of time when you could be doing physio exercises or organising your kit for an early morning run.

7 Involve the kids/dogs

If childcare or ferrying children around is a barrier to fitting in your runs, consider taking the kids with you instead. Run with a buggy or kids on bikes, hike with them in a backpack or cycle with them using a bike seat or trailer. The sooner you start, the sooner they get used to being zoomed round at Parkrun or lugged up various mini-hills, and the more likely they will accept that 'Mummy/daddy runs! Yay! Go mummy/daddy!' and be more active themselves. With dogs, this depends on the breed, age and fitness of your precious pooch, and just like humans they need gradual training to be up to the mileage.

8 Use short journeys

Not only is it great for the environment to cut down your car use for short journeys, but it's the perfect opportunity to save money and boost your fitness and time on your feet. Sometimes it can even be quicker to cycle or run somewhere, either at school pick-up time or to skip the traffic during rush hour, which does make you feel very smug.

Ultra hack – squeeze in strength

Physio and strength moves are something many of us runners struggle to prioritise despite most of us knowing that they will really help us achieve our ultra running goals! So turn dead time into exercise time – do five squats when you're waiting for the kettle to boil, 10 calf raises on each leg in a queue, stand on one leg on a rolled up towel for balance while you brush your teeth, and stretch during your favourite telly programme.

FITTING IT IN

BEING ECO-FRIENDLIER

MANY ULTRAS TAKE PLACE in beautiful countryside and mountainsides all over the world, and as people who take delight in running through them, we're also keen to reduce our impact on the planet. Here are some super-easy ways to be even more eco-friendly with your running, and often save a good few pence yourself into the bargain. We can make a difference and every little helps.

> ❝ I think nudging the system is more impactful than reducing your personal carbon footprint, and running's biggest footprint comes from racer travel. If every time a runner signs up for a race they ask the event how it's accommodating and incentivising public transport as an option, we could be on to something. And join the Green Runners! Greater numbers will give us greater power to push for change. ❞
>
> DAMIAN HALL, SPINE RACE RECORD BREAKER, CO-FOUNDER OF THE GREEN RUNNERS AND AUTHOR OF *WE CAN'T RUN AWAY FROM THIS*, @ULTRA_DAMO

Do you need to fly?

There are fantastic ultras all over the world, but as 90 per cent of an event's carbon footprint comes from the runners' travel, is it possible to race more locally or travel without flying? If you take the train or a car (especially if you car share), you drastically reduce your carbon footprint. If you do fly, can you tie it in with a longer trip or family holiday to make it even more worthwhile? Many ultras have Facebook communities; head on in there to find lift shares to races or people willing to pick you up from the nearest station.

Offsetting

You can offset the carbon impact of your flying and other travel, but make sure it's a genuine company that will make your hard-earned cash work as hard as possible for the planet. I recommend Wren and Our Carbon.

Do you need that new kit?

Clever marketing (and maybe your mate Steve) makes it very tempting to get the latest gear, but ask yourself, 'Do I genuinely need this? Or have I already got one that will do?' You can also borrow things like poles, waterproofs, running packs and maybe even a whizzy GPS watch (if Steve's feeling generous) while you work out if you need to invest in your own. Second-hand gear is also a great shout: try eBay, Gumtree, Vinted, Preloved Sports, and the Facebook groups Running Gear Buy and Sell, and Outdoor Gear Exchange. One massive upside of buying second hand is that you save yourself tonnes of money, which you could put towards more races, a coach, a charity or your bills.

Can you repair it?

Looking after your gear in the first place will make it last longer (read the care instructions for how to wash, clean and reproof it properly), and when it does start to fail, have a go at repairing it or send it off to a small repair business like Snowdonia Gear Repair. If you're crafty with a needle, you can sew up small tears on backpacks, pop on a new pocket zip and patch a shoe or jacket. Spending a few minutes regularly cleaning muddy shoes is a good way to make them last longer, and some companies offer a resoling service, too.

Can you recycle it?

Before you give your old running kit to the local charity shop, consider parcelling it up and posting it to Kitsquad or Preloved Sports who will each find good homes for it with runners who really need it.

Ultra hack – email the race organiser

Millions of unwanted race t-shirts unfortunately hit landfill every year, so politely (always politely – they're already doing their best) email race organisers to suggest they offer no t-shirt and no-medal options on their entry page. Let them know that instead, they can easily give entrants the choice to plant a tree via Trees Not Tees instead. You could also encourage them to ask runners to take their own cup for water stations.

Can you eat less meat?

Having one or two meat-free days a week is an easy way to massively reduce our impact on the environment. It's also great if you buy local and in season. I cover this in the nutrition section (see p. 120), but being partly or even 100 per cent veggie or vegan is absolutely no detriment to ultra training, if you know your food basics.

Use eco-friendly nutrition

Consider making your own or buying your nutrition from companies that use recyclable or compostable packaging, like Outdoor Provisions, Supernatural Fuel, Unwrapped Bars, Nurhu and 33Fuel. As well as being careful not to drop your own wrappers, you can also feel wonderfully smug if you pick up litter along the way wherever you run.

Can you give back?

Wouldn't it be nice if every ultra runner spent as many days giving back to the environment as they raced each year? Hop on a nationwide conservation initiative, volunteering to repair footpaths, clear invasive species, litter pick and plant trees with charities like the Woodland Trust, Fix the Fells, Mend Our Mountains, Surfers Against Sewage, Moors for the Future, and local wildlife and conservation campaigns.

Share, share, share!

The more people we can encourage to make more eco-friendly choices, the more impact we have overall. Personally I feel it's very important to do this in a friendly, non-judgmental and enthusiastic way to get people onside rather than shaming them, and to be encouraging to cynics who think small changes aren't worth making. Send out your eco-joy on social media; chat to other runners, friends and family; lobby the government; sign petitions; and get involved with positive climate action.

ULTRA HACK

SPEND LESS!

There are plenty of ways to save money in ultra running, including: race more locally, lift share, volunteer in return for race places, create your own DIY ultra, make your own race nutrition and use supermarket fare rather than fancy sports nutrition. Sign up for shorter summer races with less gear on the mandatory kit list; borrow gear; buy all-rounder gear rather than three sizes of backpack or types of jacket; buy second hand; buy high-quality kit built to last; and take care of your gear and repair it. Use shoes forever (they don't collapse after 500 miles/805km, despite the clever marketing!) and join a local running club or try a social media-based one like Maverick Run Project, Black Trail Runners, Vegan Runners, Lonely Goat Runners and RunTogether. For free or a very low annual fee, you can get to know like-minded runners who will share their tips and support for races, kit, routes and training.

BASIL HEANEY, FOUNDER OF INTO ULTRA – HELPING LOW INCOME PEOPLE GET INTO ULTRA RUNNING

MY STORY

WHY I'M A GREEN RUNNER

'**I signed up** with the Green Runners within days of it launching. It was a no-brainer given my life-long interest in natural history and the environment, running being a more recent passion. My pledges are:

- **How We Move:** To run locally as much as possible and not fly solely to race
- **How We Kit Up:** To buy new kit only where necessary, mending what I can
- **How We Eat:** To continue not to eat red meat
- **How We Speak Out:** To promote green running and low-carbon choices

Being a Green Runner isn't about conforming to a single approach. Each of us finds our own way to rise to the challenge, drawing on ideas from the community. While individual actions to combat the climate emergency are important, the key changes must come from those in power – governments, corporations and the media. Acting alone, our voices are in danger of being lost, so join those who share your passion.'

MARTIN ELCOATE, MEMBER OF THE GREEN RUNNERS, @THE.GREEN.RUNNERS

BEING ECO-FRIENDLIER

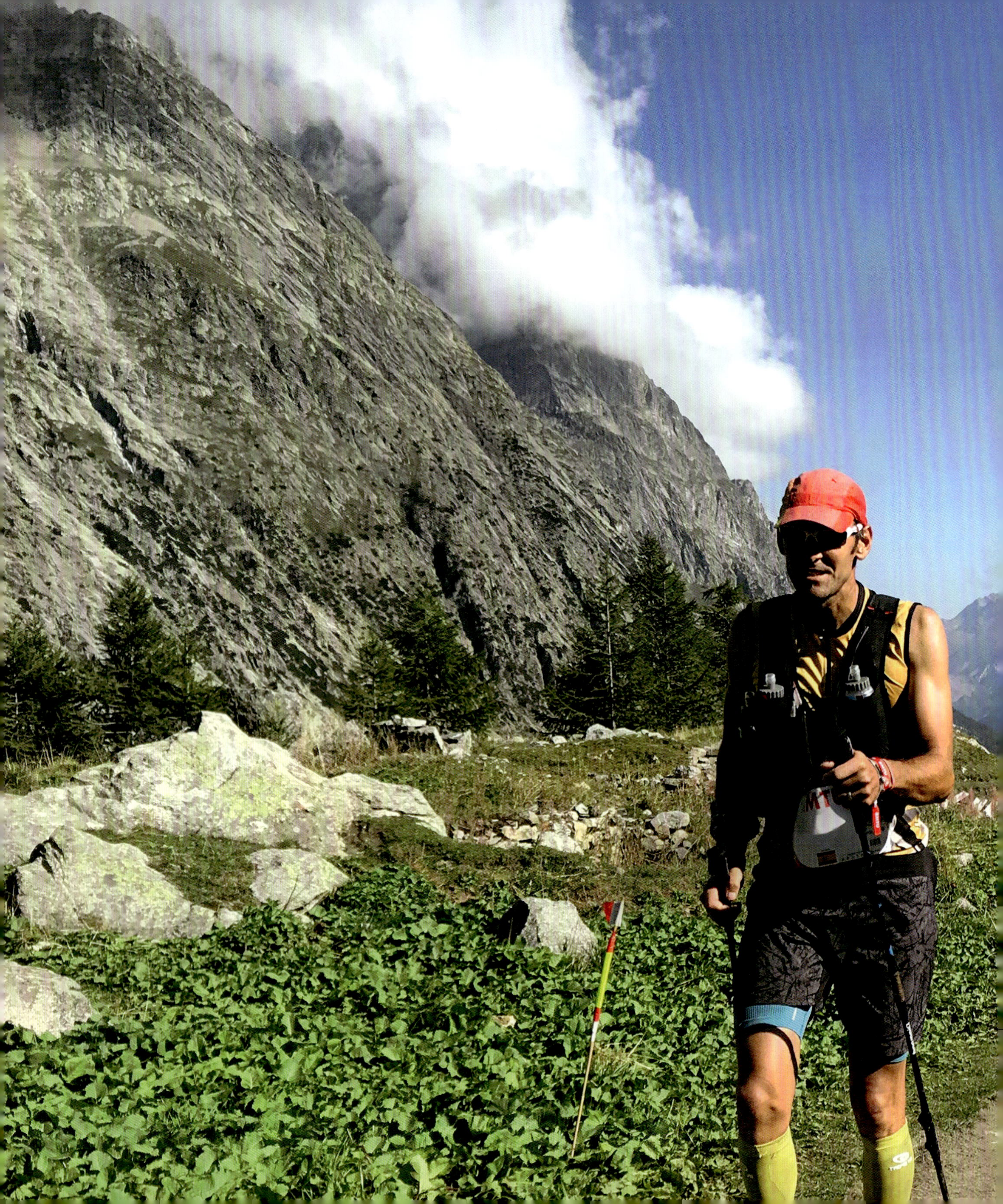

2
PREPARATION AND SKILLS

There is so much more to ultra running training than just running a lot. Ultra completion requires good nutrition, shrewd gear choice, foot care, mental strength, logistics, problem solving and sometimes navigation. Read on to fully equip yourself and give yourself the best chance of success.

TRAIN SMART – PREPARE FIRST

TEN YEARS AGO I just ran (well, *suffered* is probably the better word!) ultras with hardly any consistent or intelligent training whatsoever. I simply stuffed whatever food was at the aid station into my gob and made do with whatever kit I was currently testing from *Trail Running* magazine.

Now I'm in my 40s, the boundless energy of youth is not on my side. I'm sleep deprived from a night-screeching toddler and when I'm not working, I'm zooming tiny toy cars along the sofa and into a box again, and again, and again… For anyone with limited training time, here are 12 cunning ultra running preparation tips and tricks to maximise your chance of success and they don't involve any extra time on your feet.

> *Make sure when you stand on that start line you are so well prepared you can go into autopilot and minimise the amount of higher-level thinking required The brain uses a ton of energy, too; save that for the legs!*
>
> TIM PIGOTT, PHYSIO AND COACH FROM HP3 COACHING AND TEAM SCARPA ELITE ULTRA RUNNER, @TIMPIGOTTHP3

ULTRA HACK

PLAN A, PLAN B AND PLAN C

When planning the timings for your ultra, it's useful to think in terms of a Plan A – your ideal race time; Plan B – your back-up race time if something goes wrong, you are ill or you can't train as planned pre-race; and Plan C – how to just get round before the time limit by hook or by crook. This can help you not to feel too disappointed if things aren't quite going to plan, and remind you that it's an impressive achievement just to finish an ultra, let alone race it.

1 Make your race plan

This was a complete game-changer for me – doing this makes you feel so much more prepared and in control, especially if you think you might be grazing the cut offs, as I was when I first got back to ultra running after having a baby. Print out a gradient profile or map of your race from the event website. Write on it the distances between each checkpoint, the cumulative race distance, what fuel is available, and where and any drop bag or support crew locations. Then add the cut-off times, and your estimated times to reach each aid station and the tops of any significant climbs. Seal this plan in a clear plastic bag or wallet and keep it handy, so you can refer to it during the run and pace yourself accordingly.

HOW LONG WILL EACH SECTION TAKE?

Planning your timing for each leg of an ultra is a rough prediction that depends massively on your fitness, the terrain, the ascent, the total distance and the weather conditions; however, it is very useful to have an estimate to work from. As a mid-pack runner, I estimate using 15 minutes per flat mile (4mph/9.3mpk) plus five minutes for every 100m (328ft) ascent as a rough guide. This translates to roughly 15–20-minute miles (9.3–12.5-minute kilometres) as a doable mid-pack pace over a hilly 50-mile (80km) ultra without too much rocky terrain underfoot to slow me down.

Checking your current pace on your watch during the ultra itself is not usually very helpful as it will vary so much – so using these time estimates between checkpoints and high points is much more useful. If in doubt, slightly overestimate, which will make you feel like a hero during the race when you come in earlier than expected.

2 Research the aid station fuel

Research what food and drink will be supplied at aid stations and practise with that in training. Many events give a more detailed list nearer the time, or you can email the race organiser in plenty of time before the race (please never contact an RO just before a race unless it's an emergency: they're a tad busy). This helps you plan what fuel to pack or put in your drop bag and what you can pick up on the way round. Organise your own fuel into bundles for each section of the race, using elastic bands or transparent bags to keep them together. Stick inspirational quotes or messages from loved ones on your race nutrition and write motivating words or the first letter of them on the backs of your hands or arms to keep you going strong.

3 Be aware of cut offs

Some cut offs (the time limit to get to certain checkpoints) can be really brutal, especially earlier on in the race, so find out what these are and make sure you know how long you have to get to (and out of) each checkpoint – in some races the cut-off time is when you need to leave the checkpoint, not arrive. Being aware that you will have to get a move on in the first half before relaxing into the second is useful. For your first few ultras it's wise to pick events with generous cut offs, while you get used to everything. Knowing how long you have to get round each section makes you more prepared and in control. If you think you might be chasing cut offs, add these to your race plan (see point one above), so you can check at a glance whether you're on track during the race.

4 Plan for when sh*t happens

Think about some of the things that you're worried might affect you in the ultra. Write them all down (start a note page on your phone and add to it as your worries come to you) and then write down potential solutions. Thinking of solutions ahead of time will allow you to respond to any problems more quickly and confidently during the race itself. For example, if you're worried about blisters, make sure you know where they might appear, pre-cut kinesiology tape (also known as K-tape, or just tape) to size and dress/lube your feet in advance or once you begin to feel a hot spot. If you're worried about stomach issues, start testing out different nutrition ideas, products and strategies in your long runs well before the race.

5 Know some things are out of your control

We can be as well prepared as possible, but the weather and course conditions underfoot might have other ideas. Keep an eye on the weather forecast 1–2 days before the race and watch out for any last minute changes from the race organisers. There might be a course alteration, shorter route, change of start time and additional mandatory kit due to changed weather conditions. The earlier you can receive this information and process the new details, the more settled you will feel on the start line. In rare cases a race might be cancelled altogether – this wasn't so rare in Covid times, but under normal circumstances the race organisers will do everything in their power to make sure their event goes ahead safely.

6 Learn from mistakes

If you've had bad races or got some DNFs under your belt, these experiences can actually help you immensely rather than being a negative thing. Write down everything that has ever made things difficult, physically and mentally, for you in the past. You might start to see a pattern or stop sweeping a particular problem under the rug and sort it out. Ask yourself, 'Why did it hurt at that time or in that place? What slowed me down and when?' You might realise you need to start fuelling earlier, start more slowly, learn how to care for your feet better, improve your navigation or spend less time in aid stations. Make a plan for being super efficient through the aid stations, practise eating race food on your longer runs, practise taping your feet up, do some orienteering or plan and navigate a new running route locally to you to improve your navigation skills.

MY STORY
I'M STILL LEARNING

'I had two DNFs and a DNS (Did Not Start) in the last three years involving the Hardmoors 55, Hardmoors 60 and the Montane Lakeland 50. Injury in two of them and then one being timed out. I have taken a year off to concentrate on strength training and building a better aerobic base. We'll see what happens next year on the Hardmoors 55 in March...'

TONY MCGONNELL

7 Absorb course info

If you have time, recce-ing the course, especially night sections, will make you quicker, more confident and give you a better chance of finishing. A 100-mile (160km) route can often be broken down into four 25-mile/40km (ish) sections that you can tackle over a couple of weekends, and many races offer guided group recces of the route in a similar fashion. If you can't do this, watch YouTube videos of the route wherever possible; listen to podcasts about the event or similar races – using headphones on your long run to kill two birds with one stone and ignite that training fire within you on tougher days; and read blogs and race reports rather than doom scrolling through social media before bed. This will help you feel more confident in deciding what kit to take, how much fuel to carry, what shoes to wear and whether you should order, say, a cowboy hat, to adhere to that year's race theme. Not kidding – this was my fancy dress for the Western-themed Montane Lakeland 50 in the summer of 2023.

MY STORY
DON'T COMPARE YOURSELF

I felt daunted coming back to ultra running after having my son Finley in January 2021; even 18 months post-birth I was finding building up to a steady 10 miles (16km) for a couple of autumn half marathons ridiculously tough. This distance had been easy pre-pregnancy, but my fitness seemed to have gone. How on earth was I going to write this book about ultras? It was hard not to compare myself to amazing mums who bounced back to ultra running so much sooner – Jasmin Paris pumping breast milk at checkpoints during her incredible overall Spine Race record, the unstoppable Sophie Power making headlines breastfeeding her three-month-old second son during the UTMB and the amazing Katie Kaars Sijpesteijn making the GB Trail Running team within a year of her daughter's birth. What I lost sight of was that these three were all elite athletes! I'd never compared myself to them prior, so why was I now? So I tried to focus more on just doing what I could, through the lack of sleep, exhaustion and parent-guilt/stress/worry that now gripped my daily life. I DNF-ed my first ultra post-Finley (Manx Mountain Marathon, 50km/ 31 miles), which taught me a great deal, and has actually been fantastically useful for this book, too. So the first one I completed (Ultra-Trail Snowdonia by UTMB 50K) made me feel really proud. I've since run several ultras successfully and those comparisons have stopped plaguing me. It's easy to look back now and think I shouldn't have worried, so hopefully sharing my story will help you if you are experiencing similar doubts. Don't compare yourself to others; focus on your own ultra journey.

ACE IT PRE-RACE

- Pack your kit a couple of days before, and look at the mandatory kit list in case you need to beg, steal or borrow any last-minute items.
- Check the event address, check where registration is and plan to arrive early.
- Set off in plenty of time, park, register and drop your drop bag.
- Attach your race number where the race organiser specifies and so it doesn't flap annoyingly.
- Check you have filled your water bottles and have your fuel.
- Go to the loo one final time before heading to the start.
- Smile and chat with others on the start line to ease any race nerves.
- Eat a sugary snack if that's part of your nutrition plan.
- Enjoy the pre-race briefing/band/banter.
- Listen out for the starting gun – and go! (not too fast!).

HARNESS RACE DAY NERVES

Training for an ultra, especially your first one or one you've been building up to for years, can fill you with equal parts excitement and dread. Here's how to harness those pre-race nerves and enjoy your grand day out.

1 Being a little nervous is actually a good thing – it means you care and you're not being blasé about the race.
2 Viewing your ultra as 'just a long hike' can help, as can thinking back to any other races you've done in the build-up to your big day that have prepared you for event logistics, registering and standing there on the start line.
3 Think about all the training and preparation you have done (or if lack of this is your concern) and revisit the prep section of this book (see p. 40) to help yourself as much as you can without extra physical training. Most people don't think they've done enough training, so you might be surprised to find that what you have done is enough.
4 Finally, take the pressure off yourself, trust in your training and run your own race. Ultra running is supposed to be enjoyable, so share your worries with a friend or have light-hearted chatter on the start line and treat race day as an exciting adventure to be enjoyed as much as possible.

46 2. PREPARATION AND SKILLS

8 Replicate race sections

As you absorb that course info, you will come to a better understanding of the terrain and hilliness involved, so start replicating sections of it locally as much as you possibly can in your long run. Say the first leg is 11 miles (18km) with 300m (984ft) of ascent followed by 9.5 miles (15km) with 770m (2526ft) of ascent – plan a local route with similar stats and over race-like terrain if possible. It might involve more planning, a lot of hill repeats and running on grass verges next to pavement in an effort to reproduce uneven terrain underfoot, but doing this will give you a feel for what's coming and prepare your body and mind fantastically well.

9 Use lightweight kit

Get the scales out and weigh up your options – can you take a lighter-weight spoon, hat, base layer or jacket without compromising safety with the climate or predicted weather conditions? Can you do without that spare pair of socks until you are reunited with your drop bag at half way? Do you need to carry so much food if the aid points are well stocked? Do you really need that cuddly toy mascot on the back of your running pack? The answer to that last one is undoubtedly, YES! But there might be other bits of kit you can cut the labels off (every gram helps!) or ditch altogether. Pack your kit into small, light, transparent sandwich bags rather than thick, heavy, opaque dry bags, so it all stays dry (from sweat or rain) and you can easily dig through your bag to find the item you need.

ULTRA HACK

BOOST YOUR CONFIDENCE

Ultras are often called races, but if you run ultras for enjoyment and exploration rather than pushing yourself to the extreme by actually 'racing' them, you might prefer to call them 'events', 'challenges' or even 'hikes' to take the pressure off. I often told myself, 'It's just a long hike', when I felt worried about my lack of training before the Montane Lakeland 50, and once you realise that, for the majority of us, ultra running is a great deal about jogging and hiking, that mind-shift can make these long distances seem much more attainable.

ULTRA HACK

EVERY LITTLE HELPS

Walk or run as many errands as possible, and make it all part of your training. You can also up the ante here by wearing a weighted backpack (or child) where possible. It takes a little organisation, but filling a few water bottles and popping them into a spare running pack or backpack that can easily be grabbed before you head out makes it easy to increase the intensity of a lunch time screen break or dog walk.

10 Join the Facebook group

Many of the bigger races have well-established Facebook groups that you can join to find out more info about the course, get ideas for clothing and gear, hear epic stories of previous race disasters and generally join in the fun banter. It is here that you might learn you don't have to carry much food because the aid stations are so well stocked, or you might decide to take a spare head torch rather than just spare batteries. These groups really are a mine of useful information and great motivation. Search for queries like yours within these Facebook pages by using the search bar on the top right instead of being the 20th person to post the same question and getting weary, tongue-in-cheek replies.

11 Use mind power

Especially in the longer ultras that take a whole day or several, the power of your mind becomes even more important. The majority of runners will find things hard towards the end of a race and there might be setbacks and low points along the way, too. Aching muscles, swollen feet, blisters, chafing, energy lows, sleep deprivation, cut-off time stress, gear blunders, drop bag woes and navigation errors (boy, doesn't it just make you want to enter an ultra right now?) all play their parts to nudge that little piece of your brain (possibly the one that chose your sofa) into saying, 'You know, you could just stop, no one really cares if you do this apart from you.' So barring injury or danger, unless you really, really, really want to finish an ultra, it can feel like there's nothing stopping you from quitting at the next aid station. Here's where your 'why' comes in. Summon all the reasons why you're at that event for the determination to never give up.

EXPERT ADVICE
RECOVERY ISN'T JUST NOT RUNNING

'One of the most common mistakes I see is ultra runners not recognising the impact of non-running related activities and lifestyle factors on their recovery. For example, it might be a scheduled lighter training week, but the next week they are surprised when their runs do not feel any more energetic than before. But the runner has not factored in that they had a week of work travel to a different time zone with some stressful workplace decision-making and less sleep than normal, followed by a weekend of on-the-go activities with their children. Just because they have run less, they think that they should feel better on their runs on that following week, but [they] have not factored in how overloading easier run weeks with other things that are equally mentally and physically taxing does not equate to rest.'

ELLIE GREENWOOD, TWO-TIME WINNER AND FORMER COURSE RECORD HOLDER OF THE WESTERN STATES 100 AND COACH AT SHARMAN ULTRA, @ELLIEJGREENWOOD

MY STORY
RACE RECCES REALLY HELP

'I recce-ed the parts of the Montane Lakeland 100 that I figured I'd be running at night. I ran them in the day rather than in the dark to make it a pleasant day out, but even that really helped me not to go off-course during the race itself. If you can, I would highly recommend recce-ing at least part of the route for a 100-miler, especially the parts where you're likely to have tired legs and be sleep deprived.'

FIONA MARTIN, FOUR-TIME LAKELAND 100 COMPLETER

12 Recovery isn't just rest

It took me a long time to realise this, but consistent strength work, gradually upping training, eating healthily and properly fuelling the long run all helps us recover much quicker. It's not just about the day or week afterwards where we rest, eat well and sleep. It sounds very obvious now, but this was a eureka moment for me. It was also very motivating – it made me fuel my long run just as I would my race rather than trying not to eat too much in case it made me put on weight, and it gave me a reason to prioritise the strength work that I had previously struggled to get motivated for.

Easy speed secrets

The top six things that make you faster that require ZERO extra physical training time or effort include:

1. Start slowly! This is the one huge tip that so many coaches and elite athletes have told me over the years and it's totally true. Mile five of a 50-mile (80km) race is not the time to set a PB (personal best time). Jog at chatting pace until there are only 5 miles (8km) to go – then go for your PB if you have any juice left in your legs!

2. Keep eating and start early! Lots of runners wait until they feel a bit tired or hungry to eat, but if you start with bites of sugary snacks from 30 minutes into the race and prioritise eating small bites and sipping your drink every 30 minutes or so during the race, your body doesn't have to play catch up and always has energy. Set a reminder timer on your watch if it has that feature.

3. Be more efficient in aid stations – cut faff for a faster time. Think about what you'd like to eat, drink and do in the aid station before you get there. Aim to arrive holding your recently fully drunk water bottles with tops off for a fast fill up; have a spare sandwich bag ready to fill with snacks to put in your pocket and munch on in the next section; toilet out on the trail if the loo queue is too long; or eat snacks and drink fluids in the queue, have your cup or bowl and spoon ready for a hot meal to eat or drink on the way out. Beware the chair!

4. Improve your navigation – GPS watches are great tools, but on certain races, being able to read a map, too, will massively improve your race time. See p. 68 for more tips and then plan a new route for your long run to brush up on your skills.

5. Run with people – boost your motivation and morale, especially on night sections or when you feel tired or sick. You don't even need to be chatting if you don't feel like it. Soon the miles will be zipping past, especially if you're in the mood for sharing a story or three with a likeminded long-distance runner/hiker/crawler.

6. Use a waterproof jacket one size bigger or with a special extended back that fits over your running pack. This way you can get it on and off without stopping to take off your pack, and stow it in an easy-to-access pocket or reach around to stuff it into the main compartment of your pack just behind your neck.

PACE IT RIGHT

PACING IS THE HOLY GRAIL of trail and ultra running, as you need to conserve your precious energy for the many hours, if not days, ahead. However, after a week or two of tapering before a race, it can feel so tempting to rush off with everyone else at the start, giddy with fresh legs. Now is not the time to be setting a 5k PB you'd be proud of at Parkrun, so here's how to hold yourself back and pace yourself to successful ultra completion.

> *Given ultra race intensity is low compared to shorter races, most runners push too much in the first half. A good rule of thumb is that if you even suspect you're going too hard, you definitely are.*
>
> IAN SHARMAN, FOUR-TIME LEADVILLE TRAIL 100 CHAMPION AND DIRECTOR OF SHARMAN ULTRA COACHING, @SHARMANIAN

ULTRA HACK

WHEN TO HIKE THE HILLS
On long ultras you might have a personal rule of getting your poles out and hiking all the hills, but if you plan to run the gentler gradients, notice how your breathing and heart beat change. Ease into an efficient, brisk walk when you become breathless and your heart beat thumps into overdrive. Remember all those hills add up later in the race, so it's better to take it easy early on rather than run out of steam later.

1 How slow at the start?
This is said time and time again – starting slowly is absolutely crucial to surviving a trail race or ultra without blowing up. But just how slow are we talking? Well, most coaches and pros agree that chatting pace (a steady pace where you're not going so fast you can't talk easily) is a good marker for a well-paced start. It might feel too slow, so be prepared for that, and take your mind off things by chatting to the runners around you. That said, in certain races you may need to crack on a little ahead of your comfortable cruising pace to meet strict cut-off times early on. Elites may also need to dash off at the start to avoid bottlenecks, but for most of us, slower is better. On some GPS watches you can program in a virtual pacer, which can be useful during races.

2. PREPARATION AND SKILLS

ULTRA HACK

FUEL YOUR LONG TRAINING RUNS

In the past I didn't used to eat much at all on my long training runs/hikes, thinking it'd make me put on weight. I'd return home feeling zen-like, then after a shower would be overcome with a sudden hunger to eat everything in the world immediately. This does not lead to great food choices, so when I discovered that eating every 30 minutes or so still applies to the long training run and not just the race (this also trains your gut to tolerate eating on the run), I was thrilled to notice not only a lack of slumping at the two-hour mark, but neither was I delirious on my return home. Fuelling your long run properly also starts the recovery process quicker.

2 Get to know your own pace

For ultra running it's very useful to be aware of how hard your body is working so you can ease off or push the pace when necessary. You don't need a heart rate watch or any fancy gear for this; it can all be done by rate of perceived exertion (RPE) - how hard you feel like you're pushing yourself during exercise. See the training plans on p. 105. So in your long runs, actively notice what your personal chatting pace feels like by doing a group run, talking to a friend on your headphones, singing along to a song or even talking out loud to yourself (always amusing for any passers by).

3 Pace your nutrition

Pacing your fuel intake and deciding what to eat and drink when is vital, too. Our muscles have about 90 minutes of energy stored in them before they conk out, but many of us make the mistake of not taking on any food until that point – and then it's too late. Start fuelling 20–30 minutes into the race and keep sipping and nibbling a mouthful or two of your snacks and drinks every 30 or so minutes so your body always has energy available. For more on fuelling right, see p. 147.

4 Have a rest

Assuming you have done a bit of pre-race planning and know your cut offs, significant climbs, aid stations and how long each leg should take you (see p. 43), it's absolutely fine to throw this all out of the window and stop for a rest. Especially if you're feeling low or particularly fatigued, taking 10–20 minutes to sit down, eat, sort your feet out and recharge mentally can be vital to successful completion (unless you're bang up against the cut offs, in which case, you might have to ignore this option). If you can get to the next aid station before you stop, then you can also benefit from shelter, more food, maybe a hot meal or drink, and a brain-boosting chat with fellow runners and helpful marshals.

5 Have a power nap

On longer ultras where you're running through one or two nights or more, there are often sleeping areas and even beds provided. Set an alarm in case you end up zonking out for 12 hours and missing the race entirely, or sleeping longer than the rules allow. Whether it's at an aid station or out on the trail, a 20-minute power nap can work wonders on a 100 miler, while on a multi-dayer you might treat yourself to two or three hours – luxury. Just make sure you're sheltered and have the right kit.

PACE IT RIGHT 51

USING RUNNING POLES

ESPECIALLY FOR LONGER or hillier ultras with more hiking, running poles can help you breathe more easily by keeping your lungs open with a less-hunched forward-lean posture uphill. They can encourage a good pace and rhythm on hiking sections, and ease the pressure on your leg and knee joints and feet as your upper body shares some of the load.

They suit wide, smooth, harder paths best because they're a bit trickier to place (and extricate) if the terrain is very tussocky, muddy or boggy, or when scrambling over steep, rocky ground where you may need to use both hands. They're also great for balance if you're wearing a heavy pack, negotiating some types of rocky ground or crossing rivers. If you're going to use them for your race, it really pays to get to grips with them during your long training runs to avoid shoulder, arm and hand ache, and to nail the technique for maximum efficiency.

How to fit poles:
ADJUST THE GRIP
Slide your hand through the pole strap from underneath and grip the pole handle. Adjust the Velcro or slider on the strap so it supports your hand comfortably.

GET THE RIGHT LENGTH
Stand on flattish ground with your pole next to your shoe. You're aiming for a 90-degree bend at the elbow, so adjust the height of the pole or measure accordingly if you're looking at fixed-length poles.

BEFORE YOU GO…
Be aware of people around you and keep 1–2m (3.3–6.6ft) away so as not to stab others in the heels or poke them in the head as you lift your arms to climb a stile.

Using poles:
OFF YOU GO!
Swing the poles alternately as you run, planting each one just ahead of your leading foot and pushing off when it's behind you, helping to propel you forwards. You might find that you want to take two to three steps before you place each pole down again. Try not to overthink this and it hopefully should come quite naturally. If you're finding it complicated to coordinate, slow to a walk until it feels comfortable, then slowly jog while you get the hang of how often

ULTRA HACK

CHECK THEY'RE ALLOWED!
In most ultras there's no problem with poles beyond the usual guideline of 'Don't stab the runner behind you in the eye with them as you climb over that stile,' but during your training be aware that not all events allow poles, especially fell (mountain) races in the north of England and Scotland.

you feel like planting each pole – this will change throughout your run depending on the terrain, the hills and your speed. Scan the path ahead for pole placements to avoid catching the pole tips between rocks, wooden slats and boggy bits.

IT'S GREAT FUN TO…
Plant both poles at the same time before or in the middle of a large puddle as a way of easily jumping over it.

MY STORY
POLES ARE A MUST FOR ME

'**As a 65-year-old** ultra runner, for me personally, the benefits of using poles are: assistance going uphill, balance going downhill, especially steep, rocky descents – useful for big steps down. Fording streams and boggy areas is much easier – you can use [a] pole as [a] "third leg" so you can "jump" across wider streams/bogs without falling in! When tired on long ultras, you can march much more quickly with greater range of movement (bigger stride), better posture and rhythm. It's way better than trying to jog in hunched shuffling style. It also gives me an arm "workout" and during long ultras prevents dangling, fat hand syndrome. I use them as "nettle sticks" to bash down nettles and brambles or to hold them out of the way. I have even used them to fend off dogs, cattle, horses and butting sheep!'
ANNE WADE, LONG DISTANCE WALKERS ASSOCIATION MEMBER AND ELEPHANT BEAR AND BULL 100-MILE (160KM) RACE ORGANISER

RIVER CROSSINGS
Running poles are a great help for balancing across shallow to knee-high rivers (and snow patches), but never underestimate the power of flowing water. Always go upstream to a bridge or shallower crossing place if you can. Never cross deep, wide, fast-flowing rivers unless you and your group are very experienced. If in doubt, don't cross. A longer route is preferable to not coming home at all.

Carrying poles:
PRACTISE MAKES PERFECT
Practise collapsing your poles on the run and stowing them in your running pack without stopping. There are various ways to attach poles to your running pack or waistbelt – some people wear a belt as well as a pack for their poles and more snacks. Remember you can also move or stitch on your own attachment points if needed.

DEALING WITH RACE LOW POINTS

WHILE YOU MIGHT BE ABLE to breeze round a 50k (31-miler) with a smile all the way, the further you run, hike and stagger, the more chance you have of experiencing some quite debilitating low points on your way round. Unless your downer is related to an injury, bad weather, dangerous fatigue or a health condition, there are lots of tricks you can employ to power on through to the finish line regardless.

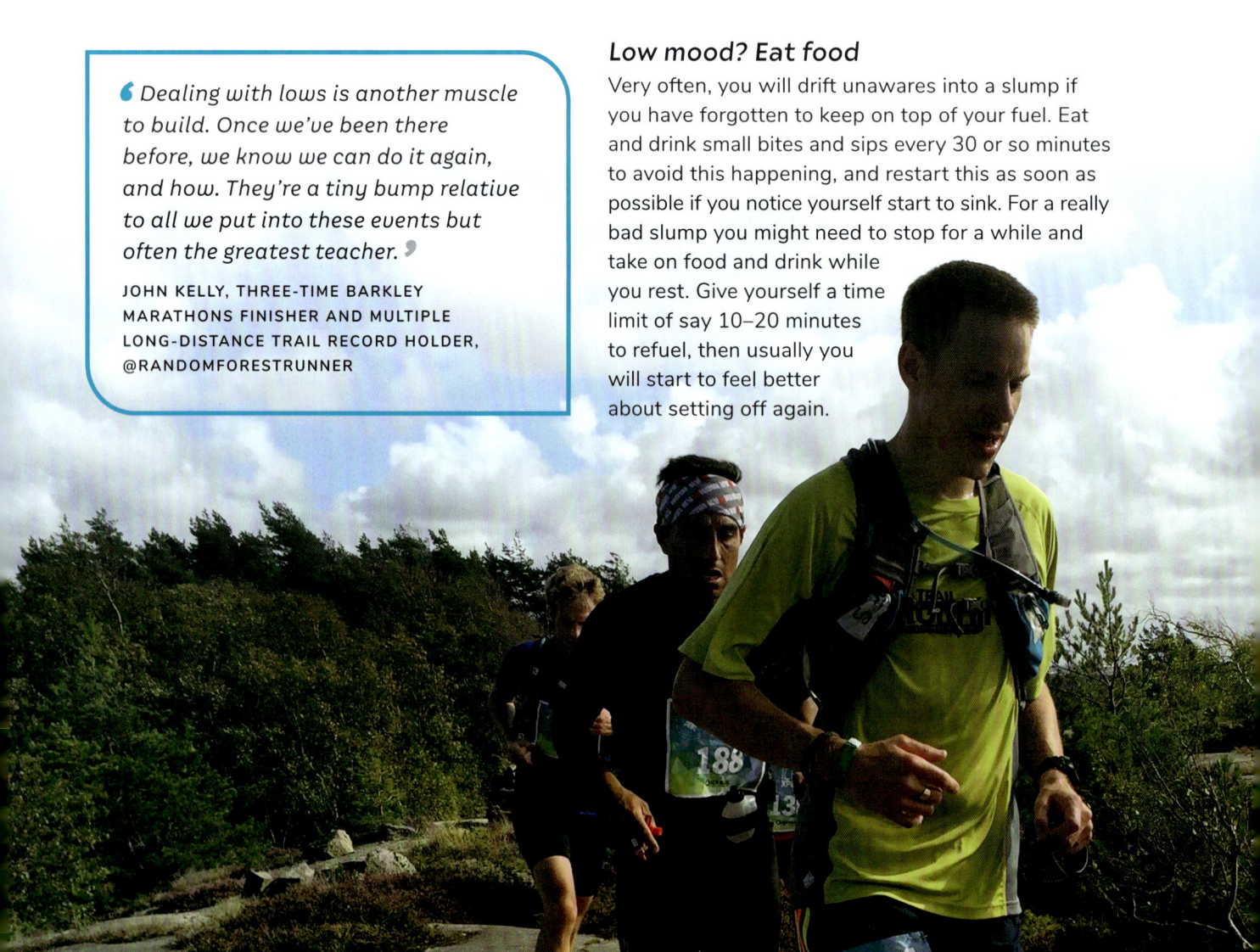

> *Dealing with lows is another muscle to build. Once we've been there before, we know we can do it again, and how. They're a tiny bump relative to all we put into these events but often the greatest teacher.*
>
> JOHN KELLY, THREE-TIME BARKLEY MARATHONS FINISHER AND MULTIPLE LONG-DISTANCE TRAIL RECORD HOLDER, @RANDOMFORESTRUNNER

Low mood? Eat food

Very often, you will drift unawares into a slump if you have forgotten to keep on top of your fuel. Eat and drink small bites and sips every 30 or so minutes to avoid this happening, and restart this as soon as possible if you notice yourself start to sink. For a really bad slump you might need to stop for a while and take on food and drink while you rest. Give yourself a time limit of say 10–20 minutes to refuel, then usually you will start to feel better about setting off again.

Remember, it doesn't always get worse
Especially on the really long distances, you can go through a whole range of different highs and lows as the hours march on, and the secret here is knowing you just have to hang in there. Experience helps here, as some people will know they are likely to have a difficult low in the early hours of the morning or before sunrise on the second night. Others might find the heat in the middle of the day difficult, or bad weather might depress others. Don't quit the first time it enters your mind. Give it time. Knowing things will probably perk up in an hour or so can help you get through.

Get to the next checkpoint
It's daunting to think of how far you've got to go, so ban yourself from thinking about how you have 70 miles (113km) left and how on earth you are going to keep going, and instead focus only on getting to the next checkpoint. Breaking down the race into manageable chunks like this and congratulating yourself on each mini-achievement on the way to your ultimate goal will make it mentally easier.

Don't quit as you arrive at a checkpoint
You might arrive at a checkpoint in a bit of a state, very down on yourself, perhaps in pain, frustrated, tired and wanting to quit immediately, but hold your horses! If you have plenty of time before the cut off, grab some food and a hot drink, sit down, chat, relax and recharge. If you need to be out of the checkpoint immediately to meet the cut off time, quickly grab all the fuel you think you'll need, refill your water and head out of the checkpoint to a sheltered place to sit down, take stock and re-motivate yourself. You may find others doing exactly the same. Make yourself set off on the next leg, give yourself a time limit or distance to test the waters and if it really isn't happening, it's not far to walk back to the security of the aid station, but hopefully you'll get the boost you need to get to the next checkpoint.

Have a trail nap
For those going through a second night or non-stop multi-dayer, power naps on the side of the trail may really help get you through when debilitating fatigue sets in. It helps to set a 5–20-minute alarm for these, so you don't oversleep and miss cut offs or risk getting cold and stiff. Even a few minutes can give you the refreshment that you need to continue to the next checkpoint. There might be a sleeping area there, too, if you have time for a longer nap.

Chat
During low points, a nice chit-chat with another runner can distract you or allow you to commiserate or problem solve together. If no one's around, maybe you have headphones you can put on with some motivating music or a podcast. If you have signal, call a loved one who can remind you of your 'why', and in checkpoints, chat to the marshals. Lastly, talk to yourself (or the sheep, or the trees: it all helps). Be your own cheerleader and say out loud your reasons why. It can help to write or stick motivational messages on your fuel packets or water bottles to remind yourself, too.

Think about the medal

As they say, pain is temporary, glory is forever, but when you're in the middle of a low point, this is easier said than done. If you're verging on quitting, think about whether you will still be happy with a DNF tomorrow morning. Spend a good few minutes nestled in your imagination, thinking about crossing that finish line and getting that well-earned medal around your neck. Think about showing it to your friends, colleagues, family, kids, grandkids, dog, cat, hamster (pets do count, even cats). And imagine all the great memories you'll have to look back on when you're too old to run.

Stay positive

Setbacks can happen, however prepared you are – perhaps you are kicking yourself about a navigation error that has added on a few bonus miles; you're behind the schedule that you trained for with such dedication; or you forgot to put your spare pair of socks in your drop bag and you were pinning your hopes on a fresh pair. Whatever happens, you're still alive, and you can maybe come back next year and have a better race. We pay to put ourselves in these situations and while challenging, they are supposed to be vaguely enjoyable and maybe even make us better humans. So be flexible, change to Plan B (a longer time goal) or even Plan C (just finish within the cut offs) and accept your new lot with grace.

DEALING WITH A DNF

Quitting a race you've been preparing for and looking forward to for ages is totally gutting, but it's all part of the ultra running experience – if it was easy, everyone would run ultras! You might feel intense disappointment and even shame after a DNF, but if you can face those feelings and look back at why you quit, learn from what happened and make changes for next time, it actually turns a DNF into a very useful experience.

GETTING THROUGH LOW POINTS

Here are some great tips to keep you from quitting, from real runners in the Montane Lakeland 50 and 100 Ultra Trail Race Community Facebook group.

'The thought of an incomplete activity on my Strava sends me crazy. I also don't want to let down friends or family who have sacrificed things in their life to allow me to be on that start line.'
KEV HARRISON

'I tell my daughter I'll bring her back a medal. I had some dark times during the 100 a couple of years ago and being tired wasn't a good enough reason to quit. "Sorry but daddy was too tired to get you a medal." Just couldn't go back with that excuse, so when I felt down and exhausted, I repeated that to myself, and finished.'
STEVE WRIGHT

'At 72, I knew this might be my final Lakeland 50 finish. I had completed it three times and WAS NOT going to fail this time. I focused on the belt buckle medal and finished 10 minutes before the official cut off, leaning seriously to the right with only my poles keeping me upright.'
DI NEWTON

'Stick to your own training plan – I got really disheartened in the first few miles, as I felt everyone was overtaking me. I was going slower than slow, as I'd done in training, but felt really out of place when everyone was leaving me behind. I caught everyone up on the first big climb though!'
CLAIRE KIRK

'I wrote on my arm "YCDHT" – "You Can Do Hard Things", and then the DOB [date of birth] of my little boy. Kept me going on the harder bits!'
SUS DAVY

NIGHT RUNNING

LONGER ULTRAS may have you finishing in the early hours of the following morning. A 100-miler (160 km) usually means running through a whole night or even two nights, depending on the start time, time of year and your speed. And in non-stop multi-dayers the days and nights may well just start to blur. Here are my top tips for running well in the night.

1 Practice

There's no need to run through the whole night in training (read the sleep deprivation section to find out why, see p. 61), but if you've picked an ultra that could have you running in the dark, regularly pop out with your head torch and do an hour or two of running with it. This will get you used to taking it out of your pack without faff, fitting it on your head and turning it to the right setting.

2 Get the right gear

Making sure you have a good head torch (see p. 197) makes night running a lot more appealing, and investing in a good-quality waterproof jacket and thermal leggings to protect you from the elements, plus some high-vis gear for any road sections, will also make it easier to get out of the door.

3 Carrot and stick

Think about ways to make yourself get out of the door, for example, have the heating come on later in the evening so you're not tempted to get comfy on the sofa when you get home, and have rewards for afterwards like your fave meal, a beer, a hot shower, a Netflix show you like, a new head torch, a night race, your choice!

4 Keep it simple

Run a familiar route so you are confident finding your way, and if you can time your run to coincide with sunrise or sunset, that offers a massive potential bonus to see that beautiful orange glow melt across the horizon surrounded by pink clouds. The soft cloak of darkness makes any boring, old, familiar run into an adventure. This is a new dimension to explore by torchlight – what will you see tonight?

> **EXPERT ADVICE**
> **HONE YOUR NIGHT RUNNING TECHNIQUE**
>
> 'Slow down slightly because darkness alters your perception of speed. This allows you to absorb your surroundings and reduces the risk of tripping over tree roots that come out of nowhere. Then scan ahead regularly with your head torch, focusing on the path directly ahead of you as well as terrain further down the trail to identify potential hazards and give you a better reaction time.'
>
> ANDY PYE, TRAIL AND FELL RUNNING COACH AT TRAIL RUN WEST MIDLANDS, @TRAILRUNWESTMIDLANDS

5 Scared?

Training and racing in the dark or through the night can be frightening for all sorts of reasons – both real and imagined. Taking a four-legged friend, or joining a friend or a running club, can quell the fear of training alone in the dark, as can waiting at an aid station until you can leave with a group of runners during an event. You might be able to take detours to avoid certain areas that cause you concern, such as subways, forests and tunnels, or wait for another racer to come along. You could even run back towards the last checkpoint until you find a fellow runner to team up with.

NIGHT RUNNING

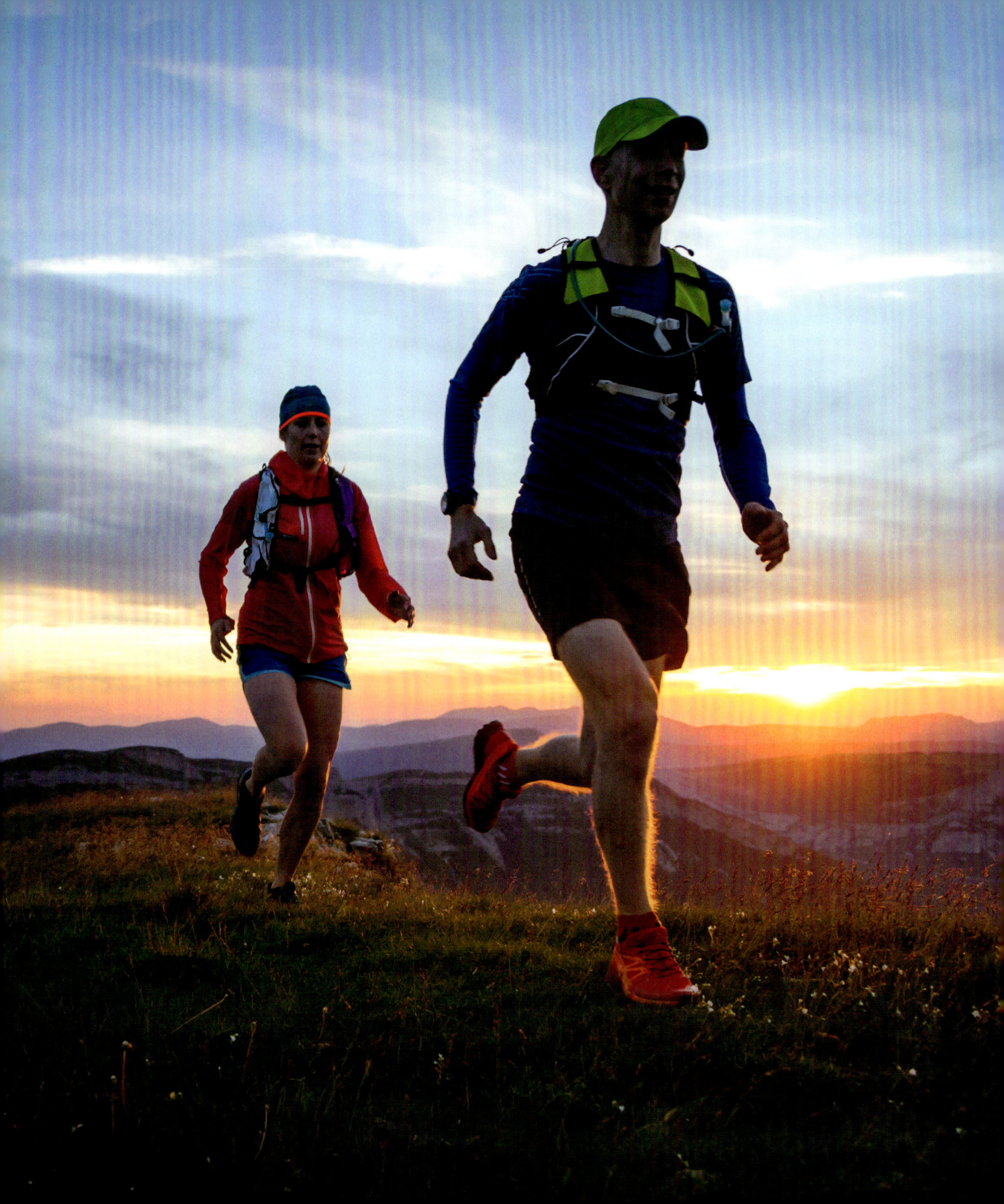

SLEEP DEPRIVATION

WHILE YOU CAN'T TRAIN for sleep deprivation in the same way you can train your muscles, you can gain useful experience during events and work out your own personal strategies for coping better.

1 Sleep well beforehand
This isn't always possible, so don't worry if you don't sleep well beforehand, especially the night before the race if you suffer from nerves; the human body is amazing and can really overextend itself if the brain tells it to. But if you can, get a few early nights and/or have a few lie ins a couple of weeks before the race.

2 Don't train for it
This is a tricky one because although you cope better with sleep deprivation through experience, cutting out sleep during training doesn't make for the best performance and damages your recovery. Maybe if you're super worried and have time to recoup the sleep, a training run through the night might help you feel more confident, especially if you're also practising your navigation skills and testing your head torch. But regular sleep deprivation is not advantageous to training and also feels quite different to during the event itself, so it's not usually recommended.

3 Know what might be coming
Many ultra runners experience a slump during the night-time, especially a second one. This could be in the early hours of the morning, or just before the sun comes up at dawn. If you're mentally prepared for when you personally might feel most tired based on previous experience, it's easier to push on through, or perhaps it's the time to take a power nap (see p. 62).

> **MY STORY**
> ### HALLUCINATIONS AHOY!
> 'I saw Captain America and Laurel and Hardy in the stone walls on the Lakeland 100, as well as umpteen animals, storm troopers and all sorts of faces! Afterwards, in the shower, I noticed some hand-drawn tattoos, including a naked lady on my leg, and spent ages trying to scrub them off wondering how someone had done this to me! [I] never had anything this severe before and was almost disappointed when they finally went the next day.'
> **SIMON WATKINS**

4 Have mantras
Knowing your 'why' is especially important when you're fighting the urge to snooze, so make your reasons for completing this ultra into a few mantras that you can say over and over again in your head, or out loud, to keep your mental energy up. Some people write the first letter of their 'whys' on the back of their hand or arm as a visual reminder, too.

5 Keep up your fuelling
As covered in the fuel section (see p. 147): low mood, eat food – remembering to keep on top of your nutrition during the night can be much harder than during the day, as your body tries to hunker down for its normal rest and digestion fast.

ULTRA HACK

YOU DON'T HAVE TO!

If you really hate sleep deprivation, or you're already sleep deprived from having young kids, work stress, family situations or insomnia, there are plenty of shorter ultras that you can get done before nightfall. Ultras are supposed to be an enjoyable challenge, not a sufferfest (unless you want them to be). That said, maybe you'd be pretty great at a non-stop multi-dayer if you're already used to being sleep deprived!

6 Use caffeine

Caffeine delays tiredness and is the only legal performance booster you can take to help with sleep deprivation and keep you alert. This can also help you navigate and remember to eat and drink for a triple whammy. How it works is very personal and it takes race experience to get it right. You might start with a caffeine gel, as the dosage is clearly labelled, for example 60mg at 3a.m. on the second night. The guidelines from Science In Sport gels are that '1–2mg/kg bodyweight every 60–90 minutes might be effective during the later stages of a 50k–50-mile race or during the overnight hours of a 100k–100 miler.' The aim is not to use caffeine until you really need it, and to find out the lowest dose that works for you, and when and how often to take it. Too much and you risk anti-ultra running symptoms like a headache, a stomach upset, needing to pee more, fast heartbeat, muscle palpitations and mood changes.

7 Splashing water

Splashing water on your face can help to wake you up, alleviate tiredness and feelings of grogginess, and boost your alertness. Keeping hydrated can also help with the same, so make sure your water is always easily accessible, so it's not hard to keep sipping it when you feel tired and can't be bothered.

8 Get a good head torch

Some headlamps kick out brilliant white-blue light, while others adopt a sunnier, yellow hue, which gives a more natural light. Try both to find out which you prefer, and get a light bright enough that you can fool your circadian rhythms into thinking the sun hasn't really set!

9 Power nap

The longer the ultra, the more essential these start to become. It is entirely possible to complete a 100-miler through two nights without napping at all, but some people might benefit from a 5–20-minute power nap. For races longer than 36–48 hours you might take multiple 5–20-minute power naps in aid stations or on the trail, and 2- or 3-hour sleeps on non-stop multi-dayers. You might have a vague plan for when you might take these naps, but for each race it will be a fine balance between mood, hunger, pain, weather conditions, time of day, upcoming terrain and the distance to the finish that will influence your decision.

10 It's personal

What works for your friend or that elite athlete you read about may or may not work for you, so getting to grips with managing sleep deprivation can take a fair bit of experience and maybe even a DNF or two before you finally nail it. Even then it can change race to race, hour by hour, so being flexible and adapting to the conditions and your own mood is key.

TOILETING OUTDOORS

MANY ULTRAS HAVE PORTALOOS at aid stations and the best have sanitary products in them in case you unexpectedly get your period during a race. But what do you do on long training runs in the wilds, or if you're caught short between aid stations? Here is the latest best practice on pooping and peeing on the trails.

Peeing

I don't think anyone needs to explain to men how to pee outdoors; with their enviable, in-built spout system it's easy enough to turn round and wee with enough modesty. While there are a few ladies brave enough to bare all and squat on the start line or on the trail (I've been impressed to see the first and have done the latter myself), most will feel more comfortable out of sight behind dense vegetation or a wall.

WHERE TO PEE?

Regardless of what kind of bits you have down there, avoid peeing near water sources so as not to contaminate them, and avoid buildings or shelters so as not to make everything smell like a urinal. In the UK the official advice from the British Mountaineering Council is to go 30m (100ft) away, 60m (200ft) in the USA. Carry loo paper or wet wipes in a dog poo bag or ziplock bag, and a spare for the used items.

SHEWEE?

A Shewee is a plastic, fake-penis tube women can pee into. It takes a bit of practice at first: in the shower is a good idea. One of these can be handy in races (and festivals), especially if there are plenty of urinals and a big queue for the loos. However, owning one means you have to carry it, clean it and not lose it, which can be more faff than it's worth.

PANTYLINERS

To save taking loo paper into the wilds and carrying it out again (you must carry it out, so take a small ziplock plastic bag), some ladies swear by a disposable pantyliner to catch drips, changing them when needed and carrying them out as well.

Pooping

The guidance here has changed over recent years from leaving your poop in a 15–20cm (6–8-in) -deep hole dug with a trowel, stick or stone 60m (200ft) away from water, paths, buildings and any kind of shelter, to carrying the poop and the paper/wet wipes out entirely in a poo bag just as you would for a dog. This is to avoid contaminating the soil and water sources with the bacteria, protozoa, viruses, chemicals, hormones and antibiotic-resistant bacteria now found in human faeces. You can then dispose of it in a dog poo bin.

ULTRA HACK

THE PRE-RACE POOP

A caffeinated beverage an hour or two before a race can really help wake up your digestive system for that otherwise elusive pre-race poo. Better out than in, eh!

MY STORY

WE WERE POOPED!

'I was encouraging a fellow first-timer on the Lakeland 100 to sleep at the penultimate checkpoint, as he was struggling with sleep deprivation. He refused, but 500m (1640ft) after leaving he said he wanted to sleep and proposed napping in the bracken by a wall. I said, "Ugh, it stinks here." Lying down, I noticed some flies; turning round I saw loo roll littered around me and that I had lain in a human poo and it was on my hand and all over my bag and coat. Exhausted and totally grossed out, we left. Managed to wash most of it off in a stream, but it still stank for the final 10 miles [16km]. Disgusting!'

ALICE LEE

Sanitary products

Period gear also has to be carried out rather than buried because it contains either non-biodegradable or very slow to biodegrade waste. Even if you're using a menstrual cup, it's best to tip the blood into a nappy bag or dog poo bag to leave no trace.

KEEPING CLEAN

A small bottle of anti-bacterial gel is super handy, as are wet wipes (and remember to carry these out with you).

MULTI-DAYERS

MULTI-DAY ULTRAS come in two forms – non-stop and stage races. Non-stop is where everyone tries to get to the end in the shortest number of days and hours possible, trading a good night's sleep for a jog and the odd power nap. Stage races have a set distance each day and everyone stops in the same place for the night to have a hot meal, some chit-chat and a good kip. You can probably tell from this intro which one I prefer! But whichever floats your ultra running boat, here are some golden nuggets of information for success over these longer distance races.

> *Play the long game – start steady, go strong... go long. Strong does not mean speed but efficiency and pacing. Look after your feet, stomach and head and the finish will be yours.*
>
> JOE FAULKNER, FOUR-TIME DRAGON'S BACK RACE COMPLETER AND DIRECTOR OF NAV4 ADVENTURE NAVIGATION AND SAFETY TRAINING AND COACHING, @NAV4ADVENTURE

1 Avoid overtraining
The biggest mistake multi-day hopefuls make is overtraining the month and week before the event. Every year a certain number of folk will fail to make the start line (DNS) because they've picked up a late injury through panic overtraining in the last month before the race. Ideally you need a whole year to prepare and train for a long, expedition-style race with a slow and steady build-up, rather than cramming it in at the end.

2 Set off slowly
Hello! We're here again. Setting off slowly and pacing oneself does seem to be one of the key elements to successful ultra running, and in the case of a multi-dayer this can mean reining in the pace over the first two to three days rather than just the first few hours of the first day. Anyone can win the first day of an eight-day ultra, but not everyone will get to the end in one piece. Chatting pace is the ideal in these monster races.

3 Be more ladylike
It has been noticed amongst ultra race organisers that female participants on longer multi-day races seem to be more successful than males as a percentage of finishers. It is thought that women are less likely to get caught up in the competitiveness of the start which can lead to runners going too fast too soon and conking out later on.

4 Mix sweet and savoury
If it's a stage race, this might be less important, as you satiate your savoury yearnings morning and evening at camp. Depending on the day's distance it may be doable on gels and jelly babies, with minimal savoury and salty snacks. With longer stage days or in a non-stop race you'll definitely want to have access to sweet and savoury food throughout as you create your own nutritional strategy, especially if the aid stations are very far apart. For ideas on sweet and savoury foods see page 134.

5 Take kit for all conditions
If your race is a week-long one, the weather can change rapidly, so it's important to pack for every condition just in case the forecast isn't right, and when

---

ULTRA HACK

FOOTCARE IS KING

If you haven't got feet, you can't run an ultra. This is what I found by day four of the Cape Wrath Ultra in 2018. I quit and became a non-competitive (NC) runner, then after three days' rest, I forced my swollen toes into my tent mate's three-sizes-bigger shoes to complete day eight, but how I wish I'd cared for my feet better on that race, and taken a pair of shoes a size bigger. It would have made the race much more enjoyable and possibly even doable...? Who knows, I'd love to have another crack at it in a fitter, foot-better, future life.

is it ever right? It's important to have all the mandatory kit the organisers ask for at all times, too. On a stage race you will have access to a drop bag overnight (see p. 194 for drop bag essentials), so extras can be packed in there while you dress for each day. On a non-stopper you'll have to carry more on your back unless there are very regular drop bag locations.

6 Admin is the priority

On a stage race, at the end of each day, eat as much as you can, air your feet, sort any hots spots or blisters, get packed for the following day, eat some more, then lie down and relax or sleep early. It's very tempting to mill around spending extra time on your feet chatting to everyone and before you know it it's 11p.m. and you've a 6a.m. start time. Take ear plugs for communal sleep spaces, too. On a non-stopper, being efficient at checkpoints can shave hours off your race, so much like the advice for single-day ultras, know what you need to do before you get there, crack on with replenishing your supplies, and if you're not planning to rest or sleep, eat while you walk along the trail.

7 Calm navigation

Don't rush the navigation, even if you're tired and pressured by looming cut offs. Taking just 10–30 seconds more to make sure you've made the right decision can be the difference between going the wrong way and becoming timed out or even more exhausted, and finishing the race.

8 Know your 'why?' inside out

The longer you're in the ultra running zone, the higher the chance that you will experience some challenging low points, so it's even more important to know why you put yourself through these gruelling races. Write the initials of your reason on your arm in marker pen, have messages from loved ones written on your fuel, have a photo of your beloved kids/dog/cat/hamster laminated and snuck into an easy-to-reach pocket.

RUN YOUR OWN MULTI-DAY ULTRA

Organised ultras and multi-dayers are fantastic, but they can be long, gruelling and require a high level of fitness and a specific time commitment. Instead you could consider running these routes under your own steam over a longer timescale or making up your own DIY challenge. For example, the coastal path of an entire island over six days like the 100-mile (160km) Raad ny Foillan on the Isle of Man. You need to be confident in your navigation skills and/or use the OS Maps app, or you can hire a running guide to lead you. Grab a group of running friends and invent your own unforgettable running holiday at the right level for you.

> *Ultrarunning can often feel like it's for "other" people – people who wear short shorts and can gallop up mountains without breaking a sweat. But the beauty of a long-distance journey is that you can make it your own. Go your pace. Run the route you want to and make your own precious, unique memories along the way.*
>
> ANNA MCNUFF, ADVENTURER AND AUTHOR OF RUNNING BOOKS *BAREFOOT BRITAIN* AND *THE PANTS OF PERSPECTIVE*

NAVIGATION AND GPS

MANY OF THE LONGER ULTRAS rely on self-navigation, as it would be such a mammoth task to waymark the whole course. The race organisers might give you a map, a route description booklet, a GPX file of the course for your GPS watch or a combination of all three. Some might be very straightforward to follow, for example, along a well-signposted National Trail or a coastal path with the sea to your left, while some require more map-reading skills.

Whichever you choose, it's a good idea to gain some basic navigation skills so you can plan interesting training routes, recce the course and feel secure if your GPS batteries fail on the race. Here are some easy navigation pointers to get you started.

1 Orientate the map

It's natural to hold the map with north pointing away from you and all the writing the right way up, but you need to rotate it to match up with the way you're going. You need to turn it around so that the features on the map line up with what's around you in real life. For example, if you want to run along a path with a river to your right, turning left when you get to a building on your left, turn the map until the river is on the right hand side of the path, leading to the building on the left, followed by the junction.

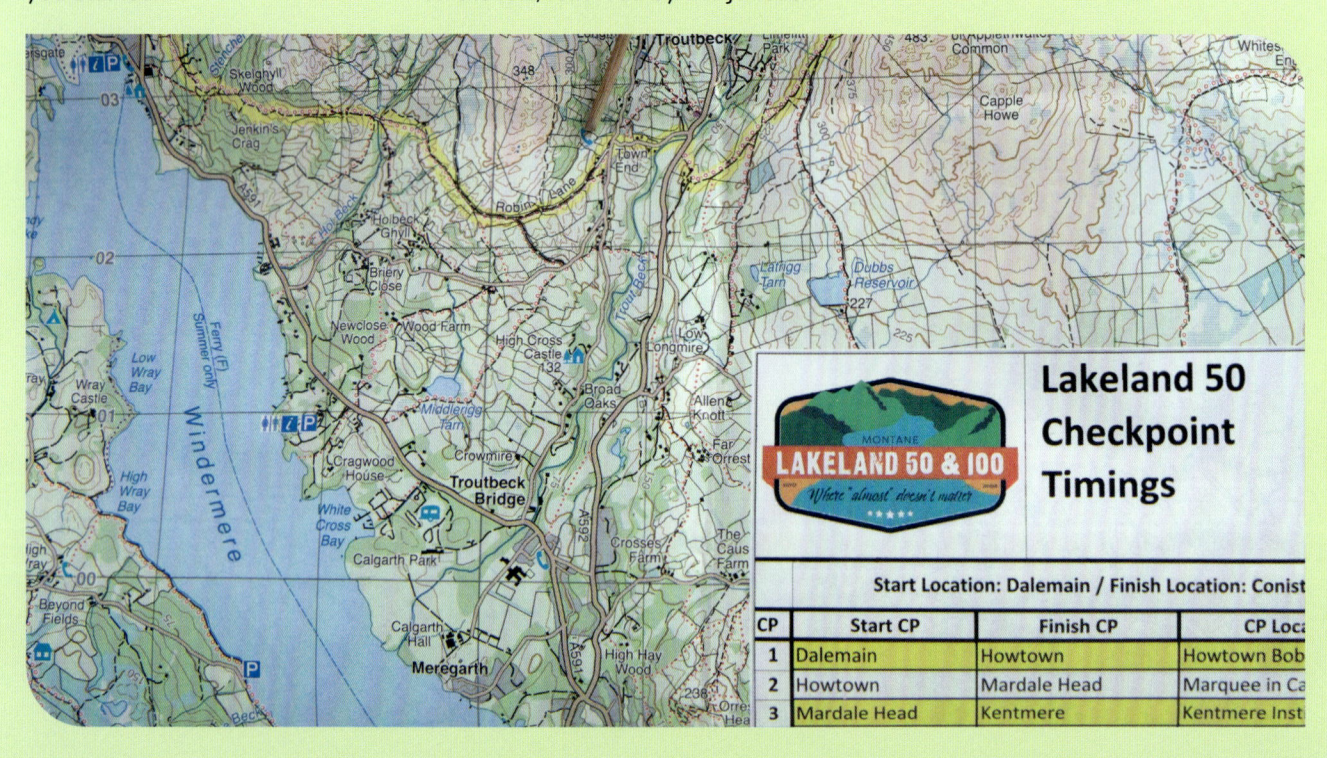

68   2. PREPARATION AND SKILLS

2 Tick off features

Now you have the map the right way round, look at what lies ahead on it – for example, you're following a river until you see a building, then there should be a junction where you turn left, then you will start going uphill away from the river, coming out of the forest and meeting another path at the top of the hill. All these features will be marked on the map (familiarise yourself with the legend or key to work out what they all are), so you can tick them off as you run along. Be aware that some features may have changed since the map was created, like forest boundaries, walls and fences.

3 Thumb the map

As you tick off each feature on the map, slide your thumb along the route as you progress, in the same way as your sat nav locator arrow moves. This enables you to look down at the map and quickly pinpoint where you are without having to stop, think and work it out each time.

4 Understand contour lines

Contour lines are the little brown lines all over the map that represent how high the land is above sea level. If you're crossing them, you're going uphill or downhill, and if you're running along one, you're staying at the same height, also known as contouring a hill. The closer they are together, the steeper the gradient, and a good way to tell if they're going up or down is to look for a large-ish river, which will be at the bottom of a valley with the hills rising up all around it. The more practice you get at relating the contour lines on the map to the hills around you, the more you will be able to look at a map of any landscape and create an image in your head of the hillside it represents, which is very useful for navigating.

NAVIGATION AND GPS 69

6 Use distance and timings

One nice, simple piece of info you should know about Ordnance Survey (OS) and Harvey maps is that whatever their scale, the distance horizontally or vertically across one grid square equates to 1km (0.6 miles) in real life. Diagonally it's 1.5km (0.9 miles). This gives you an idea of how far you will be running until you reach the next feature or path junction, and on many compasses there's a measuring scale, so you can easily work out smaller distances within those squares. This takes a little practice and experience, but you will soon learn roughly how long it takes you to run 1km on the flat or hike 1km up a steep hill. Then you can estimate timings so you know when to start looking out for features or junctions and don't turn off too early or too late.

5 The compass is not scary

Many compasses have an air of being complicated, with their swivel dial and all the numbers round the side, but to start with, ignore all of that. Unless you're learning how to navigate in thick mist or the dark, all we're interested in for ultra running is the red north arrow. This will help you to orientate your map (see point one) and confirm you're heading off in the direction you think you are! So once you've orientated your map using the features, double check by getting the compass out and seeing if the red north arrow points in the direction of the grid lines that run northwards. These are the grid lines that run vertically up the map when you hold it with the writing the right way round. If the features match up, bravo! If not, rotate the map until north on the map matches up with north on the compass, and look again. Equally you can double-check the path direction. If the path on the map runs south east, get the compass out and check the one you're on is headed in that direction. See, easy! Remember, you almost certainly also have a compass on your smartphone.

7 Use catching points

It's super handy to know when you've run too far very early on, to save running extra miles that turn your 100-miler into a 110-miler! So have a quick look on the map to see what features will alert you to overshooting your mark. Perhaps the gradient steepens, or a river will start to bend left if you go too far on the track or take a wrong turn. Being aware of what you're not expecting to see can be just as handy as knowing what you should see on your route.

8 Map memory

Especially for running faster or using poles, it's really useful to be able to memorise the route so you don't have to refer to the map as often. This definitely takes practice and is much harder when you're tired or hungry, but if you can

70   2. PREPARATION AND SKILLS

manage it, this will save a lot of time. Divide your route into small sections that you can remember, especially for downhill sections so you don't waste gravity's free boost. For example, 'Down to forest edge, straight on to river, footbridge, turn right, uphill, wall on right.' Try to memorise the next leg as you slow down for the climb.

9 Escape routes

Since you can never tell exactly what the weather might do or when fatigue or injury might strike, be aware of points on your route where you could safely descend, avoid a summit or rocky section, or cut the route short if needed. Always check the forecast before you head out, and in races don't be blinded by the mandatory kit list alone – take more, if needed, to keep yourself safe, like extra layers, an extra 500ml soft water bottle and a survival bag.

10 Night nav

Navigating at night ironically can be easier in a large race as you simply follow the head torch lights ahead (hoping they're all going in the right direction of course!). Recce-ing the part of the course you are most likely to face at night is a bonus if you have time. If navigating by GPS is allowed, have a practice in the dark locally to make sure you know exactly how your watch and headlamp work ahead of time. If you have to navigate old-school style, practice as much as you can on night runs locally. Get used to picking out features in the dark with your head torch and paying more attention to timing so as not to under- or overestimate distances to the next feature or turning.

ULTRA HACK

GO ON A COURSE

It's so much easier to improve your navigation if you attend a course pitched at the right level for you. There, a real-life person will answer all your questions, help you work out which way round to hold the map and have you confidently navigating by the end of the session. I haven't covered taking bearings for more intricate orienteering and running in the mist and dark, because I think it's really hard to explain via words only, so my advice is definitely to go on a course to learn these things, and then practice, practice, practice.

TRAIN RIGHT FOR YOUR AGE

THE AVERAGE ULTRA RUNNER is in their early 40s according to the State of Ultra Running 2020 survey by Run Repeat, and it's wonderful to know that age is more on your side for the longer distance. While it's pretty frustrating to know for a scientific fact that muscular strength starts to wane and recovery slows down with age, ultra runners can more than make up for these downsides by a whole host of other very important aspects like preparing well, fuelling right, pacing wisely and navigating well. Better still, if you're a newcomer, whatever your age, your performance can improve with experience. Here's the best advice from your 20s to your 80s and beyond.

> *Think of yourself as a classic car, like an E-Type Jaguar. Spend time strengthening old parts (muscles), make sure you think about the fuel you're using – protein will be your new friend here. And forget what the speedo (your watch). Instead enjoy the moment.*
>
> PAUL LARKINS, FORMER SUB FOUR-MINUTE MILER, FORMER EDITOR OF *TRAIL RUNNING* MAGAZINE, SPORTS EDITOR OF *SAGA* MAGAZINE

In your 20s

The main risk here is burn-out as you have tons of energy and aren't afraid to use it! You might also not have developed the stamina and endurance of an older runner, so you may be best at shorter races right now. You might not even stop growing until your mid-20s, so make sure you get a lot of sleep, eat well, be aware of the signs of overtraining and get into good habits, such as listening to your body, making sure you eat well and prioritising strength work.

In your 30s

Despite there possibly being a decrease in available time due to family and work commitments in this decade, this is the prime of life for many ultra runners. What you lose in strength and recovery times you gain in experience, pacing and stamina, and commitment to hard or 'boring' sessions like strength, speedwork, tempo runs and hill reps. Again, though, watch out for signs of overtraining while you ride this high.

In your 40s

So many ultra running greats are in their 40s – this decade can be the best for long-distance runners, as your wisdom and experience distils into pacing, navigation skills, good fuel and gear choices, race strategy and endurance. You may start to notice you take longer to recover and get injured more easily, so warm up well before fast sessions and weight training. Cross-train, prioritise sleeping and good nutrition, and keep up your strength and speedwork to maintain your endurance and pace.

In your 50s

The more you stay active and ramp up your strength work, the more muscular strength you will maintain in this decade, although most runners will unfortunately start to see a decline in time. But stay positive – this could be the decade to start running even further! Never neglect strength training and continue your speedwork – you don't have to just plod along, unless you are happy with that. It's even more important to rest well, eat well, stretch, crosstrain and get niggles seen to before they turn into injuries.

In your 60s

Some people start running in their 70s, even their 80s, so at 60 you are still a spring chicken. If you've been running for a long time, you may see old injuries rearing their ugly heads, but focusing on strength work and cross-training combined with plenty of sleep and a healthy diet will help with that – especially calcium-rich foods. Joint supplements such as cod liver oil can also make a difference, as can using poles. Speedwork sessions and shorter races will help you maintain your pace, too. For more on using poles see page 52.

In your 70s

It's fantastic when you see runners in their 70s; we all aspire to be you! The same applies as in your 60s, and better still, you possibly have way more time to train as hopefully you are retired by now (or sooner!).

> **ULTRA HACK**
>
> **USE IT OR LOSE IT**
>
> One of the best ways to slow age-related muscle-wastage is resistance training, so the older you become, the more important it is to do at least 20 minutes of strength work three times a week. Follow the workouts in this book on p. 90.

Regular strength work will maintain your muscles, joint supplements can oil your bendy parts, while eating healthily and sleeping well will boost your energy and recovery. Plenty of hiking with poles will get you round the longest courses, but you may need more mental energy to chat to all the other runners who keep striking up conversations about how incredible you are.

In your 80s and beyond!

There really is no reason to stop doing ultras if your mind and body are still going strong at this age, which we all very much hope will be the case. It will please you to know that the oldest person to complete a 100-mile (160km) event is a 90-year-old US dude called Don Jans (at the time of writing). It might be that you spend more time hiking with poles and more energy replying to fellow ultra runners saying, 'Wow, you're amazing!' Strength work, a healthy diet, joint supplements, cross-training, plenty of recovery time and sleep are your best buddies here.

> **MY STORY**
>
> **I'M 87 AND STILL RUNNING ULTRAS**
>
> '**My ultimate challenge** is 100 ultras before my 100th birthday. I'm doing all this for the animals, fundraising for vegan charity Viva! I became a vegan in my 60s and at the same time my arthritis disappeared, so I started exercising again. After months running around a track in my garden in lockdown and doing daily press-ups (I'm aiming for one million by my 90th), I discovered ultra running. My first was in July 2021, Minehead to Dawlish over two days. I remember climbing Dunkery Beacon – in torrential rain and high wind (some other runners got hypothermia) and saying, "There's nowhere else I'd rather be!" I felt so alive. I was addicted and have now completed 12 ultras, both races and virtual events. The only supplement I take is two 400mg shots of beetroot juice concentrate, one before the start of a race and one halfway through. No matter how tough it gets on the trail, it's much harder for the animals – so I just keep going. I aim to show that, as a vegan, you can be fit and healthy into old age – should I ever get there...'
>
> **PAUL YOUD**, VEGAN RUNNER, AGED 87

WOMEN'S RUNNING (ALSO VERY HELPFUL FOR MEN TO READ)

THERE ARE SPECIFIC HORMONAL and bodily changes for women that have a big impact on running and they vary enormously from person to person. Periods, pregnancy, postpartum, peri-menopause and the menopause all have an effect on training and racing. It's brilliant that these topics have become much less taboo over recent years, resulting in more talking, research and advice, but there is still much to be done. There are whole books on each of these very important topics, but here are the essentials in a nutshell for ultra runners.

Menstruation

Most women can run long distances throughout their menstrual cycle. The effect of the cycle on energy levels, pain tolerance, strength and performance is finally becoming better researched. Exercise can help ease or deal with premenstrual and menstrual cramps and tension. Some studies indicate that different phases of the menstrual cycle are better for training or injury risk than others. However, there is a long way to go to increase the quality of this research and every woman is different. So it's best to track your cycle and note any symptoms so you can identify your own personal patterns, trends and ideal training schedule. It might also please you to know that women have won Olympic medals during all phases of the menstrual cycle.

> *If your run doesn't go to plan, take some time to reflect on it and think why this could be. Poor nutrition, not [being] recovered enough, doing a session you're not yet ready for, stress, [the] phase of your menstrual cycle or accumulated fatigue, or maybe it was just a bad session that you need to move on from. Figure it out, dust yourself off and go crush your next session.*

CARLA MOLINARO, ULTRA RUNNER FOR TEAM HOKA, LAND'S END TO JON O'GROATS FEMALE WORLD RECORD HOLDER, RUNNING COACH AND FOUNDER OF SCY (STRENGTH, CONDITIONING AND YOGA) FOR RUNNERS, @CARLAMOLINARO

WHICH PRODUCT?

Using a tampon or menstrual cup rather than a sanitary towel or period pants can make running more comfortable, less sweaty and less messy. If you have a very heavy or irregular flow, you might feel more secure using a panty liner, sanitary towel or period pants as well as a tampon or cup. The menstrual cup and a light period pant in case of leaks is a great option for ultra running because you don't need anything else. To clean the cup before reinsertion on the trail wash it with water from your bottle (taking a mouthful and squirting the desired amount of water on the cup can be quicker than trying to coordinate the squeeze valve, amount and direction of flow from a floppy, possibly half-empty soft bottle) or use an alcohol wipe (and carry this out, too).

ALWAYS CARRY TAMPONS - MEN TOO

Starting your period during a long run or an ultra can vary from inconvenient and uncomfortable to messy and painful depending on your flow, so it's a good idea to carry a spare pad, tampon or your menstrual cup with you at all times. I am forever finding odd tampons stashed in all my various running packs and backpacks and if I'm due to start my period I pack my Mooncup. Some races have started providing period products in the aid station Portaloos, which is excellent. In the first aid kit list in this book (see p. 192) you will find tampons, and this applies to men, too. Wouldn't it be great if you could go up to anyone, male or female, knowing that there was a good chance they'd have a spare tampon to help you out? Be a real ultra running hero, guys!

LOSING YOUR PERIOD

Training too much and not fuelling enough (also known as RED-S, see p. 127) can lead to losing your period (known as amenorrhea) due to hormone disruption. It might sound handy not to have periods as a runner, but training this way poses very serious health concerns with debilitating symptoms including low energy, persistent illness, lack of performance, low libido, irritability, poor concentration, depression, eating disorders, body dysmorphia, difficulty conceiving and an increased risk of osteoporosis.

Birth control

Your choice of birth control is very personal, and some ultra runners will get on with one method or product while it isn't convenient or produces unwanted side effects in another. Talk to healthcare

---

EXPERT ADVICE
UNDERSTAND YOUR OWN MENSTRUAL CYCLE

'Talk about it – chat periods and menstrual cycles with health care providers and other runners of all ages and sexes, especially if you're a coach. This will help end those ridiculous taboos, it's just blood after all.

'Knowledge is power – track your cycle along with your performance, as a specific period-phase-related recommendation, won't work for everyone. Look for patterns and trends in how you feel and how you perform. Simply being aware of your cycle and associated symptoms makes it easier to manage and mitigate.

'Reframe it – yes there are unwanted, painful symptoms, but periods are here to stay, so let's focus on the positive aspects to menstruation. The goal is to educate and empower, not to limit.

'Wait for it – more research needs to be done to better understand how menstruation affects ultra running, so focus on what works for you first and foremost.'

CORRINE MALCOLM, ELITE ULTRA RUNNER, COACH AND EDITOR-IN-CHIEF OF *FREETRAIL*, @CORRINEMALCOLM

professionals, other runners and coaches about the effectiveness and the potential side effects of the different types of protection available.

Abortion

Depending on how you feel mentally and physically with any prolonged bleeding and soreness, you may want to wait anything from a couple of days to a week to start running again after having a medical or surgical abortion. Start gradually with low intensity workouts and light weights until you feel completely recovered. There is no right way to feel after an abortion and you may feel a combination of emotions at once, numb or overwhelmed, so running and exercise is a really good way to care for yourself, distract yourself, or talk with supportive friends.

Fertility and infertility

More research is needed in this area, as studies can be conflicting, but it is generally agreed that regular, moderate exercise and a healthy lifestyle free from too much stress can increase fertility and chances of conceiving. So running should be fine for most women trying for a baby, but pushing your body to the extreme may reduce fertility. Overtraining, under-eating and long-term stress can lessen your chances (see Losing your Period, p. 77), so listen to your body even more while trying to conceive. During IVF treatment cycles women are advised to reduce exercise, and some doctors will advise no running whatsoever, but while the jury is still out scientifically, it's personal choice as to which will give you the least stress – running or not running. Running, jogging and hiking are also excellent ways to process difficult life events, including conception struggles and infertility.

Pregnancy

Every pregnancy is different, so listen to your body and run according to how you feel. Keep an open mind and be flexible. If you've never run an ultra before, during pregnancy isn't the time to start, but if you feel good and have the energy, it's perfectly possible to run your usual distances, cross-train and resistance-train with baby on board. However, most of the advice you will hear is to run at a lower effort level until your bump becomes uncomfortable, depending on breathlessness, fatigue, pain, nausea and/or the persistent need to pee. Keep well hydrated and ventilated, take a snack and mix running with lower-impact sports such as brisk walking, swimming and cycling. Stop running if you feel faint, dizzy

> **REAL LIFE STORY**
> ### PREGNANCY RACE DEFERRALS
>
> **There is a very famous,** viral photo of Sophie Power breastfeeding her three-month-old son during the iconic Ultra Trail du Mont Blanc (UTMB) 105-mile (169km) race through the Alps. While all runners are permitted to defer their UTMB entry due to injury, because they consider pregnancy to be 'planned' the UTMB did not accept this reason. Sophie had already missed one UTMB in having her first son, and was determined to race in 2018 with her second. Her experience led her to set up the organisation SheRaces whose guidelines help race organisers make their events more inclusive for female runners. It's down to Sophie and her team that the UTMB, London Marathon, Ironman and many other road, trail and ultra races, and triathlons now offer pregnancy deferral policies that also extend to partners, adoptions and surrogacy. The SheRaces guidelines also include using more inclusive imagery, language and cut offs, appropriate toilet and changing facilities, women's fit t-shirts, outside help allowances for breastfeeding athletes, equal media coverage, equal prizes and prize money. Thank you Sophie, I think we all owe you a pint or three.

WOMEN'S RUNNING 79

or have chest pain, or if you have any pregnancy complications and have been advised not to run. If you have abdominal pain, bleeding or a reduction in the movement from your baby, call your emergency maternity number.

Miscarriage

It doesn't make it hurt less to know that miscarriage is very common, but hopefully it helps to know that scientific research shows it is not caused by running and exercise. According to Tommy's pregnancy research charity, one in four pregnancies end in miscarriage within the first three months and most are due to unpreventable chromosomal abnormalities that mean the foetus is not developing as it should. After a miscarriage, the pregnancy hormones take a few weeks to go down, so you may still feel the same effects when you run. Run as soon as you like once the bleeding, cramps and any other symptoms become manageable. Be kind to yourself, ease back in and gradually increase your training when you feel ready. Running can also be good therapy for loss.

Postpartum

Again, every woman and every pregnancy is different. You hear of incredible women breastfeeding on the race finish line and expressing milk at checkpoints

> **ULTRA HACK**
>
> **POWER HIKING**
> Brisk walking, or power hiking as it's more glamorously called, is an essential part of ultra running, especially uphill. So, walking as much as you can is a fantastic way to maintain both physical and mental fitness for ultra running when trying to conceive, during pregnancy and postpartum.

MY STORY
RUNNING AS THERAPY FOR BABY LOSS

'**I ran my first 50-miler** during the three months between miscarriage and my current pregnancy. I found running to be a very healing part of the process. I would have loved to stumble upon a section in a running book on loss while going through that.'
ELLIENNE NOONAN

'**I had four miscarriages** in a year before having my now five-year-old. I had to cut back on intensity and distance, but running was always an important part of mental and physical health. Now I have two happy healthy kids.'
CANDICE TIPTON SAWYER

for 100-mile (160km) ultras, and while this is fantastic and can obviously be done, don't feel under any pressure to make this part of your journey if you're having a hard enough time getting back to a jog. Try not to compare yourself to other running mums, and return when you personally feel able to; six weeks is a guideline, but some mums take a year, or more. If you are able to afford it, it's well worth getting a Mummy MOT with a specialist postpartum physio, keep up your pelvic floor exercises and strengthen your abs as they part when the uterus expands (diastasis recti). Avoid the plank and sit-ups while you rebuild these muscles with pelvic floor and diaphragm exercises.

Pelvic floor and diaphragm exercises
TOP THREE PELVIC FLOOR EXERCISES

Activate your pelvic floor at the start of each of these exercises – pull your stomach in and imagine you are stopping yourself going for a wee and holding in a fart.

Cat cow
Kneel on all fours, breathe in and arch your back. Hold for 3 seconds. Breathe out as you lower your back and hold again for 3 seconds. Repeat 10–15 times.

Superman
Kneel on all fours, raise your right arm straight out in front and at the same time raise your left leg straight out behind you. Hold for 3–5 seconds, then back to all fours. Repeat with the other arm and leg. Do 10–15 on each side.

MY STORY
RUNNING AND THE MENOPAUSE

'**I'm 53** and have found ultra running, and the training helps with menopause symptoms so much. When I don't run my hot flushes and night sweats are awful but [on] run days they are so much less – I can really notice the difference. Running helps with my mood as well.'
ANITA BULLEN

'**I consider my menopause** experience generally positive. At 54 now, post menopause, I've never had hot flashes/night sweats, and no typical symptoms, except perhaps fatigue and weight gain (gained 5lb abdominal fat with no dietary/activity change). I've slowed about a minute per mile, but I still love being out there. I did my fifth 50k (first post menopause) earlier this year and felt good after, mainly I think because I took up heavy lifting, and maybe I've learned a few things from experience. I try to avoid comparison to premenopause me, I keep signing up for new-to-me events, and practise gratitude for being out there. Every story is different for sure!'
CELESTE DECKER

Glute bridge

Lie down on your back, knees up, soles of the feet planted on the ground. Lift up your hips so you make a straight diagonal line with your torso and legs. Lift one foot off the floor and hold the whole leg out along this diagonal line. Hold for 3–5 seconds. Swap the legs. Repeat 10–15 times on each leg.

Peri-menopause and menopause

The word peri-menopause means 'around menopause' and it's when you start heading towards the menopause (the natural cessation of your periods). It can be noticeable for anything from a few months to 10 years (whoopee!) as you start to get less frequent or irregular periods. You may or may not also get symptoms like hot flushes, brain fog, sleep problems, mood changes, anxiety, low self-esteem, decreased fertility, increased fat-storage, heart palpitations, migraines, dry and itchy skin, vaginal dryness and recurrent UTIs. None of this is sounding great is it? But don't despair, not everyone is affected, and if you are, help is at hand in the form of, you guessed it, running! Running, cross-training and strength work are all brilliant treatments for many of these symptoms. And also getting the right HRT (hormone replacement therapy) can be a blessing for many.

> **FURTHER READING**
>
> New women's health research is gradually taking place and the information on each aspect of women's running can fill a whole book in itself, so I recommend *Roar* by Stacy Sims, and *Period Power* and *Perimenopause Power* by Maisie Hill.

> **ULTRA HACK**
>
> **DEALING WITH HOT FLUSHES**
>
> As runners, at least we're nice and used to getting hot and sweaty, but hot flushes are just yet another thing to deal with on an ultra. Wearing a light, technical vest top or T-shirt as your base layer helps to wick the sweat away and dry quickly, and looping your jacket through your running pack strap, under the arm, means it's quickly accessible for multiple on-offs.

WOMEN'S RUNNING 83

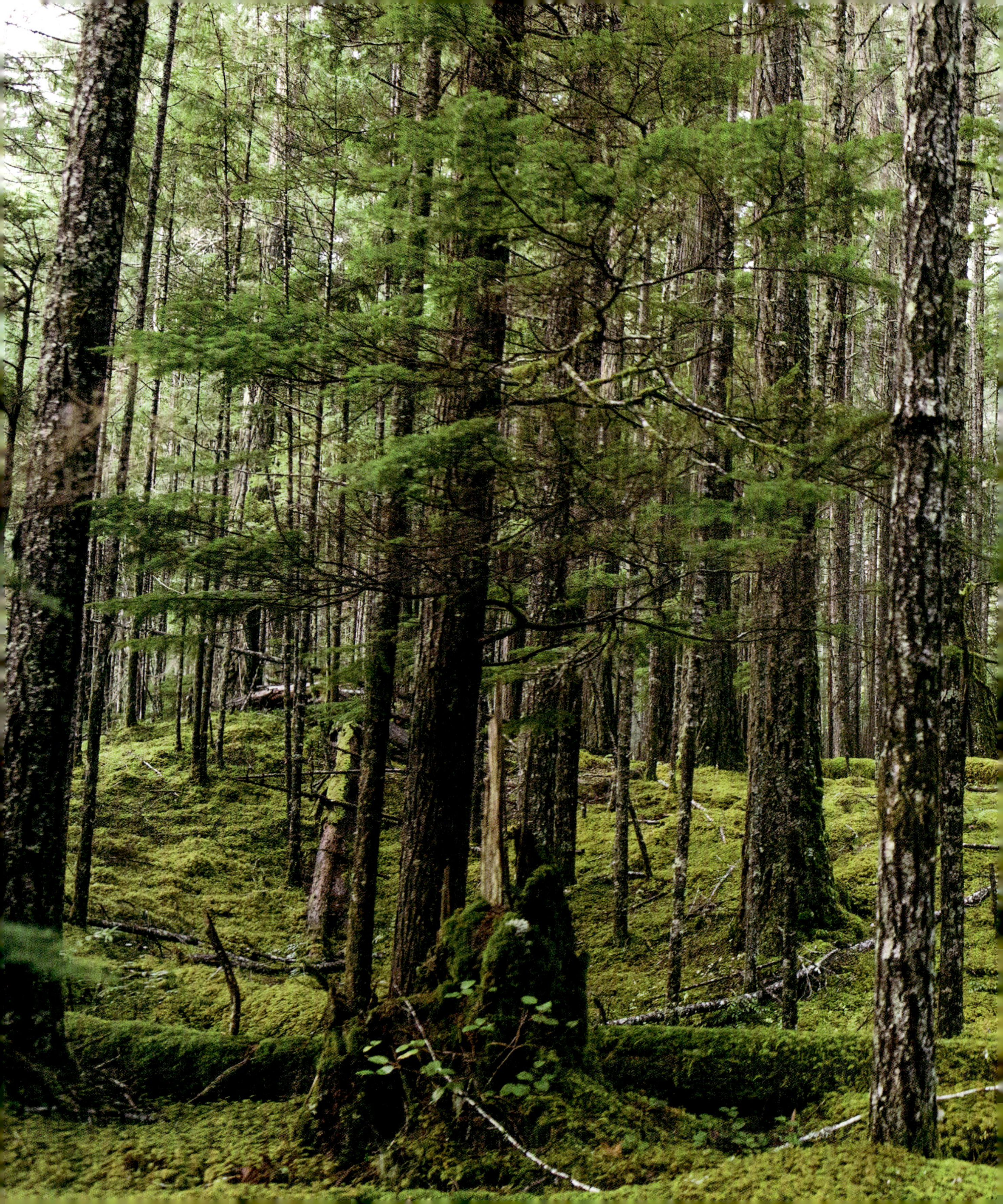

3
PHYSICAL TRAINING

Here are strength workouts and training plans for everyone, whether you're a complete beginner, time poor or ready to push your body to the limits.

STRENGTH TRAINING IS ESSENTIAL

I'VE STARTED WITH STRENGTH in this section because for some reason, myself included, the vast majority of ultras runners prefer to just run, and run, and run some more, rather than doing the regular (ahem, boring) strength work that we know logically will save us from the gaping jaws of injury, make us run more efficiently and recover quicker. This neglect of strength work is unfortunate, because the further and more frequently we want to run, the more vital strength work becomes as the foundation from which ultra runners can build on.

Whether you are new to ultra running or an experienced ultra runner, you will only see positive benefits from strength training, including being able to run for longer without feeling tired, reducing your risk of injury and enjoying running even more.

MEET THE EXPERT
NICK KNIGHT

Podiatrist Nick Knight is the clinical director of NK Active, an expert podiatry and injury rehabilitation practice based in Hampshire that also offers global appointments online. A keen hockey player and runner, Nick was a sports podiatrist at the London 2012 Olympic and Paralympic Games and has been an expert footwear advisor for Salomon.

Three essential strength moves

Every runner's personal needs will differ, but first, here are Nick's three essential moves.

WHILE YOU BRUSH YOUR TEETH
Crab walk: glutes (bum muscles)

Put a resistance band around your feet, bend your knees slightly, keep your feet shoulder-width apart and walk sideways up and down your kitchen and hall. It will feel easy at first, but soon your glutes will be on fire. This is also a great warm-up exercise to activate your glutes before you go for a run. When it gets easy, switch up to a stronger resistance band.

WHILE THE KETTLE BOILS
Straight and bent leg calf raises: soleus and gastrocnemius (calf muscles)

Stand on the edge of a stair or step with the ball of one foot. Keep this leg straight, then raise the heel up and down, lightly holding the banister for balance. Repeat on the other leg. Then isolate the smaller but very important soleus muscle by performing the same move with the knee bent on the active leg. To help you bend the knee more towards 90 degrees during this move, you can use a towel around a banister to balance. Make it harder by wearing a weighted backpack.

WHILE YOU WATCH TV
Bulgarian split squat: all leg muscles

Stand on the floor in front of a chair (or sofa), lift one foot and place it on the chair behind you. Keeping the back straight and as upright as possible, squat down with the leading leg so the knee of the leg on the chair moves towards the floor. Then push back up. This works the whole posterior chain, including your glutes, hamstrings and quads, and gives you a bonus hip flexor stretch, too. Make it harder by carrying a backpack or a couple of bags for life loaded with weighty kitchen items (some can carry a whopping 65kg!). Placing a cushion underneath the foot on the floor also makes it harder from the unstable surface.

STRENGTH TRAINING IS ESSENTIAL   **87**

How many and how heavy?

To start with, just get used to fitting these exercises into your life – doing two moves per day is better than none per day. Then for maximum strength-building efficiency, you want to start using a weight that gives you an RPE (rate of perceived exertion) of seven, where zero is no effort at all and 10 is maximal effort. Do no more than five sets of eight repetitions. Doing 20 of these moves at an RPE of five will build endurance but not strength, so once you can do the move with correct form, it's more efficient to up the weight and do fewer repetitions.

> ❛ If you only find time to do one or two strength exercises that's a great deal better than doing nothing. Finding regular time slots for these that fit in with your life helps. ❜
>
> PODIATRIST NICK KNIGHT FROM NK ACTIVE, @NKACTIVECLINICS

ULTRA HACK

STRENGTH IS FOR LIFE, NOT JUST FOR ULTRA

The World Health Organisation (WHO) have updated their weekly exercise recommendation to include 18 minutes of strength work three times per week in addition to their recommendation of 30 minutes of cardiovascular activity three times per week, because it has such a fantastic impact later on in your life, leading to less risk of falls and a longer life expectancy. Believe me, your 80-year-old (still ultra running?) self will thank you for doing the moves in this book.

3. PHYSICAL TRAINING

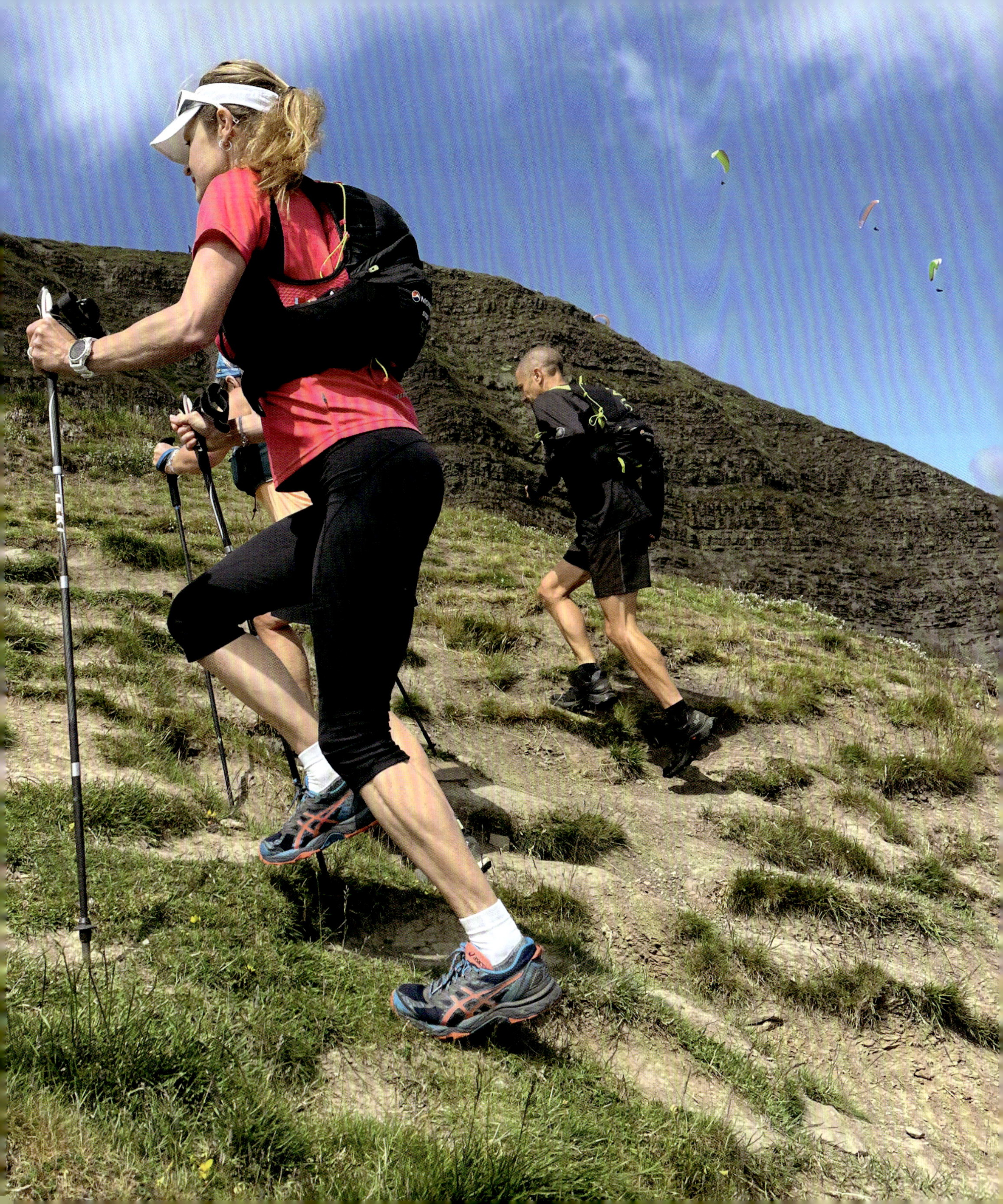

20-30-MINUTE STRENGTH ROUTINE TO BEAT INJURY

IF YOU'RE THE RARE ULTRA RUNNER who is committed to doing more regular strength training to keep yourself strong and injury-free for ultras, here are four more moves taking around 20–30 minutes, which you can add to the 10 minutes of crab walks, bent and straight leg calf raises and Bulgarian split squats described on p. 87 for a longer session. Start by doing this once a week, then build to twice. Go on you hero!

How many should I do?

Start with one set of five repetitions, building slowly up to five sets of eight repetitions. Start with no weights or lighter weights, then once your form is right, slowly increase the weights and resistance bands. The most efficient way to build strength from these exercises is to do them at 7 out of 10 RPE, where 0 is very easy and 10 is maximal effort. When you get to the eighth and final rep, you should only just be able to perform the exercise with correct form.

ULTRA HACK

BREAK IT DOWN!
If you have to break this session up into chunks throughout the day to spare the time, that's totally okay – remember the best exercise is the one that actually gets done.

Squats: leg muscles

Stand with your feet shoulder-width apart. Bend both knees and stick your bum out, keeping your back straight, to lower into a squat. Squeeze your bum muscles as you push back up to standing. Hold hand weights or filled bags for life or wear a weighted pack for more resistance.

Walking lunges: leg muscles and balance

Stand with your feet hip-width apart. Step one leg forwards and bend each knee 90 degrees to lower into a lunge position, with your lower knee just above the ground. Power upwards and step your back foot forwards, then repeat the lunge on the alternate leg. Hold hand weights or filled bags for life or wear a weighted pack for more resistance.

Step-ups: leg muscles and balance

Step one leg up on to a chair, bench or the second step of a staircase. Raise the knee of your other leg, then set it down on the floor again. Repeat on the same leg before switching to the other leg. Hold hand weights or wear a weighted pack to make this harder.

Glute bridges: glutes, hamstrings, core

Lie down on your back with your knees bent and feet on the floor. Push your hips up into the air until your thighs are straight in line with your body, then lower them. Repeat 8 times. Make it harder by holding a weight over your hips and/or placing your feet up on a chair or sofa.

Russian twists: core

Sit down with your legs out in front of you, then bend your knees through 90 degrees and lift your feet just off the floor. Clasp your hands together in front of you and twist from side to side, tapping your fingertips down on the ground each time. Hold a weight to make this harder.

Press up

Place your palms on the floor, arms straight, body straight out behind, balancing on your toes. Engage the core muscles by holding your stomach muscles in, bend the elbows to drop your body downwards until the chest almost touches the ground, then push back up again. Make this one easier by dropping your knees to the floor and rock forwards on them (still keeping the back straight) when performing the press up action. Make this harder by wearing a weighted pack.

MY STORY
STRENGTH WORK SAVED ME

'**I recently took part** in my first 100-mile (160km) event; it was tough of course, but I arrived at the start line feeling strong and with no injuries. The last 12 miles (19km) were particularly challenging and mentally I lost it, BUT my body just kept going, one foot in front of the other, and I crossed that finish line! The most amazing thing, though, was my recovery in the days post-race; I was out walking, albeit very slowly, the next day with not too much trouble and with no injuries to speak of. Brilliant! After events in the past, before I introduced strength work into my routine, I have been in a much worse state before, during and after races, often turning up at the start line injured. This is just one experience that has proven to me the many benefits of strength work; it got me to the start line fit and ready, through the race to the finish and helped my recovery like nothing else!'

MELISSA MASON, COACH AT MAMA-MEL FITNESS, SPECIALISING IN PRE- AND POSTNATAL FITNESS, @MAMAMELFITNESS16

10-30-MINUTE STRENGTH ROUTINE FOR SPEED

IF YOU WANT SOMETHING a little more exciting than your usual interval session or hill reps to nudge you along that course a little faster than before, try these explosive plyometric moves. Warm up before you start (see p. 96). You can get through a few repetitions of each in about 10 minutes, building to a 30-minute session with the full recommended sets and repetitions. Do these once or twice a week for a stronger, faster performance, better balance, protection from injuries and a quicker recovery.

WHAT IS PLYOMETRICS?

Plyometrics is basically a posh word for jumping around, which is super fun to do on your own in the garden, in a running group and especially with kids (and it tires them out too!). You build strength and speed with each quick, powerful jump. Good form and balance are more important than how far or high you jump, and you should aim to land in a soft, controlled manner each time. Shouting the word, 'Boing!' has also been scientifically proven to make you jump higher…

Ankles and feet
HOP AROUND THE CLOCK
Imagine a large clock face on the ground and carefully hop on one foot, in a controlled manner from numbers 12 to 3, to 6, to 9. Change to the other leg and repeat. Vary from clockwise to anticlockwise. Get a friend or your kid to shout the numbers out at random and hop onto the corresponding spot. Doing this barefooted on soft, uneven ground promotes proprioception further. Start with 3 rounds of the clock on each leg, and build to 3 x 5 repetitions.

Calves and shins
SKIPPING
Steal your kid's skipping rope if it's long enough or find an old washing line in the garage and skip for 30–60 seconds. Once you remember how to skip and feel coordinated enough, make this harder by continuously propelling the rope round and jumping faster, rather than doing the easier jump, stop rope, go again, jump, stop rope, go again motion. Start with 30 seconds of continuous skipping, then aim for 5 x 60 seconds with 30 seconds of rest between each set.

Quads and hamstrings
JUMP SQUATS
Stand with your feet shoulder-width apart. Bend both knees and stick your bum out, keeping your back straight, to lower into a squat. Jump up as high as you can, driving your arms upwards for propulsion. As you land, sink back down into the squat position. Make it harder by travelling forwards as well as jumping upwards; jump as far as you can across the room or garden, using your arms together to propel you forwards. Start with 3 jumps, build to 3 x 12–15 repetitions.

Glutes and hip flexors
ALTERNATING SPLIT SQUAT JUMP
Stand with your feet hip-width apart. Step one leg back and bend through 90 degrees in each knee to sink down into a lunge position, knee hovering just above the ground. Jump up, driving upwards with your arms for balance and propulsion, swap the legs over in the air and sink down into a lunge on the opposite leg. Get your balance, go again. Try 6 initially on alternate legs, then increase to 3 x 12–16 repetitions.

Everything!
BOUNDING
Standing on one foot, leap forward with one leg outstretched as far as you can, in a bounding, running motion. Keep your eyes front, back straight and drive forwards with your arms; focus on a balletic movement and soft landing. Switch to the other foot and repeat. Try 6 bounds on alternate legs to begin with, then increase to 3 x 12–16 repetitions.

Arms and shoulders
SHOULDER-TAP PRESS-UPS
In the press-up position, toes on the floor, hands on the floor with straight arms under your shoulders, bend your arms to perform a regular press-up, but as you come up again, lean slightly to one side switching the weight to one hand while the other rises up to tap the opposite shoulder. Use a wider arm stance and/or take your weight on your knees instead of your feet to make this easier. Start with 8 on alternate arms, then move to 3 x 12–16 repetitions.

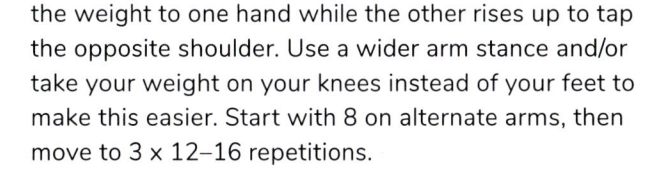

10-30-MINUTE STRENGTH ROUTINE FOR SPEED

WARM UP AND COOL DOWN

BEFORE A STEADY RUN, it's not essential to do any particular warm-up routine beyond starting at an easy pace. For speedwork or hill reps, you need to prepare your body for the intense exercise to come, so an easy couple of miles' jog or cycle to the start of the hill and back again is best for performance and injury prevention.

Before strength work, however, warm up with a combination of pulse-raising jogging on the spot and these mobilisation moves to prepare the joints and limbs for resistance training. After a run, it's advisable to walk briskly for a few minutes then do a few of the stretches on p. 101 to cool down more effectively than sitting straight down at a desk or driving a car for example. This will reduce your chances of injury and boost your recovery time.

1 Heel kicks
Place the back of your hands on your butt cheeks and kick your heels up to meet them.

2 Knee raises
Put your hands out in front, palms down, and raise your knees up high, to 90 degrees if you can, to meet them.

3 Leg swings
Stand with your feet shoulder-width apart and hold a wall for balance if needed, while you swing one leg outwards to the side then inwards across the body in a controlled manner. Then swap legs.

4. Shoulder rolls and shrugs
Roll your shoulders forwards and backwards at the same time and alternate directions. Then shrug them up and down.

5. Arm circles
Circle your arms one at a time forwards and backwards, then together, if this works for you.

6. All fours ad lib
On all fours, move your body around however feels best, paying attention to any areas that feel tight and in need of waking up. You might arch and lower your back, bend at the elbows, move your head up and down or move into downward dog for a stretch of the legs.

GOOD TO KNOW
WHY BOTHER WARMING UP?

Your muscles are a bit like Blu Tack. Imagine taking some Blu Tack straight from the fridge and trying to stretch it. What happens? It snaps. Now mould it in your hands, letting it get warm and pliable, then stretch it. Stretches like a dream! No snapping. Think of your muscles in the same way before strength training and you will never miss your warm-up again.

WARM UP AND COOL DOWN

STRENGTH YOGA AND PILATES

YOGA AND/OR PILATES is absolutely brilliant for ultra runners, as both can improve your balance and co-ordination, strength, flexibility and range of movement. Try this dedicated running strength Pilates routine to improve your ultra agility, balance and endurance.

Arabesque balance

WHY? Works on balance and the whole of the leg chain, increasing strength to help prevent shin, plantar and Achilles pain.

DO IT Stand tall with your feet hip-width apart. Lift one leg slightly off the ground while maintaining a slight bend in the standing leg. Hinge forwards at the hips, lowering your upper body and extending the lifted leg straight out behind you. Keep your back straight and stomach pulled in throughout, arms out for balance if needed. Slowly lower your torso until your upper body and lifted leg are parallel to the ground, then return to the start position. Repeat slowly 5 times, then swap legs. Hold a weight in your hands to make this harder.

Superman

WHY? Boosts your core strength for better running economy for longer.

DO IT Get on your hands and knees, hands directly under shoulders, knees under hips. Keep your stomach pulled in to engage your core, and keep your back in a neutral, straight position. Steadily extend your right arm straight out in front of you at the same time as you extend the left leg out behind you, both limbs parallel to the ground. Engage your glutes, keep your hip and back level without arching, twisting or sagging, gaze directed downwards, and hold for 3–5 seconds. Return the hand and knee to the floor. Repeat slowly 5 times, then swap limbs. Hold a weight in your extended hand to make this harder.

Side plank leg raise

WHY? This move especially helps if you experience back pain when running, walking or standing for a long time.

DO IT Lie on your side, propped up on one forearm, elbow directly under the shoulder. Stack your legs on top of each other and lift your hips off the ground, creating a straight, diagonal line from head to feet. Engage your core, pelvic floor and glute muscles for balance. How? Pull in your stomach, stop yourself going for a pee, stop yourself farting, clench your butt. Hold for 20–30 seconds. Once you have this move dialled in, add 5 hip dips and 5 leg lifts. Repeat on the other side.

Glute clam

WHY? Activates the gluteus medius butt muscle, which can switch off from sitting down for long periods of time.

DO IT Lie on your side, legs stacked on top of one another, knees bent to form a right angle in front, heels in line with your bum. Slowly lift the top knee, keeping the feet together, in a slow and controlled movement, engaging the hips and upper buttock muscles. Repeat 5–10 times until you feel a burn in your glute (bum) muscles. If you can do more than 5–10 of these, you are doing the move wrong and using the leg muscles instead of the glutes to lift; focus on engaging the glutes by putting your hand on your bum and feeling as the muscle activates. Switch sides. Make these harder by using a resistance band just above the knees.

EXPERT ADVICE
MORE EFFICIENT TECHNIQUE

'We often always concentrate most on training our engine – the heart, legs and lungs that power us along – but actually, technique has a massive part to play in creating more efficient movement so we can run faster for longer. It's worth getting your running technique analysed by a specialist, but most of us can improve with these three simple adjustments:

1 Keep the head up, eyes on the horizon rather than hunching over
2 Run with shorter, quicker strides for a higher cadence, around 175–185 steps per minute. Watch the cadence film on Wild Ginger Running YouTube channel for a demo.
3 Land with your whole foot rather than the mid-foot or the heel by thinking tall and striking the ground with your foot under your hip rather than ahead of your body.'

RUNNING MOVEMENT SPECIALIST AND AUTHOR OF *THE LOST ART OF RUNNING*, SHANE BENZIE.

STRENGTH YOGA AND PILATES

Hip opener

WHY? Gets the hips moving more freely and increases range of motion, important when running longer distances.

DO IT Start in a press-up position, hands shoulder-width apart. Step your right foot forwards, placing it outside your right hand. Lower your left knee to the ground, keeping your right foot flat on the floor. Rotate your upper body to the right, reaching your right arm upwards. Keep your stomach held in, breathe deeply to relax into the stretch and hold it for 3–5 seconds. Repeat on the other side. Alternate until you've done 5 on each side.

Inchworm

WHY? Builds strength in the core, chest, shoulders and arms to improve your endurance when using poles and carrying a heavier running pack.

DO IT Stand up tall, hinge from the hips, with a slight bend at the knees if needed, and reach your hands down to the floor. Walk your hands forwards as far as you can into a plank position with straight arms, keeping your back straight and stomach pulled in to engage the abs. Hold this position for 3–5 seconds before walking your hands back to your feet. Repeat 10 times.

> '*Pilates wakes up any muscles that tend to become weak and lazy, which is great because a stronger body also helps us run more efficiently over longer distances.*'
>
> EOIN EVERARD FROM EVERARD PILATES

ULTRA STRETCHING ROUTINE

IMPROVE YOUR BALANCE and range of motion with these stretches after any strength workout or run. You can also do them lounging around in front of the TV, on and off while minding the kids or a bit at a time during breaks at work. If you're doing them from cold (i.e. not warmed up from prior exercising), start off with gentle mobilisation movements to warm up the body first.

GOOD TO KNOW
HOW LONG TO HOLD?

It's really beneficial to hold each of these stretches for at least 30 seconds or longer if you have time. This allows the muscles time to relax and ease into the stretch, and you may find that after holding for this time you can move further into a deeper stretch. Always move slowly and gently to avoid this, but if you start to feel pain or it's very uncomfortable, ease off immediately into a less intense stretch.

Calf stretch (back of the lower leg)

Stand on a step or stair. Move one foot back until the ball of the foot is on the edge, then dip the heel down to feel a stretch down the back of the lower leg. Repeat with the other foot.

Shin stretch (front of the lower leg)

Kneel down on a mat or carpet, bum on heels, feet pointed rather than flexed, hands on the floor for support where it's comfortable for you on each side. Lean gradually back, hinging at the hips, to intensify the stretch in the shins; move your hands back as you lean, for balance.

Hamstring stretch (back of the thigh)

Bend over with a straight back (don't bend that back) and see if you can touch your toes; if that's easy, place your hands on the floor. Feel the stretch down the back of your thighs. If you're tired, you can do this in a sitting position with your legs straight out in front of you: stretch your hands towards your toes, keeping your back straight.

Quad stretch (front of the thigh)

Stand on one leg, bend the other at the knee and hold your ankle behind your bum with the same-side hand; hold the wall if you start to wobble. Keep your thighs together and push your hips forwards to deepen the stretch down the front of your thigh, keeping a straight posture, shoulders up and back. Repeat on the other side. If you're tired, you can do this lying down on your side instead.

Hip flexor stretch (around the hips)

Stand with your feet hip-width apart and step one leg forwards. Drop your back knee down to the ground in a full lunge position, moving your front foot forwards or backwards, as needed, so your knee doesn't go over your toes. Keep your back straight, look up, then move your hips forwards to feel the stretch in the hips. Repeat on the other side.

Glute stretch (buttocks)

Stand tall; holding the wall for balance, slightly bend at the hips with a straight back, and grasp your right foot with your right hand, then place your ankle on top of your left knee. Stick your bum out, keep your back flat and bend your left knee to feel the stretch in your bum. Repeat on the other side. You can also do this lying on your back, if you're tired: bring your right foot over your bent left knee, thread your hands round the back of your left thigh and gently pull your legs towards your chest.

Abs stretch (stomach area)

Lie on your stomach and place your hands under your shoulders. Looking forwards, slowly push until your arms are straight; you should feel the stretch down the front of your body all the way to your hips.

Shoulder and back stretch
Clasp your hands together and push your arms straight out in front of your chest. Drop your head slowly downwards to feel a stretch in your upper back and shoulders. Slowly move your hands towards your feet, rounding your back, to feel the stretch travel down. Holding a weight can intensify this stretch, if you feel the need.

Shoulder and triceps stretch
Bring one arm across your chest and hold it with your other arm, drawing it into your body; you should feel the stretch mainly in the back of your arm but also in the shoulder area. Repeat with the other arm.

Chest and shoulder stretch
Clasp your hands together behind your back at the base, then lift up as far as you can without bending forward and push out your chest so you feel a stretch across your upper chest and shoulders. Drop your head to intensify the stretch.

Chest and bicep stretch
Place both hands behind your head and move your elbows backwards for a lovely underarm stretch that nicely opens up the chest. You can also do this in an office chair for stress release. Sway left and right to intensify the stretch on each side.

ULTRA STRETCHING ROUTINE 103

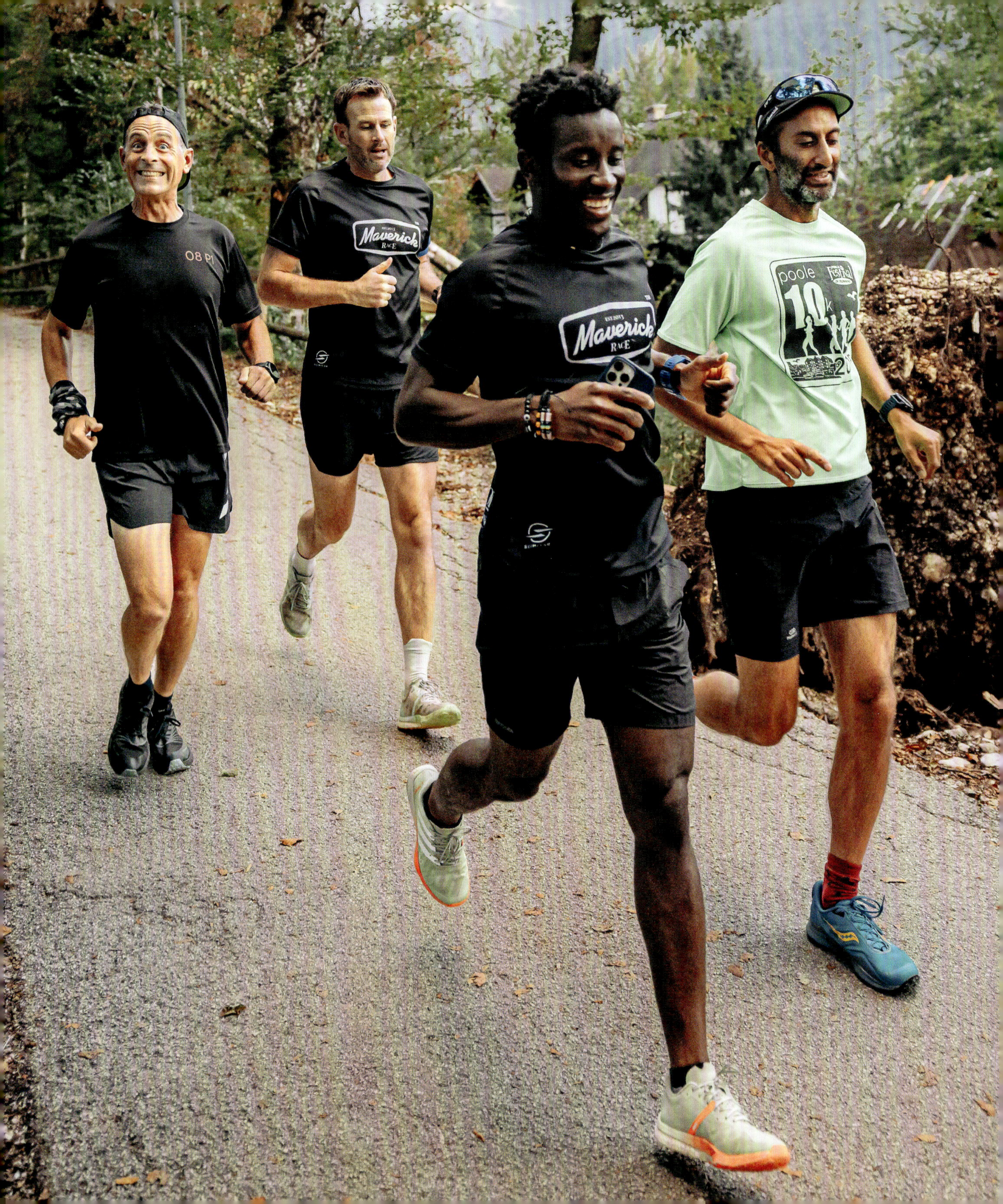
Maverick
RACE
Maverick
RACE
poole
10k

TRAINING PLANS

HERE YOU WILL FIND general training plans for 50k, 50-milers/100k and 100-milers. For each there's an 'Enjoy it' plan for beginners, the time poor and those just wanting to complete events in an enjoyable manner, and a 'Push it' plan for improvers and more experienced ultra runners looking to get faster, make races more of a challenge and push their limits.

> *To achieve your best and have a fulfilling season you need to decide how you want it to end and what you want to achieve over the course of the season. Remember, this should push your limits but not be impossible! What are three things you want to achieve over this season that will push you to the limit?*
>
> TIM PIGOTT, PHYSIO AND COACH FROM HP3 COACHING AND TEAM SCARPA ELITE ULTRA RUNNER, @TIMPIGOTTHP3

Multi-day training

For an undulating three-day multi-dayer just over the marathon distance each day, use the 50-mile/100k training plans. For anything more gruelling, use the 100-mile training plans. Refer to p. 65 for more multi-day advice and preparation.

Caveat

The variation between ultras is vast, so it's impossible to provide a perfect training plan for each race and each runner here. These training plans are for undulating ultras on reasonably good trails. If you're heading to steep, rocky mountains, up the ante with the vert (amount of ascent) in each plan, and vice versa for flat, canal path or running track ultras.

Training plans explained

REST – Rest is an essential part of training, allowing your body to recover and build back up stronger with each week. If you feel tired, listen to your body and don't push it, not even with active recovery if you feel completely drained. Eat nutritious, healthy food, hydrate and wait for your energy levels to start to come back.

SESSION WORDING – If the session says '1 hr easy, incl. 2 x 10-min tempo efforts', it means run mainly at an easy pace during this hour-long session, apart from doing two tempo efforts of 10 minutes each during the middle. It doesn't mean one hour of easy running followed by an additional two 10-minute tempo efforts.

EASY – Easy, recovery running effort. Able to talk in full sentences and breathe through only your nose. Feels very, very easy. Rate of perceived exertion (RPE): 1–4 out of 10. It should feel overly slow at first, and as you build fitness, you will be able to go faster for the same effort.

STEADY – Steady running effort. Able to talk in full sentences and breathe through only your nose. A pace you could maintain all day. RPE: 4–6 out of 10.

UPPER AEROBIC – A strong running effort but not breathless. Able to talk only in short sentences. A pace you could maintain for your fastest half marathon. RPE: 6–7 out of 10.

TEMPO – Hard running effort. Only able to say a few words at a time. Not comfortable. A pace you can only maintain for your fastest 5k or 10k. RPE: 7–8 out of 10.

MAX – Your maximum running effort. Very hard. Unable to talk. A pace you are able to maintain for only a minute or less. RPE: 9–10 out of 10.

STRIDES – These encourage a quicker leg turnover (rather than only plodding) and promote muscle strength without overloading the cardiovascular system. On flattish, smooth ground, run at a flat-out effort for 10–20 seconds, recover by dropping to a jog until your heart rate has dropped back down, then repeat. Do these in the middle or towards the end of your run so you are nice and warmed up.

HILL EFFORTS/REPS – If your goal race is hilly, make any upper aerobic or tempo efforts as uphill as you can. This doesn't have to be a sharp incline – a long, gentle slope is fine. After warming up by running a couple of miles or so to the base of a runnable hill (i.e. not so steep, muddy and rocky that you can't run quickly up it), run up for the time in the training plan, note where you get to, then jog back down, getting in control of your breathing. Stop at the bottom if needed, or turn straight around and go again, aiming to reach the same spot on each rep. Do these without wearing a running pack to reduce unnecessary impact at speed.

FARTLEK – Swedish for 'Speedplay', this is a loose effort session of running or cross-training according to how you feel – surging up a hill or to a certain tree, then easing off, playing around with the terrain and having fun pushing yourself and dropping back again.

MEET THE EXPERT

These training plans are based on ones supplied by Tim Pigott, director of HP3 Coaching. Tim is is a sports physio, university lecturer and endurance coach (pictured right) with 30+ years of race experience, including winning and setting records on 100km (62-mile) and 100-mile (160km) ultras. He has 20+ years of experience working with beginners right through to international and Olympic athletes from a multitude of sports. Tim is sponsored by Scarpa, Sidas, Precision Fuel & Hydration, and Supernatural Fuel. If you want more personalised training plans, workouts visible on your watch via connected apps, strength exercises specific to your weaknesses or a previous injury, tailor-made nutrition targets, technique tips and recovery advice connect with Tim via his website www.hp-3.co.uk
MORE TRAINING PLANS FROM TIM: WWW.TRAININGPEAKS.COM/COACH/TIMPIGOTT

ULTRA HACK

FITTING IT IN

The runs in these training plans don't necessarily have to be done all in one go. If needed during time-poor weeks, weave them into your day with a few miles here and there on errands or bobbing about with kids/dogs. Any extra walking you can add to these training plans is also a bonus, especially weighed down with a backpack slightly heavier (no more than 1-2kg) than your intended race pack.

STRENGTH – This is a VITAL workout for all ultra runners wanting to reduce the risk of injury, be strong and efficient over longer distances and recover quicker afterwards. Pick your moves from the strength routines (see pp. 90–95), follow a YouTube video and/or work on your own specific weaknesses in this session. If you don't have 30 minutes at a time, break it down into 10-minute sessions done throughout the day or across the week.

CROSS-TRAIN – This can be just brisk walking split up during the day, being active with kids and pets, swimming, biking, clog dancing, gardening – any other activity than running. It all counts.

LONG, STEADY RUN/HIKE – This is your longer, continuous, all-day type of effort at an easy, chatting pace – jog the flats and downs, hike the ups (with poles, if you plan to use them). Test out all your race gear and nutrition – fuelling the run/hike as you would your event. Carrying 1–2kg more than you plan to carry in your event also gives you a strength boost and will make race day feel a tad easier. Replicate race terrain as much as possible, so if you've signed up for a flat canal towpath event, off you go around the roads and canal paths avoiding any inclines; if your goal is a hilly, rocky ultra, seek out hills (or hill reps) and rocky trails. If you can recce the race or head closer to race terrain on your long run, then fantastic; if not, it can definitely be done with a lot of local hill reps and a good podcast for company. Make notes on your phone during your long run: food you fancied, food that didn't work, gear to swap or try, mental things that help, things to buy, spare things to pack.

TAPER – Before the race, these training plans reduce the intensity, duration and frequency of training to enable your body to recover for peak performance on race day.

ENJOY IT!
50K/30-MILE PLAN

WEEK	Mon	Tues	Wed	Thurs	Fri	Sat	Sun
1	Rest	1 hr easy, 4 strides	30 min strength	40 min easy	Rest	1 hr walk	1 hr 45 min long, steady run/hike
2	Rest	1 hr 10 min easy, 5 strides	30 min strength	1 hr 10 min easy	Rest	1 hr walk	1 hr 55 min long, steady run/hike
3	Rest	1 hr 10 min easy, 5 strides	30 min strength	1 hr 10 min easy, incl. 2 x 8-min upper aerobic efforts	Rest	1 hr walk	2 hr 15 min long, steady run/hike
4	Rest	40 min easy	30 min strength	40 min easy	Rest	1 hr walk	1 hr 20 min easy
5	Rest	1 hr 15 min easy, 6 strides	30 min strength	1 hr 10 min easy, incl. 2 x 10-min upper aerobic efforts	Rest	1 hr walk	2 hr 15 min long, steady run/hike
6	Rest	1 hr 10 min easy, 6 strides	30 min strength	1 hr 10 min easy, incl. 2 x 10-min upper aerobic efforts	Rest	1 hr walk	2 hr 40 min long, steady run/hike

This plan is for beginner ultra runners, the time poor, and joyful ultra runners/joggers/hikers just wanting to get round a 50k event. It builds on previous experience from road or trail half marathon and marathon fitness. With a minimum of only three runs (including one longer run/hike) and 30 minutes of strength work per week for three months, you can get fit enough to complete and enjoy a 50k ultra at a nice, steady pace. See *The Ultimate Trail Running Handbook* for shorter distance training plans.

WEEK	Mon	Tues	Wed	Thurs	Fri	Sat	Sun
7	Rest	40 min easy	30 min strength	40 min easy	Rest	1 hr walk	1 hr 20 min easy
8	Rest	1 hr 15 min, 6 strides	30 min strength	1 hr 10 min easy, incl. 2 x 10-min upper aerobic efforts	Rest	1 hr walk	2 hr 45 min long, steady run/hike
9	Rest	1 hr 20 min easy, 6 strides	30 min strength	1 hr 10 min easy, incl. 3 x 8-min upper aerobic efforts	Rest	1 hr walk	3 hr long, steady run/hike
10	Rest	45 min easy, 5 strides	30 min strength	1 hr 10 min easy, 4 strides	Rest	1 hr walk	1 hr 20 min long, steady run/hike
11	Rest	40 min easy	20 min strength	40 min easy	Rest	1 hr walk	1 hr 10 min long, steady run/hike
12	Rest	40 min easy, 4 strides	30 min walk	Rest	Rest		RACE WEEKEND!

ENJOY IT! 50K/30-MILE PLAN

PUSH IT!
50K/30-MILE PLAN

WEEK	Mon	Tues	Wed	Thurs	Fri	Sat	Sun
1	Rest	50 min easy (route with rolling hills)	30 min strength, 1 hr 30 min steady	35 min easy	Rest	30 min strength, 1 hr 10 min steady	1 hr 45 min steady
2	Rest	1 hr 10 min easy, incl. 5 x 10 sec strides	30 min strength, 1 hr 10 min steady	1 hr 10 min easy, incl. 2 x 8-min upper aerobic efforts	Rest	30 min strength, 1 hr 10 min steady	1 hr 55 min long, steady run/hike, incl. 3 x 8-min upper aerobic efforts
3	Rest	1 hr 10 min easy, incl. 6 x 10 sec strides	30 min strength, 1 hr 15 min steady	1 hr 10 min easy, incl. 2 x 8-min upper aerobic efforts	Rest	30 min strength, 1 hr 10 min steady	2 hr 15 min long, steady run/hike, incl. 3 x 8-min upper aerobic efforts
4	Rest	35 min easy	30 min strength, 40 min easy	35 min easy	Rest	30 min strength, 35 min easy	1 hr 20 min easy
5	Rest	1 hr 15 min easy, incl. 6 x 10 sec strides	30 min strength, 1 hr 40 min steady	1 hr 10 min easy, incl. 2 x 10-min upper aerobic efforts	Rest	30 min strength, 1 hr 20 min steady	2 hr 15 min long, steady run/hike, incl. 3 x 20 sec strides
6	Rest	1 hr 10 min easy, incl. 8 x 10 sec strides	30 min strength, 1 hr 40 min steady	1 hr 10 min easy, incl. 2 x 10-min upper aerobic efforts	Rest	30 min strength, 1 hr 20 min steady	2 hr 40 min steady, incl. 3 x 20 sec strides

This plan is for those familiar with the 50k distance who are looking to push themselves and improve upon a previous time for an undulating trail ultra. It builds on previous 50k experience on similar terrain and ascent to your goal race. For a mountain ultra with a lot of ascent, the upper aerobic work needs to be uphill, and the long run needs to be hilly and/or mountainous. Vice versa for a flat ultra. With five runs and 60 minutes of strength work per week for three months, you can get fit enough do your fastest 50k ultra yet.

WEEK	Mon	Tues	Wed	Thurs	Fri	Sat	Sun
7	Rest	35 min easy	30 min strength, 50 min steady	35 min easy	Rest	30 min strength, 35 min easy	1 hr 20 min easy
8	Rest	1 hr 15 min easy, incl. 8 x 10 sec strides	30 min strength, 1 hr 40 min steady	1 hr 10 min easy, incl. 2 x 10-min upper aerobic efforts	Rest	30 min strength, 1 hr 20 min easy	2 hr 40 min long, steady run/hike, incl. 3 x 30 sec strides
9	Rest	1 hr 20 min easy, incl. 10 x 10 sec strides	30 min strength, 1 hr 40 min steady	1 hr 10 min easy, incl. 3 x 8-min upper aerobic efforts	Rest	30 min strength, 1 hr 20 min easy	2 hr 40 min long, steady run/hike, incl. 3 x 30 sec strides
10	Rest	45 min easy, incl. 4 x 20 sec strides	30 min strength, 1 hr 40 min steady	1 hr 10 min easy, incl. 6 x sec strides	Rest	30 min strength, 1 hr 10 min steady	1 hr 20 min long, steady run/hike, incl. 6 x 30 sec strides
11	Rest	45 min easy, incl. 4 x 20 sec strides	30 min strength, 1 hr 10 min steady	35 min easy, incl. 6 x 30 sec strides	Rest	35 min easy	1 hr 10 min long, steady run/hike, incl. 6 x 30 sec strides
12	Rest	45 min easy, incl. 4 x 20 sec strides	1 hr 10 min steady	Rest	Rest	RACE WEEKEND!	

PUSH IT! 50K/30-MILE PLAN

ENJOY IT!
50-MILE/100K PLAN

WEEK	Mon	Tues	Wed	Thurs	Fri	Sat	Sun
1	Rest	1 hr easy, 6 strides	30 min strength, 30 min walk	1 hr 30 min easy, incl. 5 x 3-min tempo efforts	Rest or 1 hr cross-training	1 hr walk	2 hr long, steady run/hike
2	Rest	1 hr easy, 6 strides	30 min strength, 30 min walk	1 hr 30 min easy, incl. 5 x 3-min tempo efforts	Rest or 1 hr cross-training	1 hr walk	2 hr 15 min long, steady run/hike
3	Rest	1 hr easy, 6 strides	30 min strength, 30 min walk	1 hr 30 min easy, incl. 5x 3-min tempo efforts	Rest or 1 hr cross-training	1 hr walk	2 hr 30 min long, steady run/hike
4	Rest	1 hr easy	30 min strength, 30 min walk	1 hr 30 min steady	Rest	1 hr walk	2 hr long, steady run/hike
5	Rest	1 hr easy, 6 strides	30 min strength, 45 min walk	1 hr 30 min easy, incl. 5 x 4-min tempo efforts	Rest or 1 hr cross-training	1 hr walk	3 hr long, steady run/hike
6	Rest	1 hr easy, 6 strides	30 min strength, 45 min walk	1 hr 30 min easy, incl. 5 x 4-min tempo efforts	Rest or 1 hr cross-training	1 hr walk	3 hr 30 min long, steady run/hike
7	Rest	1 hr easy, 6 strides	30 min strength, 45 min walk	1 hr 30 min easy, incl. 5 x 4-min tempo efforts	Rest or 1 hr cross-training	1 hr walk	4 hr long, steady run/hike
8	Rest	1 hr easy	30 min strength, 30 min walk	1 hr 30 min steady	Rest	1 hr walk	2 hr long, steady run/hike

This plan is for first timers, the time poor and/or the joyful ultra runner/jogger/hiker just wanting to get round a 50-mile (80km) or 100km (62-mile) event. It builds on previous 30-mile/50k event experience. With a minimum of only three runs (including one longer run/hike) and 30 minutes of strength work per week for four months, you can get fit enough to complete and enjoy a 50-miler or 100k ultra at a nice, steady pace.

WEEK	Mon	Tues	Wed	Thurs	Fri	Sat	Sun
9	Rest	1 hr steady, 6 strides	30 min strength, 60 min walk	1 hr 30 min easy, incl. 5 x 5-min tempo efforts	Rest or 1 hr cross-training	1 hr walk	4 hr 30 min long, steady run/hike
10	Rest	1 hr steady, 6 strides	30 min strength, 60 min walk	1 hr 30 min easy, incl. 5 x 5-min tempo efforts	Rest or 1 hr cross-training	1 hr walk	5 hr long, steady run/hike
11	Rest	1 hr steady, 6 strides	30 min strength, 60 min walk	1 hr 30 min easy, incl. 5 x 5-min tempo efforts	Rest or 1 hr cross-training	1 hr walk	5 hr long, steady run/hike
12	rest	1 hr easy	30 min strength, 30 min walk	1 hr 30 min steady	Rest	1 hr walk	3 hr long, steady run/hike
13	Rest	1 hr easy, 6 strides	30 min strength, 30 min walk	1 hr 30 min easy, incl. 5 x 4-min tempo efforts	Rest or 1 hr cross-training	1 hr walk	3 hr long, steady run/hike
14	Rest	1 hr easy, 6 strides	30 min strength, 30 min walk	1 hr 30 min easy, incl. 3 x 2-min tempo efforts	Rest or 1 hr cross-training	1 hr walk	2 hr long, steady run/hike
15	Rest	1 hr easy, 6 strides	30 min walk	1 hr steady	Rest or 1 hr cross-training	1 hr walk	1 hr easy
16	Rest	30 min easy, 6 strides	Rest	30 min easy	30 min easy	RACE WEEKEND!	

PUSH IT!
50-MILE/100K PLAN

WEEK	Mon	Tues	Wed	Thurs	Fri	Sat	Sun
1	Rest	1 hr easy, 6 x 10 sec strides, 30 min strength	1 hr 30 min steady, incl. 3 x 6-min tempo efforts	1 hr easy, 6 x 10 sec strides	30 min strength	1 hr 30 min easy, incl. 6 x 5-min hill efforts	2 hr steady
2	Rest	1 hr easy, 8 x 10 sec strides, 30 min strength	1 hr 30 min steady, incl. 3 x 8-min tempo efforts	1 hr easy, 8 x 10 sec strides	1 hr easy cross training, 30 min strength	1 hr 30 min easy, incl. 7 x 5-min hill efforts	2 hr 30 min steady
3	Rest	1 hr easy, 10 x 10 sec strides, 30 min strength	1 hr 30 min steady, incl. 3 x 10-min tempo efforts	1 hr easy, 10 x 10 sec strides	1 hr easy cross training, 30 min strength	1 hr 30 min easy, incl. 8 x 5-min hill efforts	3 hr steady
4	Rest	45 min easy, 30 min strength	1 hr 30 min steady	45 min easy	Rest	1 hr 30 min easy, incl. 3 x 10-min tempo efforts	2 hr steady
5	Rest	1 hr 15 min easy, 6 x 20 sec strides, 30 min strength	1 hr 30 min steady, incl. 3 x 8-min tempo efforts	1 hr 15 min easy, 6 x 20 sec strides	1 hr easy cross training, 30 min strength	1 hr 30 min easy, incl. 3 x 8-min tempo efforts	3 hr steady
6	Rest	1 hr 15 min easy, 6 x 20 sec strides, 30 min strength	1 hr 30 min steady, incl. 2 x 15-min tempo efforts	1 hr 15 min easy	1 hr easy cross training, 30 min strength	2 hr easy, incl. 3 x 8-min tempo efforts	3 hr 30 min steady
7	Rest	1 hr steady, 30 min strength	1 hr 30 min easy, incl. 1 x 20-min tempo effort, 1 x 10-min tempo effort	1 hr 30 min steady	1 hr easy cross training, 30 min strength	2 hr easy, incl. 30-min tempo effort	4 hr steady
8	Rest	1 hr steady, 30 min strength	1 hr 30 min easy, incl. 2 x 20-min tempo efforts	1 hr steady	1 hr easy cross training, 30 min strength	4 hr 30 min long, steady run/hike	2 hr hilly, long, steady run/hike

114 3. PHYSICAL TRAINING

This plan is for those familiar with the 50-mile (80km) or 100km (62-mile) distance looking to push themselves and improve upon a previous time for an undulating trail ultra. It builds on previous 50-miler and/or 100k experience on similar terrain and ascent to your goal race. For a mountain ultra with a lot of ascent, the tempo work needs to be uphill, and the long run needs to be hilly and/or mountainous. Vice versa for a flat ultra. With five runs and a total of 60 minutes of strength work per week for four months, you can get fit enough do your fastest 50 miler or 100k ultra yet.

WEEK	Mon	Tues	Wed	Thurs	Fri	Sat	Sun
9	Rest	1 hr 30 min steady, 30 min strength	1 hr steady	1 hr 30 min easy, incl. 2 x 20-min tempo efforts	1 hr easy cross training, 30 min strength	2 hr easy, incl. 3 x 15-min tempo efforts	3 hr hilly, long, steady run/hike
10	Rest	1 hr 30 min steady, 30 min strength	1 hr 30 min easy, incl. 2 x 20-min tempo efforts	1 hr 30 min steady	1 hr easy cross training, 30 min strength	2 hr easy, incl. 20-min tempo effort	4 hr long, steady run/hike
11	Rest	1 hr steady, 30 min strength	A.M. – 1 hr easy P.M. – 1 hr easy	A.M. – 1 hr easy, P.M. – 1 hr easy, incl. 20 min continuous uphill	1 hr easy cross training, 30 min strength	Trail marathon steady – event or own test of nutrition & kit	2 hr 30 min long, steady run/hike
12	Rest	1 hr easy, 10 x 10 sec strides, 30 min strength	1 hr 30 min steady	1 hr 30 min easy, incl. 2 x 20-min tempo efforts	1 hr easy cross training, 30 min strength	2 hr easy, incl. 2 x 20-min tempo efforts	3 hr long, steady run/hike
13	Rest	1 hr easy, 10 x 20 sec strides, 30 min strength	1 hr 15 min steady	1 hr 30 min easy, incl. 2 x 20-min tempo efforts	1 hr easy cross training, 30 min strength	5 hr long, steady run/hike - test out all race kit	3 hr long, steady run/hike
14	Rest	1 hr easy, 10 x 30 sec strides, 30 min strength	1 hr easy	1 hr 30 min easy, incl. 30-min tempo effort	1 hr easy cross training, 30 min strength	3 hr long, steady run/hike with finalised race kit	3 hr long, steady run/hike
15	Rest	1 hr easy, 10 x 30 sec strides, 30 min strength	1 hr 15 min steady	1 hr easy	Rest	1 hr 30 min steady	1 hr steady
16	Rest	1 hr easy, incl. 2 x 10-min tempo efforts	30 min easy	Rest or 30 min walk or easy run	Rest or 30 min walk or easy run	RACE WEEKEND!	

PUSH IT! 50-MILE/100K PLAN

ENJOY IT!
100-MILE PLAN

WEEK	Mon	Tues	Wed	Thurs	Fri	Sat	Sun
1	Rest	1 hr easy, 6 strides	30 min strength, 30 min walking	1 hr easy	30 min strength, 60 min easy cross training	1 hr 30 min steady	1 hr long, steady run/hike
2	Rest	1 hr easy, 6 strides	30 min strength, 30 min walking	1 hr easy	30 min strength, 60 min easy cross training	1 hr 45 min steady	2 hr long, steady run/hike
3	Rest	1 hr easy, 6 strides	30 min strength, 30 min walking	1 hr easy	30 min strength, 60 min easy cross training	2 hr steady	3 hr long, steady run/hike
4	Rest	45 min easy	30 min strength, 30 min walking	45 min easy	Rest	1 hr 30 min steady	2 hr long, steady run/hike
5	Rest	1 hr easy, 6 strides	30 min strength, 45 min walking	1 hr easy	30 min strength, 60 min easy cross training	2 hr steady	3 hr long, steady run/hike
6	Rest	1 hr 15 min steady, 6 strides	30 min strength, 45 min walking	1 hr easy, incl. 8 x 60-sec max efforts	30 min strength, 60 min easy cross training	2 hr 20 min steady	3 hr 30 min long, steady run/hike
7	Rest	1 hr 30 min steady, 6 strides	30 min strength, 45 min walking	1 hr 10 min easy, incl. 6 x 90-sec max efforts & 5 x 60-sec hill efforts	30 min strength, 60 min easy cross training	2 hr 40 min steady	4 hr long, steady run/hike
8	Rest	1 hr easy	30 min strength, 30 min walking	1 hr easy, incl. 10 x 60-sec max efforts	30 min strength, 60 min Fartlek cross training	3 hr steady	2 hr long, steady run/hike

116   3. PHYSICAL TRAINING

This plan is ideal for first timers, and the time poor and/or the joyful ultra runner/jogger/hiker just wanting to get round a 100-mile (160km) event. It builds on previous 50-mile (80km) and 100k (62-mile) event experience. With four running days and a total of 60 minutes of strength work per week for four months, you can get fit enough to complete and 'enjoy' an 'easy' 100-mile ultra with generous cut offs at a nice, steady pace. Adjust the long run according to the demands of the course – for example, for a mountain 100-miler, more vertical gain is required, and vice versa.

WEEK	Mon	Tues	Wed	Thurs	Fri	Sat	Sun
9	Rest	1 hr 30 min steady, 6 strides	30 min strength, 60 min walking	A.M. – 1 hr easy P.M. – 1 hr 30 min steady	30 min strength	3 hr 30 min run/hike	3 hr long, steady run/hike
10	Rest	1 hr 30 min steady, 6 strides	30 min strength, 60 min walking	A.M. – 1 hr easy P.M. – 1 hr 15 min easy, incl. 8 x 2-min hill efforts	30 min strength, 60 min Fartlek cross training	3 hr steady, incl. 20 min tempo effort	4 hr long, steady run/hike
11	Rest	1 hr 30 min steady, 6 strides	30 min strength, 60 min walking	A.M. – 1 hr easy P.M. – 1 hr 20 min easy, incl. 8 x 5-min hill efforts	Rest	Trail marathon steady – event or own test of nutrition & kit	3 hr long, steady run/hike finalising race kit
12	Rest	1 hr 30 min easy	30 min strength, 30 min walking	1 hr 10 min easy, incl. 6 x 3-min hill efforts	1 hr easy	2 hr easy, incl. 3 x 10-min tempo efforts up 3 big hills	2 hr long, steady run/hike
13	Rest	2 hr steady, 6 strides	30 min strength, 30 min walking	A.M. – 1 hr easy P.M. – 1 hr 20 min easy, incl. 8 x 5-min hill efforts	Rest	30-mile (50km) long, steady run/hike	3 hr long, steady run/hike with all race kit
14	Rest	1 hr easy	30 min strength, 30 min walking	A.M. – 1 hr easy P.M. – 1 hr 10 min easy, incl. 6 x 3-min hill efforts	Rest	3 hr 30 min steady with all race kit	2 hr long, steady run/hike with all race kit
15	Rest	1 hr 20 min steady	30 min walking	1 hr easy	45 min steady	1 hr steady with all race kit	1 hr long, steady run/hike with all race kit
16	Rest	1 hr easy, 6 strides	Rest	30 min easy, 4 strides	Rest	RACE WEEKEND!	

ENJOY IT! 100-MILE PLAN

PUSH IT!
100-MILE PLAN

WEEK	Mon	Tues	Wed	Thurs	Fri	Sat	Sun
1	Rest	1 hr easy, 6 x 10 sec strides, 30 min strength	45 min easy – focus on fast cadence	1 hr easy, 6 x 10 sec strides	30 min strength, 60 min steady cross training	2 hr steady	1 hr long, steady run/hike with race kit
2	Rest	1 hr easy, 8 x 10 sec strides, 30 min strength	45 min easy – focus on fast cadence	1 hr easy, 8 x 10 sec strides	30 min strength, 60 min steady cross training	2 hr 20 min steady	2 hr long, steady run/hike with race kit
3	Rest	1 hr easy, 10 x 10 sec strides, 30 min strength	45 min easy – focus on fast cadence	1 hr easy, 10 x 10 sec strides	30 min strength, 60 min steady cross training	2 hr 40 min steady	3 hr long, steady run/hike with race kit
4	Rest	45 min easy	45 min easy – focus on technique	45 min easy	Rest	2 hr steady	2 hr long, steady run/hike with race kit
5	Rest	1 hr 15 min easy, 6 x 20 sec strides, 30 min strength	1 hr easy – focus on technique	1 hr 15 min easy, 6 x 20 sec strides	30 min strength, 60 min steady cross training	3 hr steady	3 hr long, steady run/hike with race kit
6	Rest	1 hr 15 min easy, 6 x 20-sec strides, 30 min strength	1 hr 5 min easy, incl. 8 x 60 sec fast with 2 min easy recovery	1 hr 15 min easy	30 min strength, 60 min steady cross training	3 hr 15 min steady	2 hr long, steady run/hike with race kit
7	Rest	1 hr 30 min steady, 30 min strength	1 hr easy, incl. 10 x 60 sec fast with 60 sec easy recovery	1 hr 30 min steady	30 min strength, 60 min steady cross training	3 hr 30 min steady	2 hr 30 min long, steady run/hike with race kit
8	Rest	1 hr 30 min steady, 30 min strength	1 hr 5 min easy, incl. 8 x 2-min hill efforts	1 hr 30 min steady	30 min strength, 60 min Fartlek cross training	3 hr steady	3 hr long, steady run/hike with race kit

118 3. PHYSICAL TRAINING

This plan is for those familiar with 80–100-mile (129–160km) events looking to push themselves and improve upon a previous time for an undulating trail ultra. It builds on previous 50–100-mile experience on similar terrain and ascent to your goal race. For a mountain ultra with a lot of ascent, the tempo work should be uphill, and the long, steady run/hikes need to be hilly and/or mountainous. Vice versa for a flat ultra. With five running days and a total of 60 minutes of strength work per week for four months, you can get fit enough do your fastest 100-mile ultra yet.

WEEK	Mon	Tues	Wed	Thurs	Fri	Sat	Sun
9	Rest	1 hr 30 min steady, 30 min strength	A.M. – 1 hr easy P.M. – 1 hr 30 min steady	1 hr 30 min steady, 30 min strength	Rest	4 hr long, steady run/hike with race kit	2 hr long, steady run/hike with race kit
10	Rest	1 hr 30 min steady, 30 min strength	A.M. – 1 hr easy P.M. – 1 hr 15 min easy, incl. 10 x 2-min hill efforts	1 hr 30 min steady	30 min strength, 60 min Fartlek cross training	3 hr easy, incl. 20-min tempo effort	3 hr long, steady run/hike with race kit
11	Rest	1 hr 30 min steady, 30 min strength	A.M. – 1 hr easy P.M. – 1 hr 20 min easy, incl. 8 x 5-min hill efforts	A.M. – 1 hr easy P.M. – 1 hr easy, incl. 20-min continual hill climb	Rest	Trail marathon steady – event or own test of nutrition & kit	5 hr long, steady run/hike with race kit
12	Rest	1 hr 30 min steady, 30 min strength	1 hr 10 min easy, incl. 6 x 3-min hill efforts	1 hr 30 min steady, incl. 30-min continual hill climb	30 min strength, 60 min Fartlek cross training	3 hr easy, incl. 3 x 20-min tempo efforts up 3 big hills	5 hr long, steady run/hike with race kit
13	Rest	2 hr steady, 30 min strength	A.M. – 1 hr easy P.M. – 1 hr 20 min easy, incl. 8 x 5-min hill efforts	A.M. – 1 hr easy P.M. – 1 hr easy, incl. 30-min continual hill climb	Rest	30-mile (50km) test run – replicate course conditions	4 hr long, steady run/hike with race kit
14	Rest	1 hr 30 min easy, 30 min strength	A.M. – 1 hr easy P.M. – 1 hr 10 min easy, incl. 6 x 3-min hill efforts	2 hr steady	30 min strength, 60 min Fartlek cross training	3 hr 30 min steady run with race kit	2 hr long, steady run/hike with race kit
15	Rest	1 hr 20 min steady, 30 min strength	2 hr easy, incl. 3 x 10 min tempo efforts	1 hr easy	Rest	2 hr long, steady run/hike with race kit	1 hr long, steady run/hike with race kit
16	Rest	50 min easy, incl. 2 x 10-min tempo efforts	40 min easy, incl. 6 x 20 sec strides	Rest	30 min walk or easy run	RACE WEEKEND!	

PUSH IT! 100-MILE PLAN

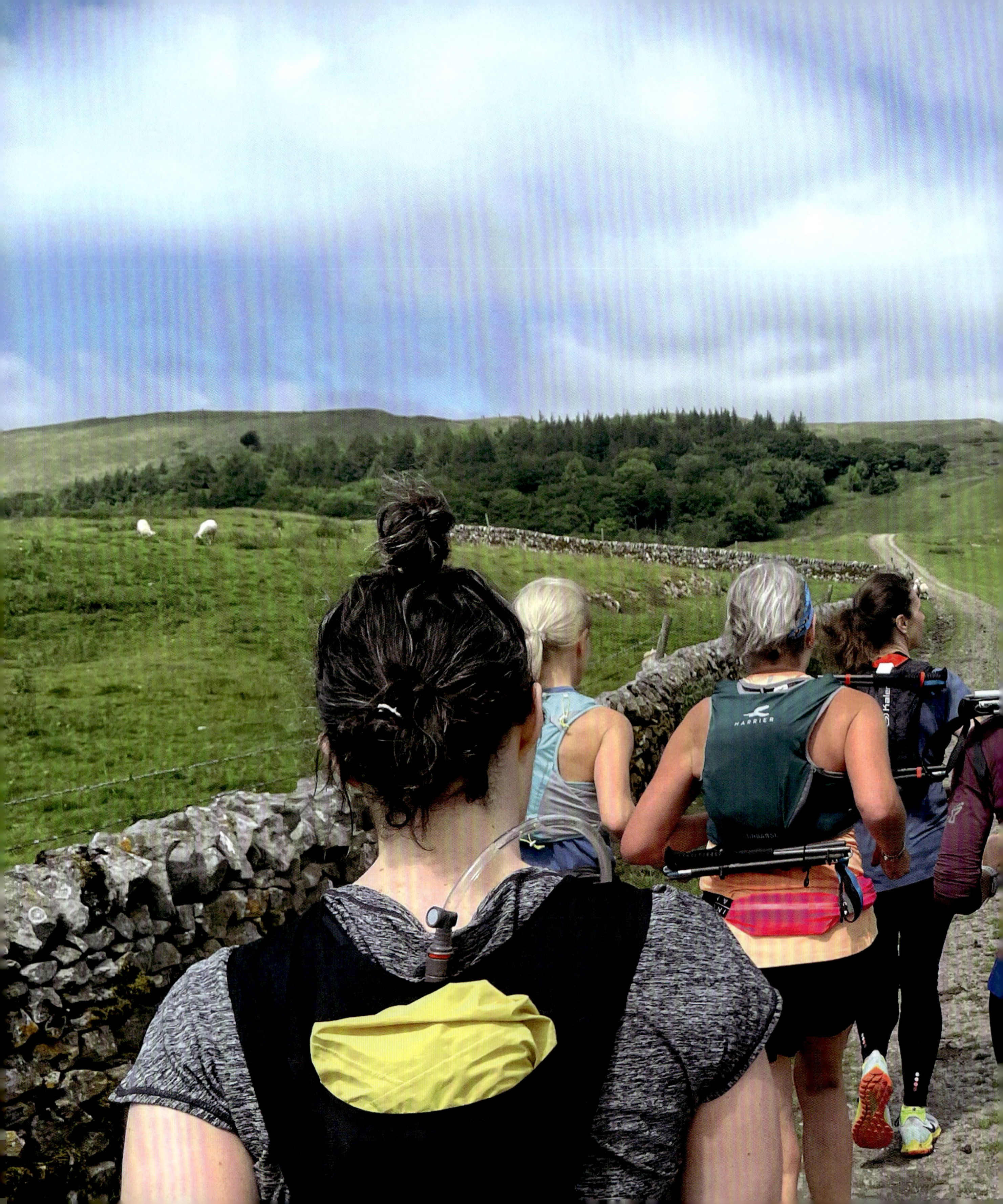
HARRIER

4

NUTRITION AND HYDRATION

What you put inside your body can have a tremendous impact on your enjoyment and performance on ultras. Here's what to eat when and why, and plenty of tasty, real food snack ideas.

FOOD MADE SIMPLE

ULTRA RUNNERS NEED TO EAT or drink high-sugar snacks during longer training runs and ultra events. We also need to have enough carbohydrate, fat, protein, vitamins and minerals in our diets to cope with the demands of weekly training. Paying attention to where that nutrition comes from and aiming to eat good-quality food will help your body build and recover in the best-possible way.

In a massive nutshell, eating healthily for ultra runners means eating nutrient-dense carbohydrates like oats, rice, sweet potatoes, beans and lentils; including lots of different coloured vegetables and dark, leafy greens; eating lean protein like fish, chicken and pulses; and having 'healthy' fats like avocado, nuts and cheese. In this section Dr. Howard Hurst explains nutrition in terms of ultra running.

MEET THE EXPERT
DR. HOWARD HURST

Ultra runner and triathlete Dr. Howard Hurst is director of and performance nutritionist at Proform Sport Science and a senior lecturer in Sport, Exercise and Nutritional Sciences at the University of Central Lancashire. He is the author of *Nutrition for Junior Athletes: A Practical Guide for Parents and Coaches*. He works with athletes and teams from beginner to professional level, including elite and amateur and ultramarathon runners.

WWW.PROFORMSPORTSCIENCE.CO.UK, @PROFORMSPORTSCIENCE

Carbohydrates

ARE CARBS EVIL?

Due to recent diet trends involving 'cutting out carbs' or 'going zero carb', many people have been encouraged to view this food group as the enemy and mistakenly assume it consists of only beige items like bread, pastry, potatoes, rice, pasta, biscuits and cakes. In truth carbohydrates are not evil, they're actually essential to ultra runners, especially in their high-density, portable forms – for example gels, jelly babies and energy drinks, both before the race to make sure your stocks are full and during the race itself. Carbs are sugars, starches and fibre that naturally occur in a huge variety of foods from bread, rice and pasta to fruit and vegetables. Only meat, fish, seafood and oils contain zero carbs – there are even very low amounts in cheese, eggs and butter. No food group or its sub-groups are inherently bad for us, it's overconsumption that is the problem. So if you want to treat yourself to a cake, go for it, just don't make it a daily habit. Scientific research shows it's damaging to the body and immune system to completely cut out carbs long term and a low carb high fat (LCHF) diet isn't recommended for ultra runners (see p. 128 for more information).

HOW MUCH CARBOHYDRATE DO ULTRA RUNNERS NEED?

As a general rule of thumb, according to Dr. Howard, ultra runners typically need a carb intake of 3–12g/kg/day (or 60–70 per cent of total energy intake) depending upon training volume and intensity, and an intake of 30–110g/hr (1–3 1/2oz/hr) during events. Studies have shown the upper end of this range to be more beneficial; however, sufficient time during training to practice higher intake is needed to train the gut and reduce the risk of gastrointestinal issues such as bloating, stomach cramps and diarrhoea come race day.

ULTRA HACK

PROTECT YOUR TEETH

We're all used to thinking about the effect of sugars on our energy levels and overall nutritional health, but ultra runners also need to be aware of the damaging effects of sugary drinks, snacks and things that stick in the teeth (like crisps and biscuits) during long training runs and races. A small toothbrush and travel-sized toothpaste in a pocket or drop bag is great for preventing tooth-decay and mouth ulcers, and it can really refresh you, too.

Protein

DO ULTRA RUNNERS NEED PROTEIN SUPPLEMENTS?

No, humans in general don't need huge amounts of protein, even for ultra running, so you can get everything you need from real food. Unless your everyday diet is severely limited or you're pushed for time on certain days, you don't need to use protein supplements. However, things like protein bars and shakes can come in handy at events, as you'll see in the next section.

DO VEGAN ULTRA RUNNERS NEED PROTEIN SUPPLEMENTS?

No, it's perfectly possible to get all eight essential amino acids from quinoa, soya beans and hemp seeds and by combining a varied range of plant proteins, including lentils, beans, peas, tofu, nuts, seeds, seaweeds and wholegrains like porridge oats, if consumed in the right amounts. Vegan runners may need to eat larger portions of these items to consume the same amount of calories and protein.

HOW MUCH PROTEIN DO ULTRA RUNNERS NEED?

Protein helps to build and repair muscles and body tissues and it's found in meat, fish, sea food, eggs, pulses, grains, beans, peas, lentils, nuts, seeds, dairy products and seaweeds (soya beans, hemp seeds and quinoa are good sources for vegans). How much you need per day depends on your bodyweight and training load, but based on most data on well-trained and elite ultra runners, daily protein intake should be 1.6–2g of protein per kg of bodyweight. So that's 104–130g (3½–4½oz) for a 65kg (143lb) runner, divided fairly equally between meals. However, during periods of very intense training they may need 2.5g/kg. If you mainly bob along slowly, use the lower end of this range, but if you do a lot of speedwork and strength training and enjoy pushing your body to its limits, use the higher end. During events, ultra runners should aim to eat 5–19g/hr (¼–⅝oz/hr) because during prolonged endurance activity protein metabolism can range between 2 and 10 per cent of total energy expenditure. For ultra runners aged over 65, add on 0.4g per kg of bodyweight, as your body reduces its ability to take in protein as efficiently as you age.

WHAT IF I EAT TOO MUCH PROTEIN?

If you eat more protein than your body needs, it's not harmful to normally healthy runners; it's simply broken down and used as a source of energy. Protein also helps you feel satisfied and fuller for longer, so it's a great snack option, but take on more carbs pre-race, as too much protein may reduce carb intake due to its satiating effect.

FOODS CONTAINING ABOUT 10G (3/8OZ) OF PROTEIN

- 2 medium eggs
- 50g (1 ¾oz) fish
- 25g (1oz) cheese
- 125g (4 ½oz) Greek yoghurt
- 300ml (10fl oz) milk
- 40g (1 ½oz) chicken
- 40g (1 ½oz) steak
- 100g (3 ½oz) tofu
- 200g (7oz) quinoa
- 50g (1 ¾oz) nuts
- 25g (1oz) peanut butter

Fat

IS FAT BAD FOR ULTRA RUNNERS?

Fat has a bad rep, but the short answer is definitely no. The right kind is essential for good health and ultra running. It's a fuel source, it contains omega-3 and omega-6 (vital fatty acids that can't be made inside the body), it's part of every cell membrane including brain tissue, it transports vitamins A, D, E and K in the bloodstream and it helps make the hormones oestrogen and testosterone for healthy menstrual function. Fat is also a natural insulator – handy on cold-weather ultras but less so in hot conditions. Eating good fats (unsaturated or HDL) means chowing down on nuts, nut butters, seeds, avocados, eggs and oily fish and drizzling your many and plentiful salads with olive or rapeseed oil dressings (such as Oh-Mega home-made dressing, see p. 141).

'NOT AS GOOD' FATS?

It's unhelpful to demonise these by calling them 'bad', but fat sources to eat less of include saturated and trans fats. Saturated fat examples are red meat, butter, lard (who eats lard?), cheese, coconut oil and palm oil, which bring a higher risk of heart disease, high blood pressure and cancer. Trans fat sources to eat less of are mainly found in processed food like anything fried, margarine, commercially baked goods like cakes, biscuits and donuts, chips (as in fries), pies and frozen pizza (darnit, pizza is my favourite ultra running savoury food...).

HOW MUCH FAT DO ULTRA RUNNERS NEED?

Nutritional guidance currently advises that fats should contribute about 25 per cent of total daily nutritional intake to support repeated bouts of endurance training. This equates to around 1–1.5g/kg per day, though heavier runners may require up to 2g/kg to ensure total caloric needs are met. The science is clear that it's best to eat mostly unsaturated fats rather than saturated or trans fats.

DO I NEED SUPPLEMENTS?

Most ultra runners can get all the vitamins, minerals and phytochemicals they need by eating a healthy, balanced diet rich in different coloured fruits and vegetables without taking supplements. However, if you're pregnant or trying to conceive, a folic acid supplement is recommended to help prevent brain and spine problems like spina bifida. Current NHS guidance also advises a Vitamin D supplement for people in the UK during the autumn and winter due to a lack of sunlight, especially if you have dark skin or clothing over most of your skin outside.

ULTRA HACK

CUT DOWN ON JUNK BY EATING LIKE AN ANIMAL

I'm not talking about the carnivore diet here, but thinking of yourself as an animal in the wild is an easy way to make healthier food choices. For example, most of us with half a brain would not feed a chimpanzee a chocolate bar or cake washed down with a can of Coke and not expect it to bounce off the walls, then crash when the sugar spike is over, so why do this ourselves? Being aware of this can help you choose natural food over tempting junk. Prepare carrot and cucumber batons to snack on before you get too hungry to make good choices, have the fruit bowl well stocked and simply don't buy any unhealthy snacks that you don't want to be tempted by.

NUTRITION MYTHS BUSTED

SOCIAL MEDIA AND THE DIET/wellness industry has a lot to answer for here, as that's where we get bombarded and bamboozled with the latest diet trends. Yet the very boring fact is that basic, healthy food advice doesn't change much (see previous section), but here are some commonly held nutrition myths we can bust for runners:

Losing weight will make me run faster
Not necessarily. Eating well combined with sensible training, including strength and speedwork, will produce the best results for running faster, not losing weight. Simply 'being lighter' does not translate directly into increased muscular strength or cardiovascular fitness, so you're better off working towards those goals and eating healthily rather than worrying about what it says on the scales. Unless you're hugely overweight (a risk to your general health), for ultra running there are so many other aspects that are far more important to speed and overall success, like strength training, staying injury-free, looking after your feet, knowing how to use your kit, fuelling right, being efficient in aid stations and not getting lost. However, if you are concerned about being genuinely overweight, weight loss (from fat) should not be more than 500g (1lb 1oz) per week. Any more and this is less sustainable and may lead to too much energy and muscle loss. With a healthy, nutritious diet and not overeating, fat loss (and therefore weight loss) will happen slowly and naturally.

You have to be skinny to have RED-S
This stands for 'relative energy deficiency in sport' and refers to a long-term calorie deficit that can affect all sports people of any age, level and bodyweight. It can happen accidentally when ultra runners underestimate their energy needs and restrict fuel consumption while still pushing their bodies hard during training. This leads to a reduction in performance, lower energy levels, a sub-optimal immune system, low bone density (which can lead to stress fractures) and hormonal imbalances, which can result in the loss of periods.

DO I NEED SUPPLEMENTS?

Most ultra runners with a healthy balanced diet will not need any supplements. There are products that claim to enhance performance and/or recovery using higher doses of legal substances like creatine, BCAAs (branched chain amino acids) and nitrate than would normally be found in foods. You can get everything you need for a top performance from a nutritious, balanced daily diet. However, there are a few natural 'superfoods' that might help you out.

Cherries boost recovery
Cherries contain a high level of antioxidants, which help protect your body's cells from damage and reduce inflammation, so eating a portion of these or drinking a shot of sour/tart cherry juice daily the week before and for a few days after a big ultra may help reduce delayed onset muscle soreness (DOMS).

Beetroots boost endurance
Beetroot contains a high level of nitrate, which helps to dilate blood vessels, increase blood flow and allow more blood to reach the muscles faster, which can improve ultra running endurance and efficiency. A shot or two a couple of hours before a race may also work for you, as in one 70ml (2½fl oz) concentrated beetroot Beet It shot there's around 400mg nitrate, equivalent to six beetroots.

Caffeine reduces tiredness
A well-known ultra running booster, caffeine is a stimulant that blocks adenosine, a chemical in the brain that makes you feel tired. It increases alertness and concentration, and lowers perceived effort, so running feels easier. It can be harnessed to boost your performance, especially on longer races that may straddle two nights. However, it can also cause a hasty trip(s!) to the loo/bushes for a poop, and if taken at the wrong time can lead to crashes later on. Timing is personal, so you need to test in training when to take caffeine and how much is beneficial to your body, though typically caffeine's effects kick in around 30–60 minutes after ingestion. The caffeine content in the most common source – coffee – is not regulated or stated, so it can vary wildly from cup to cup, so the most scientific way to manage your needs for ultra running is to use caffeine gels or bars that clearly state, for example, 60mg caffeine on the packet. Try taking caffeine 30 minutes before you think you'll need it during night sections and towards the ends of ultras. Note what worked and what didn't work for better results in future events. Current guidelines recommend no more than 400mg per day and no more than 200mg per 12 hours.

NUTRITION MYTHS BUSTED

What about special diets?

Every few months a new diet becomes trendy, like paleo, 5:2, intermittent fasting, Atkins, low carb high fat (LCHF) and even fully carnivore. They're often quite radical, requiring you to cut out whole food groups or adhere to strict timings. There's usually a book, a kitchen gadget or supplements you need to buy and/or posts by influencers with zero nutrition qualifications encouraging you to eat like they do for an Instagram-worthy body. You know the drill. Long-term adherence to fad diets can promote disordered eating and even eating disorders. Most successful ultra runners don't pay any attention to fad diets but eat a varied, healthy diet with plenty of vegetables, lean protein and quick- or slow-release carbohydrates, depending on the situation.

Do low carb high fat (LCHF) diets work?

Low carb high fat diets (similar to the Atkins diet) dramatically decrease your carbohydrate intake so that your body has to burn fat for fuel instead, which is known as ketosis or keto. While this can be a successful strategy for quick, short-term weight loss in overweight people, long term these diets are hard to stick to and unhealthy for runners because more carbohydrate is needed for energy and recovery.

Some ultra runners use the LCHF diet as a way of training their bodies to use their own fat stores rather than carrying gels and fuel, which does sound like a good plan and can be achieved with gradual practice. However, while cutting down carbs can work for running slowly, it doesn't work at all for running fast and LCHF adopters risk losing speed over shorter distances. Sticking rigidly to a LCHF diet long term can also depress the immune system and reduce recovery rates. You also have to be very careful when doing this long term because if you have no fat reserves left, your body will be forced to break down the protein that makes up your muscles for fuel – this is a last resort and very bad for your health, immunity, running performance and recovery.

Should I try intermittent fasting (IF)?

Instead of restricting what you eat, this diet is all about *when* you eat. The 5:2 method allows a regular diet on five days of the week and two days restricted to 500–600 calories while the 16/8 method restricts calorie intake to eight consecutive hours, fasting for 16 hours. Benefits may

---

EXPERT ADVICE
RAMADAN AND ULTRA RUNNING

'Ramadan is the month when those who follow the Islamic faith, like myself, fast for 30 days between dawn and sunset. This can be between 12 and 16 hours depending on where you are in the world. Abstaining from food and drink during this time is a way to purify our minds and bodies, and reminds us that others are less fortunate than ourselves. Many of us have to adjust our training programmes to cope with fasting. The main thing is to listen to your body, and it's best to stick to 30–60 minutes and avoid high-intensity training that will cause dehydration, fatigue, lowered immunity and increased risk of injury. Test out whether you feel better running after Suhoor (the meal at dawn) and not being able to refuel all day, or whether you prefer to run just before sunset and eat after, or run late in the evening after Iftar (the meal at sunset). With only a small eating window, be sure to eat high-quality, nutrient-rich foods, avoid junk food and drink plenty of water. Be flexible in your training and adjust your goals if needed. It's not advisable to run an ultra during Ramadan, but low-intensity training can continue.'

TAZ ANWAR, UKA RUN LEADER AND RUN DIRECTOR FOR JUNIOR PARKRUN, @THISHIJABIRUNS

include speedier repair as your body gets a rest from the hard work of digestion, and burning more fat with less available glycogen in the muscles. However, this only works for easy, low-intensity workouts of no more than 1.5–2 hours long. This might work if you're very overweight and eating healthily during the times you are allowed to eat, but overall, IF isn't considered a beneficial option for runners and risks stressing the body further, leading to lack of energy, lack of enjoyment and potential injury.

Are veggie, vegan and plant-based diets better?

For some runners the answer is yes, while others can find them harder to stick to and/or get the right balance of nutrients. Recently it has become easier and easier to find great vegetarian and vegan foods widely available in supermarkets, cafes and restaurants, and many ultra runners enjoy a vegetarian, plant-based (mainly plants but not fully vegan) or 100 per cent vegan diet. Eating less meat can also be a fantastic way to reduce our carbon footprint and respect animal welfare, but vegans do have to make sure they eat enough vitamin B12, calcium, vitamin D and iron – all of which are found easily in eggs, oily fish, dairy products and meat. Multivitamins, supplements, algae and seaweed products help with this. Eating more fruit and veg is never a bad thing for an ultra runner (apart from on race day itself!) so incorporating more veggie, vegan and plant-based meals is a good idea for most of us.

Are vegans getting enough protein?

Lack of protein for ultra running on a vegan diet is a complete myth – beans, lentils, tofu, grains, nuts and seeds are all excellent, easy protein sources for vegan runners. However, protein from plant sources like these are less easily absorbed and used by the body, so vegans do need to eat large enough portions from a wide variety of sources to get the full range of essential amino acids.

Should I carb-load before ultras?

Most contemporary research shows a moderate increase in carbs 24–48 hours pre-event does improve performance by as much as 3–5 per cent, but the old classic carb-loading method of doing a big carb-depleting session seven days out, then a high carb/fat diet from four days out isn't effective. You don't have to completely over-stuff yourself, as the reduced workload and training intensity from tapering pre-event will help to balance this out. Eat a normal, high-carb meal that you know you can digest easily. There are some great ideas on p. 143.

Salt prevents cramp

Runners have traditionally used salt tablets to prevent or deal with cramp, which is when a muscle, usually the calf in runners, contracts involuntarily and won't relax, causing extreme pain and hopping about trying to stretch it out. Surprisingly, however, there isn't much scientific evidence that cramp is caused by dehydration and lack of salts (aka electrolytes: sodium, chloride, potassium and magnesium). Instead, cramp is most likely to happen in tired muscles or where there is a muscular imbalance, so fuelling and hydrating little and often during races, and incorporating strength work into your training, seems to be the best way to avoid cramp.

EXPERT ADVICE
TYPE 1 DIABETES AND ULTRA RUNNING

Type 1 diabetics don't produce insulin from the pancreas so they depend on injections, either using a combination of long- and quick-acting insulin, or sometimes an automatic pump. Exercise increases a person's sensitivity to insulin, which is normally a good thing, so that lower doses can be used. However, if too much insulin is given prior to long periods of physical activity or if the exercise has been more intense than expected, blood sugar levels can become too low, and indeed be dangerous - leading to a hypo-glycaemic (low blood sugar) episode, also known as a hypo. Symptoms of a hypo are not welcome on an ultra! They include feeling shaky, disorientated, irritability or anxiousness, lack of concentration, palpitations and fast pulse, blurred vision, hunger, tiredness and a headache, worsening until cardiac arrest if left untreated. This doesn't mean that Type 1 diabetics shouldn't enter ultra events, they just need to be more aware of their blood sugar levels and carry quick-acting sugar supplies. More and more diabetics now wear a sensor on their skin that gives continuous glucose readings and will set an alarm if blood sugars are too low, which is really helpful for ultra running.

SHARON MAXTED, FORMER PHARMACIST AND RUNNER, AND THE AUTHOR'S MUM!

THE BEST ADVICE IS:

'Take extreme care managing your blood sugar levels both during and a few days after the event.
  'Consider giving 25 per cent or even less insulin than you would normally; wait for an hour and then try again.
  'Type 1 ultra runners are more likely to fail to complete an event due to low rather than high blood sugar; high blood sugar levels can impair your performance, but in the short term they are unlikely to stop you from getting to the finish line.
  'Due to stress and adrenaline, most participants with Type 1 will have high blood sugar levels at the start of the event. Be aware of correcting too early. I have learned not to correct it until at least two hours into the event.'

JAMES THURLOW, DIABETIC, FORMER RACE ORGANISER AND ULTRA RUNNER, DIRECTOR OF OPEN TRACKING, @OPENTRACKING

HYDRATION

SWEATING IS SOMETHING all ultra runners will be familiar with as the body's way of cooling down when it gets too hot, losing fluid and salts in the process, which need to be replaced. So drinking water and replacing lost electrolytes (salts) is just as important for your performance and recovery as eating, especially in hot weather. Although everyone's needs differ, hydration is mostly straightforward to get right, but there are a few things to be aware of to avoid some potentially very serious problems.

How to avoid dehydration

Lack of fluid and salts (electrolytes) reduces your performance and recovery and makes you feel tired and confused during daily life, training and racing, but everyone needs different amounts, so there's no set number of litres to drink per day. The current scientific advice is to drink small amounts often throughout the day and throughout a training run or event. If you feel thirsty, take a drink – this is the body's natural urge, but it can get overlooked if you're busy or distracted. Make sure your water bottles are easy to drink from, using straws to get the end closer to your mouth for less effort on long races. Set an alert on your watch every hour or so to remind you to drink frequently, so you don't get to the point where you're necking a pint of water like you've been lost in the desert for days. Your kidneys can only cope with so much water at a time, so most of this hastily gulped fluid ends up straight in your bladder. Day-to-day, most people will get enough salts from their meals without any special effort, but during ultra events (especially ones in hot weather), you will want to experiment with using electrolyte tablets or powders if you aren't getting them through your race food or are struggling to eat.

How to avoid overhydration

Drinking excessive amounts (of water, not just alcohol!) can be extremely dangerous because too much water dilutes the salt concentration in the blood. Drinking really excessively can cause a life-threatening condition called hyponatraemia where too much water has caused the sodium (salt) level in the blood to drop to a dangerous level. Extra water then enters the cells and makes them swell, which is particularly damaging in the brain, as it cannot expand past the skull. Don't worry, severe hyponatraemia is rare in ultra runners, but symptoms

ULTRA HACK

TAKE AN EXTRA WATER BOTTLE

If you're anticipating a hot race, no matter what the mandatory kit guidelines say, pop an empty extra 500ml (17 fl oz) water bottle in your pack. It only adds about 30g (1oz) but gives you the option to carry extra fluids if the day heats up unexpectedly and you want to drink more than usual.

---

include irritability and restlessness, nausea and vomiting, loss of energy, headache, confusion and fatigue, low blood pressure, muscle weakness or cramps, and in very rare cases if left untreated, it can lead to seizures, coma and death. Current guidelines by Hoffman, Stellingwerff and Costa (2019) suggest the typical 'no more than 2 per cent body mass loss' doesn't apply to ultra endurance in order to prevent overhydration. However, adopting a 'drink-to-thirst' strategy and avoiding excessive sodium intake in order to try to replace all sodium losses during exercise will help prevent hyperhydration.

How much salt do I need?

Salt from your meals and the salty, savoury snacks you eat while ultra running should easily be enough to replace the losses. Studies show that excessive sodium supplementation should be avoided during ultra-endurance activities because it may increase the risk of developing exercise-associated hyponatremia (EAH) (over hydration) or pulmonary edema (lung swelling). If you see salt crusting on your clothing and running pack it might also mean you have eaten more salty food recently rather than you are losing sodium more than another person.

What about alcohol?

Alcohol is a diuretic, so it makes you need to wee more, which rids you of water and electrolytes (mineral salts, such as sodium, chloride, potassium and magnesium). This is obviously not the best thing before, during or after a run or race. If you run for fun rather than peak performance, alcohol is obviously fine in moderation, but post-race it's best to rehydrate first with a pint of water or squash. Non-alcoholic beers, spirits and sparkling wines have come on in leaps and bounds in recent years, so these are a great option for that delicious taste without the downsides.

132   4. NUTRITION AND HYDRATION

Recovery snacks

All of these snack ideas are easy to obtain or prepare for those post-run and post-race 'I-can-eat-everything-in-the-world-immediately-give-it-me-now!' moments. Research points to a 3:1 carbs to protein ratio, ideally eaten within two hours after running, so if a full meal isn't due for a while, try these quick and easy carb- and protein-packed snacks.

1 GLASS OF MILK
Whole milk and soya milk contain a similar amount of protein, around 3.4g per 100ml (3½fl oz). The chocolate versions are also a fabulous recovery boost. Add a dollop of yoghurt, peanut butter, a banana and a handful of frozen/fresh cherries for a delicious smoothie, too. Long-life milk and milk-alternatives are a good treat for long ultras or multi-day races that your crew can store or you can keep in your drop bag if they fit within the weight limit.

2 GREEK YOGHURT
It's easily available from many shops and super easy to slide down your throat after running. You can also find high-protein versions, but normally a 125g (4 ½oz) pot of Greek yoghurt contains around 6.3g of protein. Frozen yoghurt is also really nice in hot weather.

3 TRAIL MIX
Your own concoction of nuts, dried fruit and seeds is the original, long-lasting source of vegan protein, quick-release carbs and healthy fats to speed up your recovery. I like cashews, almonds, walnuts, Brazil nuts and sunflower and pumpkin seeds, plus cranberries, big juicy raisins, chopped apricots and figs.

4 EGGS ON TOAST
It takes seconds to whip up scrambled eggs on toast if you're home – the original fast food. British Lion eggs quote 6.4g protein per medium-sized egg (58g). And hardboiled eggs are super easy to transport and last fairly well out of the fridge for longer ultras and multi-dayers in cool climates.

5 HOUMOUS AND VEG
Widely available, houmous is wonderfully savoury and a fantastic dip for delicious raw veg batons like carrot, cucumber and peppers. There's 8g protein per 100g (3 ½oz) houmous; add a pitta or wrap for more carbs.

6 TUNA SARNIE
You get a massive 25g (1oz) protein punch from this tinned, fishy snack (just make sure you buy the ring-pull tin or a pouch version) wedged between bread or in a wrap. If you collect packets of mayo and black pepper from service stations and restaurants, you will have a long-lasting, portable drop bag snack for long ultras and multi-dayers, too.

ULTRA HACK

HOW MUCH WATER SHOULD I DRINK?

The usual advice is to drink to thirst, but if you want to find out more accurately how much fluid your body loses on a one or two-hour training run, go for a pee, then weigh yourself naked immediately before and after the run. If you weigh less, try drinking more next time. If you weigh more, you might not need to drink as much as you think. If you weighed over 2–3 per cent less than pre-run, try drinking more next time. With ultra running especially, trying to replace all fluids lost has the potential to lead to hyperhydration/exercise-associated hyponatremia, due simply to the duration of the events and subsequent greater overall fluid intake compared to shorter events.

ULTRA HACK

SUPERMARKET SWEEP

Cruising the supermarket aisles for sweet treats is a pre-ultra must. The choice is yours – just bear in mind the following: Will it melt? Will it crumble/crush? Do I need to re-package it or chop it up into bite-sized pieces? Will it motivate me? Is it delicious? You can't always answer these questions without experimenting, so fill your basket and munch away on your long runs, all in the name of research! Think about how you'll carry your fuel if it doesn't come pre-wrapped in handy bars or bite-sized chunks - you might need to pop them in zip lock sandwich bags.

Race and long run snacks

Never try anything new on race day (unless that aid station salami and beer looks appealing...), so here are some great ideas for easily digestible, tasty snacks that you can either make yourself or buy from the sweets/biscuits/cakes/crisps aisle at the supermarket without forking out for more expensive gels and energy bars.

SWEET

Jelly babies, jelly snakes, any soft chewy sweets, malt loaf, flapjack, brownies, cake bars, chocolate biscuit bars, hot cross buns, cookies, medjool dates, baby food purees, peanut butter and jam sarnies.

SAVOURY

Cheese blocks, salty baby potatoes, crisps, peanut crunchies, salty mixed nuts, Tuc cheese sandwich crackers, savoury baby food pouches, veggie sausages and burgers (cooked at home first!), pizza, mini pork pies and scotch eggs.

FOODFAILS!

The real food that hasn't worked so well for me on ultras:

Millionaires shortbread – the shortbread crumbles and the chocolate and caramel bit melts, so sad!
Pitta, brie and chutney sandwich – tried to make it from raw components during hiking up a hill on the LAMM (Lowe Alpine Mountain Marathon, now sadly extinct), but it was way too much faff and it fell apart!
Quiche – kind of successful on the Lakes Mountain 42, but was quite hard to get out of the packet and the pastry edge fell off.
Leftover veggie burger without bun – tasted delicious half way through Scafell Skyrace, but had to stop to eat, as it was falling apart.
Vegan mushroom lentil burgers from Scott Jurek's book *Eat and Run* – absolutely delicious but quite a few hard-to-find ingredients and so much mushroom chopping! Worth it, but best to eat at home, as mine fell apart easily.

Make your own sports drinks

You can buy electrolyte, isotonic and energy powders and ready-made drinks from good-quality sports nutrition brands, but this comes at a cost both financially and environmentally with all the packaging, so here's how to make your own.

ELECTROLYTE DRINK

Add a pinch of table salt to 500ml (17fl oz) made-up squash – useful for short training runs of 60–90 minutes when you want to avoid losing electrolytes and water through sweat but don't need added energy.

ISOTONIC DRINK

Add 2 pinches of table salt and 2 tsp of table sugar to 500ml (17fl oz) squash and shake until dissolved – useful for longer runs (over 2 hours) in hot, humid conditions, as isotonic drinks have the same concentrations of salt and sugar as your blood, so they are rapidly absorbed, help maintain blood sugar levels and increase endurance.

ENERGY DRINK

Add 2 pinches of table salt and 60–110g (2–4oz) of table sugar to 500ml (17fl oz) squash and shake well – useful for runs over two or three hours long to replace salts and provide the muscles and vital organs with quick-release energy.

RECOVERY DRINK

In a blender, whizz up 125ml (4¼fl oz) of milk or yoghurt (could be plant-based), 125ml (4¼fl oz) of water, 1 banana, 125g (4½oz) of frozen berries, and a splodge of runny peanut butter – a good mix of carbs, protein and fluids for hydration and recovery post-run. Ideally drink this within a couple of hours of finishing, if you're not eating a meal for a while after the race or training session.

Sports nutrition products

Sports nutrition products like gels, energy bars and energy drink powders have the advantage of being very convenient sources of light, packable, easily opened, ingested and digested nutrition with a long storage date. They're a particularly useful addition to real food on longer, hotter ultras and multi-day races. Try them in training before depending on them in a race to make sure you like the taste and texture, and that they agree with your stomach.

GELS

As you most probably know, these are handy, easy-to-open, easy-to-eat tubes of high-energy (high-carbohydrate) gel with a huge variety of flavours and various viscosities, ranging from chocolate to lemon drizzle cake and gloopy to ganache. Some runners,

HYDRATION 135

as it's sticky to store an opened gel, if you can only stomach a mouthful at a time. However, some gels come in a larger pouch with a screw top that you can sip as required. You can also pre-squeeze them into a reusable gel soft flask, which is useful but requires a little more time and organisation.

Some gels contain more water than others and the drier they are the more water you need to slurp with them to avoid gut issues. Some find their stomachs don't get on so well with gels, so it's wise to try different brands in training to see what works best for you.

Some gels also contain caffeine to boost performance and beat fatigue, which can be handy for longer races and night sections, but caffeine can also lead to digestive issues and an urgent need for a number two.

BARS

Energy and/or protein bars are so convenient to pop in your running pack or pocket, and they last a long time and are resilient to heat and generally being jogged around. They're a very popular choice, especially on longer, slower runs when you have the time, energy and enough saliva to chew. They usually range from 40–60g (1 ½–2 ½oz) and they can taste nicer than gels, are easily eaten a mouthful at a time and feel more substantial. Although their main aim is to fill you with quick-release energy in the form of sugar, some bars contain more natural ingredients than others, so look for ones made of real foods that you recognise, such as dried fruits, oats, nuts, salts and chia seeds. Try them in training to check you like the taste, and pack a variety of flavours on your race because you never know when you'll fancy that beetroot and cocoa bar.

especially those at the sharp end pushing themselves hard, will use only gels and energy drinks (see below) for ultras up to about seven or eight hours long. Beyond this timeframe, most people find they need a bit of real food. If you're in the middle to the back of the pack like me, going at a slower pace, you will likely want to add in real food for any race longer than four or five hours.

Gels range in size and shape but are usually 30–60ml (1–2fl oz). Smaller is sometimes better,

ENERGY CHEWS
Bridging the gap between sloppy gels and solid bars, chews are the sports nutrition industry's version of humble jelly babies – easy-to-eat sweets packed with energy. The advantage of these versus normal sweets is that, like gels and energy drinks and powders, they often use a combination of different sugars like glucose, fructose and maltodextrin, which have different absorption rates, so you should get less of a sugar spike and be able to absorb more.

FUEL POUCHES
These are pouches with a screw top, often around 100g in weight, containing either gel or real, blended-up food like porridge and banana or thick sweet potato puree for more of a savoury option. They may also contain other real food goodies like dates, flaxseeds, sultanas and avocado. The screw top is handy for taking a swig and shutting it tight again, just don't lose that lid as I've yet to see one on a leash.

ELECTROLYTE TABLETS
Many gels, bars and chews contain these but electrolytes (sodium, chloride, potassium and magnesium) are also sold in tablet form, so you can add them to your water rather than combining them with energy-giving carbs. If you sweat heavily it's worth having a sweat test to gauge what your exact needs are.

DRINK POWDERS
Powders are a very handy, portable and long-lasting option to add electrolytes, carbs, protein or any combination of these to drinks before, during or after a run. They are often sold in bulk in large containers and come in many different-flavoured varieties, from 'flavourless' to chocolate to tropical fruit.

SPORTS DRINKS
Ready-made sports drinks come in various types, including low-calorie electrolyte, isotonic and energy. Electrolyte-only drinks don't contain any energy – they just replace the salts and fluid you lose from sweating. Isotonic drinks have the same concentrations of salt and sugar as your bodily fluids, so they help maintain blood sugar levels and increase endurance. Energy drinks contain sugars (often glucose, fructose and maltodextrin) to provide energy.

ULTRA HACK

COLD-WEATHER NUTRITION
I almost broke a tooth on an early-April mountain marathon in north-west Scotland biting into a frozen energy bar, so if you're heading for a cold race, pre-chop and ball up energy bars into bite-sized pieces and keep them in a plastic bag in a front pocket close to your body to keep them warm enough to chew easily. You can also get insulating neoprene sleeves for soft bottles and hydration bladders to stop your water freezing, and make sure you blow any water in any tubes back into the main bladder or soft bottle to prevent frozen pipes.

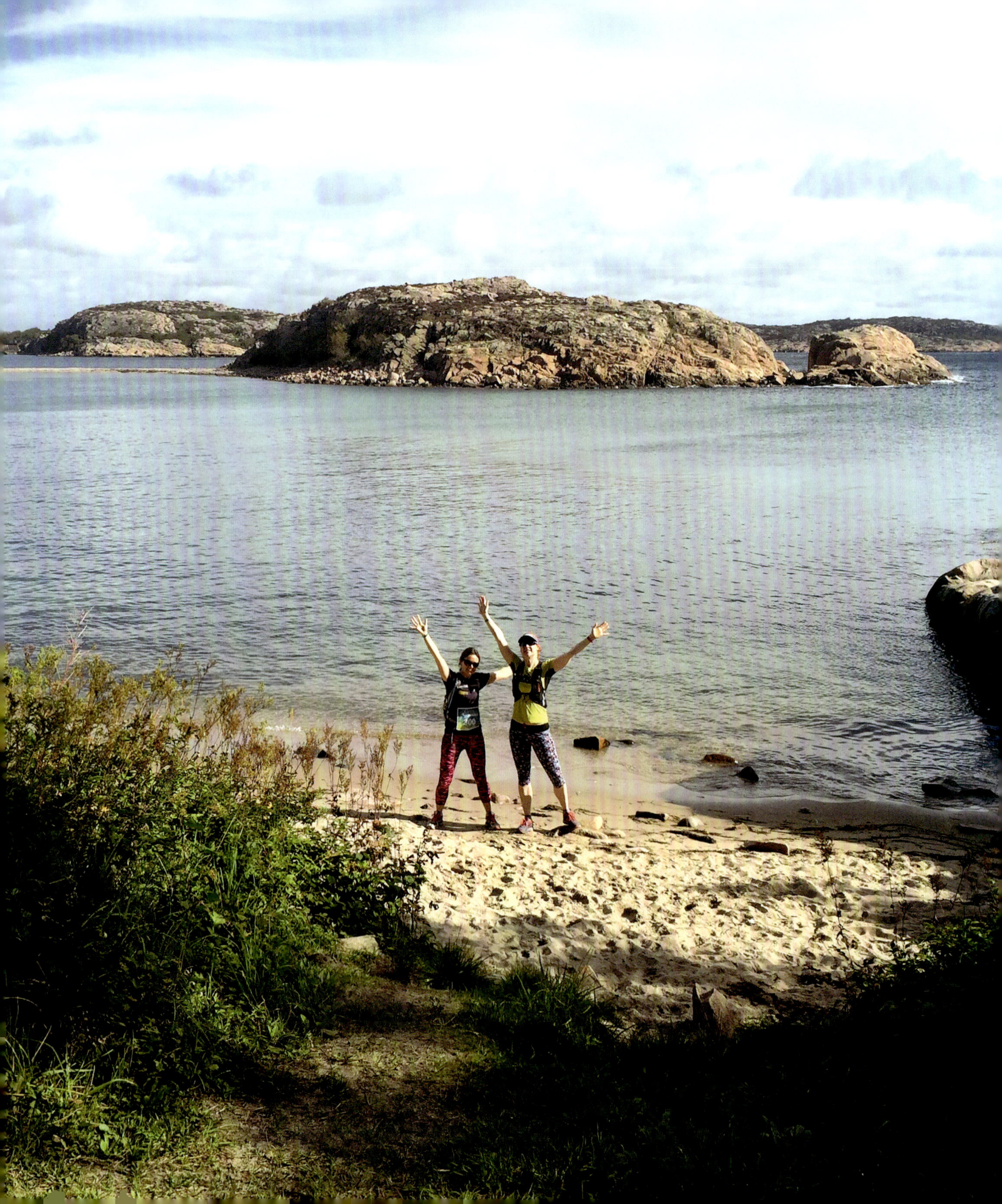

RECIPES
BEST ULTRA BREAKFASTS

Pimped up porridge

The best mix of carbs and protein to fill you up and energise you all day long.

MAKE IT — Mix 50g (2oz) porridge oats with half a sliced banana, 1 handful of raisins and cranberries, 1 tbsp mixed seeds, 1 tsp peanut butter, 100g live yoghurt and 80ml (2.7 fl oz) milk, Microwave for 2 minutes.

VARY IT — Add different fruits, such as pear, blackberries or blueberries for seasonal variety. Freezer fruits work well too – microwave first to thaw before adding.

Avocado quickie

The easiest version for those short on time, for a tasty, filling breakfast.

MAKE IT Don't bother smashing the avocado in a different bowl, simply put a couple of slices of bread (sourdough goes nicely if you have it) in the toaster and while you wait, cut a large avocado in half. Slice lengthways then widthways down the half without the stone. Butter your toast, spoon out the diced avocado and squash it down into a sandwich. Voila, smashed avocado.

VARY IT If you want to get super fancy you can sprinkle on a pinch of salt and squirt of lemon / lime juice to taste, and maybe some chilli flakes. Adding a poached egg on top looks even more exciting too.

Banana oat smoothie

Another quick one to make and go, this delicious breakfast drink will keep you full until lunch.

MAKE IT Plop 100g (or a small pot) of plain, live yoghurt, a banana, 50ml milk (any type), a handful of oats and a handful of frozen or fresh cherries into your blender. Whizz it up, add some more milk to get your desired thickness, pour into a glass or wide-mouthed bottle and off you go.

VARY IT This is basically a drinkable version of the porridge above! Add blueberries, nuts and nut butters, use different flavoured yoghurts and different milk-style products to mix this up.

Easy omelette

Even I can make this super easy eggy, veggy, cheesy concoction - slice it up, pop it in Tupperware and take it on the move with you too.

MAKE IT Chop 4 medium mushrooms and fling them in a frying pan with a blob of marg or butter. While they fry until browned, whisk 3 medium eggs. Chop 3 cherry tomatoes and lob them in with 2 generous handfuls of spinach. Stir until wilted. Pour over the eggs, crumble over some feta and cook on a low heat for 5+ mins. If the top is still wobbly raw while the base is browning, pop the pan under the grill for a few minutes until the top is firm and cooked.

VARY IT Use different fillings and cheeses like roasted mediterranean veg and parmesan.

QUICK & EASY ULTRA LUNCHES

Oh-Mega 3 salad

Pack more healthy Omega-3 fat into your life with this colourful, wholesome salad. Tip: roast twice the veg and save the extra for another meal for more economic oven-usage.

MAKE IT
Preheat the oven to 180 deg C. Dice a sweet potato, toss with oil and salt, then roast for 20 mins. Chop a few florets of broccoli and cauliflower, oil them too and pop them in for 15 mins, or until just browned. Hurl salad leaves at a bowl, plus a few cherry tomatoes and slices of cucumber. Tip the roasted veggies on top along with a drained can of tuna, add your fave dressing (see right) and enjoy.

VARY IT
Chopped up boiled eggs are a very nice swap for the tuna if you're veggies and for vegans use edamame beans.

OH-MEGA HOMEMADE SALAD DRESSING

Flaxseed or rapeseed (canola in the USA) oils are the best for Omega-3, but if you don't have them to hand, sunflower is the next best thing.

MAKE IT
Mix 2 parts oil to 1 part balsamic, wine or cider vinegar in an old jam jar. Add a few generous pinches of mixed herbs of your choice (I like thyme, sage, rosemary and oregano from our garden), a pinch of salt and freshly ground black pepper. Shake and pour over salad.

VARY IT
If you're feeling brave (and working from home?) add half a clove of crushed garlic and/or a slice of red onion finely chopped. Adding a generous dollop of Dijon mustard to a white wine vinegar version of this, along with a pinch of sugar, makes for a deliciously creamy French dressing too.

Anything soup

The beauty of this soup comes from the fact that it saves absolutely any old vegetables hanging around in your fridge waiting to die.

MAKE IT Raid the fridge, chop up that wilting old broccoli, wash and cut the brown bits out of those slightly slimy carrots in a bag in the bottom drawer, gouge the mouldy pockets out of that sweet potato (they don't last as long as white potatoes do they?). Am I giving too much away about the state of our fridge here? You get the gist – gather all the old, random veg, chop it up, fry an onion and garlic in a large non-stick pan, then add the veg to the pan along with enough veg stock to just cover them. Simmer for 20mins or until they're all soft, adding extra water if needed. Add in a packet of soft, puy lentils, a drained tin of pulses, baked beans even or any leftover meat. Whizz up and serve with a swirl of creme fraiche and parsley garnish.

VARY IT No need, it varies every time you make it!

Quinoa, beetroot and feta mess

The white feta-stained beetroot-pink looks messy but tastes wonderful, and the quinoa adds a filling, protein punch.

MAKE IT — Cook 100g quinoa in 200ml water for 20 mins with half a veg stock cube crumbled in. Throw mixed salad leaves into a bowl, chop a chunk of cucumber, 2 medium beetroots and break up a quarter packet of feta. Drain the quinoa, wait for it to cool if you have time, pour it over the salad leaves, then top with the other ingredients.

VARY IT — You could swap the feta for grilled halloumi and the beets for roasted peppers. Adding olives would be nice too, or any Mediterranean roasted veg.

The sandwich of utter delight

If you have time to make a batch of homemade pesto it's a total game-changer. If not, the poshest one from the shop might be ok...

MAKE IT — Slice half a halloumi and grill for 15-20mins, turning half way to brown both sides. Whizz up 80g basil, 50g pine nuts, 50g parmesan and 150ml olive oil (I don't use garlic in my pesto, it overpowers the taste for me, but you could add a clove if you love it). Or open a jar of shop pesto. Lay out 2 slices of sourdough bread, line with salad leaves, slim slices of big beef tomatoes and the halloumi. Drizzle on as much pesto as you can handle. Mmmm.

VARY IT — This could also be a wrap or a pitta or your choice of beige surrounding to the supremely delicious filling.

DINNERS OF WINNERS

Chicken surprise (with smoked mackerel...)

My dad used to make something like this when my sister and I went through a long phase of hating fish. He called it chicken surprise and hey presto, we ate it right up.

MAKE IT — Chop a red onion, clove of garlic and 3-4 leeks. Pop on your choice of pasta (I quite like spaghetti for this one) and heat a blob of oil in a frying pan. Saute the onion and garlic until softened, brown the leeks then lower the heat and cover to steam them for 5 or so mins until softened. While the leeks cook, grate the zest off a lemon, slice it in half and remove the pips, and de-skin the smoked mackerel if it's not tinned. Wilt 2 handfuls of spinach in the pan, pour over a tub of creme fraiche, stir in the mackerel and lemon zest, and squeeze the lemon juice over it. Heat, then serve over the pasta with parsley to garnish.

VARY IT — Swap the pasta for rice, and you can also make a lovely version with shallots, a dash of white wine and smoked salmon, but this makes it more expensive and the latter can be a less sustainable source of fish (depending on when you're reading this).

Lemony asparagus frittata

Who knew that eggs and lemon would pair so well? Also a delicious cold lunch the next day, if there's any left...

MAKE IT Chop and steam a large bunch of asparagus for 5 mins or until tender. Whisk 8 eggs in a big bowl and mix in the zest of one lemon, half its juice, a squeeze of lazy garlic paste from a tube, 60g grated parmesan, 120g grated cheddar and some freshly ground black pepper. Add a couple of handfuls of spinach to the asparagus for the final 2 mins. Pour the mixture into a frying pan, quickly stir in the asparagus and spinach then leave on a medium heat for 5-10 mins. The innards will still be wobbly, so add a further handful of grated cheddar to the top then place the pan under the grill on a medium to high heat for 3 mins or until it is firm, browned and bubbling. Mmmm.

VARY IT Broccoli, courgette and green beans also work really well with this. You could use a combo with asparagus or each individually.

Boosted shepherd pie

Buying top quality lamb mince from your local butcher can be twice the price of supermarket fare, so adding nutritious lentils makes the meat go further.

MAKE IT Chop 4 large potatoes (or 8 smaller ones) and boil for 10mins. Chop an onion and 2 cloves of garlic, and fry in oil on a medium heat until soft. Brown 500g lamb mince in the same pan, stirring often until cooked through. Add dried thyme and rosemary (or any mixed herbs) and a 250g packet of ready-cooked puy lentils, cover with veg or beef stock (I find lamb stock a bit fatty) and simmer. Drain and mash the potatoes with a knob of butter and slurp of milk. Pour the mixture into an oven dish, top with mashed potatoes and grate cheese on top. Oven cook on 180 deg C for 30-40mins until the cheese is browned. Serve with seasonal veg.

VARY IT You can use any lentils, and it's much cheaper if you used dried ones soaked overnight, I'm just never that organised! You can also make a delicious veggie version with Quorn mince.

MY STORY
I EAT REAL FOOD NOW

'**My very first ultra** was the Blues Cruise 50k. I prepared by using high-calorie, high-electrolyte sports drinks like Tailwind and Gatorade. I had been having some bowel problems on long training runs but wrote it off to other issues. About halfway through the race I began to feel the need to relieve myself, but there wasn't a toilet at ANY of the aid stations! I told my friends to go on without me as I ran 500m [1640ft] off course to find woods dense enough to conceal my desperation! Crisis resolved and now much lighter, I re-entered the course and finished with my friend Ron, who had been running behind us. With apologies to the ultra running nutrition industry (and that wooded area!), since then I have only used real food, water and crisps in my ultras, and I've never had a problem in any 30-, 40-, or 50-miler.'

JOHN GARDNER

Roasted veg & bean chili

The roasting of the veg is key to giving this hearty vegan dish its rich, deep flavour. Pop any leftovers in the freezer for a delicious home-made ready meal.

MAKE IT Pre-heat oven to 180 deg C. Settle rice to simmer in a pan according to packet instructions. Chop two baking trays' worth of mediterranean veg of your choice (I like peppers, courgette, aubergine, red onion sprinkled with a few peeled garlic cloves) into bite-sized pieces. Drizzle with oil, a few teaspoons of smoked paprika and mixed herbs. Mix on the tray to ensure all are coated. Roast for 10-15 mins, then stir and add a handful of cherry tomatoes, then pop back in for 5-10 mins if not fully cooked. Empty 2 tins of chopped tomatoes, 2 tins of pulses (I like borlotti and cannellini for this) and a few chopped sundried tomatoes into the pan, and crumble in a veggie stock cube. Slide the med veg into the pan, stir and serve over the rice.

VARY IT You can add sweet potato or butternut squash to this for an even more filling, carby all-in-one dish without having to cook rice, and vary the mix of pulses, eg chickpeas, butter (lima) beans, black-eyed peas and lentils. It's also very nice with crumbled feta on top if you're not vegan.

DINNERS OF WINNERS

FUEL TIMELINE

WHAT TO EAT when is super important for ultra running. Especially on the longer ultras and multi-day races your fuel choices and timing of consumption can make or break your race. This timeline is a good guide to keep you full of energy and well hydrated before and during an ultra, and to speed up your recovery, warding off illness and injury afterwards.

Day before
Eat normally and make sure you are well hydrated using the info on pp. 122–137.

Night before
Eat a healthy meal rich in carbs, protein and good-quality nutrients but low in fibre to prevent possible gut/bowel issues (see p. 139 for some great recipes). There's no need to stuff yourself – a week or so of tapering along with being fully satisfied will ensure all your energy stores are completely topped up. It's best not to try anything you haven't eaten before in case it disagrees with you, so if you're in a different country, maybe tonight is not the night to try the dish on the menu you don't quite understand…

Two hours before
It's best to eat a substantial meal two or three hours before your start time, so your body has time to digest it. This is often breakfast time, so have some porridge with honey or a couple of slices of toast with eggs – whatever you are used to eating before running is a good idea here. If you struggle to eat breakfast during a race, have a pre-bed high carb snack – porridge, again, is ideal. If it's not breakfast, have a small, plain meal, such as an omelette, or a houmous and cheese or chicken mayo sandwich. For more ideas, see pp. 139–145.

Thirty minutes before
You might want to have a small snack on the start line, such as a couple of mouthfuls of energy bar, flapjack or gel, as a final top-up for your muscles.

During the event
Your muscles contain about 90 minutes' worth of energy before they will need topping up, but many ultra runners like to eat a mouthful or two of an energy-rich snack every 30 minutes from the get-go to avoid any chance of depletion. The latest studies indicate that most people can absorb 60–90g (2–3oz) carbs per hour, which is roughly 12–18 jelly babies or 1–2 gels (depending on size). A glucose:fructose mix of 2:1 is often regarded as best,

> ### ULTRA HACK
>
> #### BEWARE THE CHAIR!
> In aid stations, sitting down to eat can lose you valuable time, so aim to finish off your fluids just prior to arrival and unscrew your lids as you enter the checkpoint, so you can quickly fill them and grab a few snacks to pocket and eat while walking further along your route. Not stopping can often be easier on your tired legs anyway, as getting back up from a chair feels harder. If you need the loo, head for the snacks and refill your bottles first, so you can multitask – I know its gross to eat and drink on the loo, but it does save time on an ultra!

but newer research by a few studies have shown 5:4 is better. You'll also want to mix up sweet fuel with bites of savoury real foods, so keep them handy in your pockets up front. Throughout the race, drink to thirst with water, electrolyte, isotonic or energy drinks (see pp. 131–137). On hot races replacing electrolytes is particularly important and many ultra runners have one 500ml (17 fl oz) bottle of water and one containing electrolytes, sipping each alternately. Carb absorption rates reduce by 10 per cent in hot races (possibly because you can't run as fast), so reduce your intake accordingly. On long events it can be hard to remember to eat and drink regularly, so you could put an alarm on your watch as a reminder.

Especially on foreign races you might be faced with aid station food that you've never seen before. If this is your A-race, it's best to stick with what you know, but if you're just out to enjoy the ride and absorb the local culture, dig in and enjoy that cheese, ham and beer!

Within two hours after finishing
Rehydrate with semi-skimmed milk, whole milk or fresh orange juice following exercise for more than two hours. If you aren't eating a meal within this time, speed up your recovery with a snack containing 3:1 carbs and protein (see p. 133 for ideas).

After the race
Depending on when your race finishes, you might have missed lunch and go straight on to dinner, or even breakfast the following day or two days later. So indulge your taste buds – you deserve this; have whatever you fancy! Have a beer! Have three! You've run 50/75/100 miles (80/120/160km) – you're invincible! But seriously, it's of course good to keep it healthy (see pp. 142–145 for ideas), but if you've been craving fish and chips all race, it's fine to reward yourself.

The next day
Ease back into your regular healthy eating, making sure you eat plenty of protein combined with carbs for recovery. (See p. 133 for some fantastic, easy recovery snacks.)

> ### ULTRA HACK
>
> #### ECO-SNACKS
> Instead of using new ziplock bags for your trail snacks, you can be more eco-friendly (and save pennies) by using the plastic packaging from other items, such as cherry tomatoes, dried fruits and nuts, crisps, wraps and even magazines or junk mail. Simply fold them over, tie the ends in a knot or use wire twist ties.

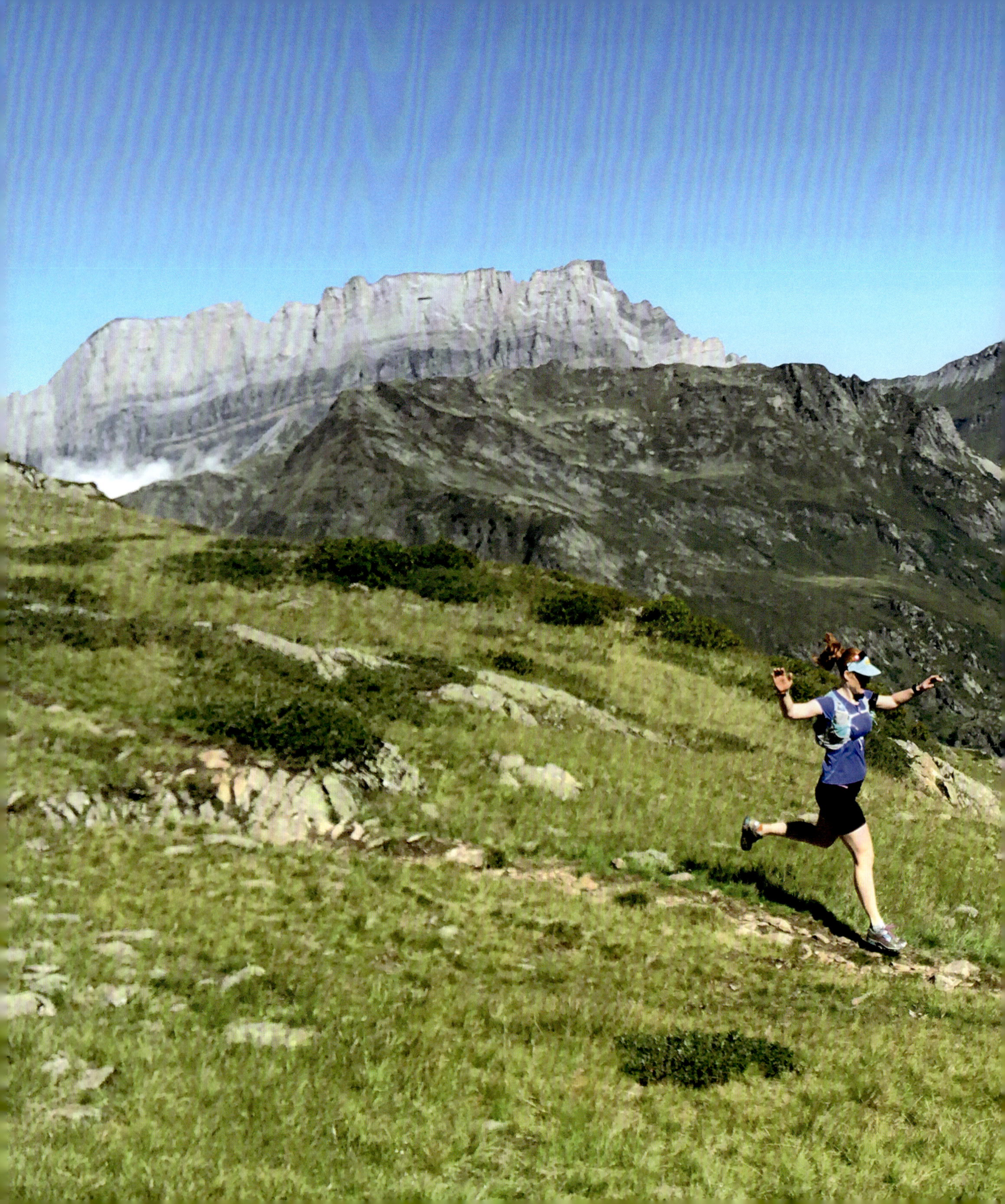

5
BEAT INJURY

Have you ever met an ultra runner without a history of some kind of injury? They're a rare gem! However, you can use this chapter to drastically reduce your chances of succumbing to injury, and help to cure yourself more quickly should the worst occur.

PREVENT INJURY

THIS IS THE HOLY GRAIL of ultra running, isn't it? Don't get the injury in the first place. And while I can't stop you falling over your own feet while sleep deprived, twisting your ankle down a rabbit hole or accidentally stabbing your leg with your own pole (I've done all three!), there are myriad things you can take control of right now to ensure you keep the risk of running injuries to a minimum.

Sleep well

It's really important to prioritise sleep because it's so vital for your body's repair processes – there's no use training hard if you don't let your body recover enough. Aim for seven to nine hours a night, and practise good sleep hygiene: avoid caffeine late in the day, avoid alcohol and large meals late at night, avoid bright lights and screens an hour before bed, take a relaxing bath. Prepare your bedroom for a peaceful night with a cool temperature and low lighting, then sink into your pillow (possibly listening to a meditation app) and let the zzzzzz commence. Take 20-30 minute power naps in the day if at all possible when you don't get enough night-time sleep.

Increase training gradually

Although it's really exciting discovering the world of ultra running or learning about a new, epic race, one of the main ways you can injure yourself is by upping your distance or the intensity of your training by too much too soon. It's boring, it's sensible, but increasing the toll on your body gradually is the best way to avoid injury – for example, make that 100-miler a three-year project rather than this summer's A-race and your body will reward you by actually toeing that start line.

> **MY STORY**
> ### TOO MUCH TOO SOON
>
> '**Lakes in a Day** was my ultra debut, but despite having run 10 road marathons, 36-mile [58km] training runs and introducing more hills, I found it much, much, harder – and it took a longer time to complete – with loads more running in the dark than I'd hoped for. I fell over twice; had bad cramping; and lost a contact lens in the last handful of miles, so that all made it a rude awakening. But it didn't put me off.... I've completed two ultras since - either would have been a more realistic debut as I did much, much better. And I've entered another three...'
> **PAUL FRANCIS GREGORY**

Avoid overtraining

Overtraining when ultra running can be difficult to spot, as you do need to stress your body in order to improve, which means you may think that feeling tired is normal. However, if you feel overly fatigued with sore muscles that don't recover after a few days, you might be overdoing it and start to pick up niggles and injuries. Other signs include plateaued or worsened performance, and feeling lethargic all the time; and your mojo might have gone and you might feel irritable or depressed. You might be gaining weight, getting ill a lot and your resting heart rate might be higher by 7–10 beats per minute. Sandwich intense or long sessions or races with rest days or active recovery such as walking and do 10 minutes of strength work every few days, or a 30-minute session once a week. Listen to your body. If you ignore the signs, overtraining can get worse, but if you take a few days' rest, sleep well, eat well and lighten your training volume and/or intensity, the effects of overtraining can be reversed quickly.

Eat well

Mmmm, I like this one. Fuelling your long run just as you would your race and eating healthily the rest of the time speeds up your recovery time and helps prevent injury (see pp. 120–147). A lack of iron (common in female runners) can lead to exhaustion, so include dried apricots, nuts, chickpeas, sardines and a small amount of red meat in your diet.

Strengthen up

Unless you have a physical job, you're likely sitting at a desk all day, which switches off your glutes (bum muscles), does nothing to engage your core muscles, and shortens your hamstrings (backs of your legs), so follow the ultra running injury prevention moves (see pp. 90–92) and ultra strength routine (see p. 90) to make sure your body is as strong as possible for the increase in mileage.

Cross-train

Doing exercise other than running uses different muscle groups, which is great for preventing overuse injuries, and if it's lower impact than running – such as swimming and cycling – it helps you keep fit without putting the same stress on your joints (see p. 164 for ideas).

Seek help early

It's always best to seek professional advice (not Dr. Google or a Facebook community) sooner rather than later. For most running-related injuries you can still keep some form of running going, unless you have a fracture. If you do have to stop running, this is a good time to cross-train and work on strength. If you do this, you're likely to come back from injury even stronger. Use the time to reflect on the build-up to the injury, sleep pattern, training, diet, etc. as this all has an impact. A lot of running-related injuries are training errors, for example running too far before you've built up to the distance, and when you reflect back you can often see the point when the problem started.

Avoid painkillers

Painkillers should be used with extreme care during ultra running. Some races don't allow NSAIDs (non-steroidal anti-inflammatory drugs, like ibuprofen) because they can upset your stomach and gut, and place a serious strain on your kidneys (especially if you're dehydrated) and on your heart. The risk increases with age and can become life-threatening. Paracetamol is safer, but still should be taken only if absolutely necessary, and stick to the correct dosage and timings. If you're regularly taking painkillers just to get through training, you're disguising what your body is trying to tell you. Taking them during an event is a risk but can work to take the edge off. Be wary of taking painkillers for headaches – this could be a sign you're dehydrated.

How many races a year?

If you have a lot of time to train and travel to races, then you might want to enter quite a few, especially if you don't 'race' them but use them to explore the world rather than push your body to the limits. But do be wary of entering more than three very long (for example, 100-mile/160km) races in one year, so as not to over-exhaust yourself. Many seasoned ultra runners and pros have two or three A-races per year where they go all out, and a few training races leading up to them to hone

> ### ULTRA HACK
>
> #### EASE OFF DURING ILLNESS
> If a friend with a hacking cough asked you if they should train today, you'd probably say no, so why do we insist on dragging ourselves out in the thick of the latest cold or bug that's going round? We don't want to miss a day on our training plan – but it's actually massively counter-productive and possibly even injury-inducing to run while you're ill because your body needs to put its energy into getting you back to 100 per cent. Eat healthily, rest (or walk or do gentle yoga, if you have to) and you will recover faster. The day you think you're ready to go running again, wait until tomorrow to recommence an easy week of training – that's the best way to ensure you're back to 100 per cent.

their strategy, gear and fuelling. In training races you can aim to relax the pace or even DNF if the plan goes awry, in favour of a quicker recovery.

Illness, stress and lack of sleep

Life can really scupper your best-laid training plans, but do not fear, ultras can still be achieved on less training than you'd like. The more important thing is to get back to training quickly, so if you're ill, if work or family life is stressful and busy or if you have been sleeping badly, take a break and prioritise sleep for recovery. Some weeks, you might not be able to train much or even at all. And mainly that's fine; ultra running training is not achieved in one week or even one month. If you're unable to train consistently for long periods, you might want to readjust your goals; ultra events will always be there when things calm down, and it takes strength to acknowledge that you may have different priorities at certain times in your life. Shorter trail and road races are also brilliant for keeping you motivated to keep active during these times, without as much pressure and planning.

DO YOU NEED RECOVERY TOOLS?

There are now myriad recovery tools on the market, from foam rollers to massage guns and from TENS (transcutaneous electrical nerve stimulation) devices to compression boots. Unless you're an elite athlete searching for marginal gains, you don't need to spend any money on these gadgets because walking, swimming and gentle cycling are also excellent ways to promote recovery. If anything, more time spent on strength work will protect you from injury and promote a faster recovery.

TREATING COMMON INJURIES

IF YOU DO GET A RUNNING INJURY, don't despair; the best thing to do is get it checked out by an expert and follow their treatment guidelines. Then continue following the advice and doing the strength workouts in chapter 3 (see pp. 84–119) to protect yourself against future running injuries. Here, podiatrist Nick Knight explains how to diagnose and cure the most common running injuries.

INJURY	What is it/they?	Cure it
Plantar Fasciitis	An intense ache pain on the inside of the heel; it can feel like you're standing on a stone in the morning. It's a pain that wears off after a few steps and eases for the rest of the day, then the pain returns after you've been off your feet for a while. It will be worse the morning after a run.	Shockwave therapy combined with foot and lower limb stretches and strengthening exercises. Rolling the foot over a bottle of icy water, and a higher drop or rocker-soled shoe may help some sufferers. Taping with rigid zinc oxide tape can provide short-term relief and/or indicates that you would benefit from an insole. There are plantar fasciitis socks, however, compliance in wearing them is poor. Steroid injections may be an option and surgery in extreme cases.
Bunions	When the metatarsal bone leading to the first big toe bone (proximal phalanx) starts to rotate outwards, then the big toe starts to point towards the other toes, which then creates a bulge on the outside of the big toe joint. Bunions are not always painful and can be hereditary. Often they are caused by footwear rubbing on the big toe. A bunion is different to arthritis of the toes.	Use wide-fit shoes; wear shoes with a super-soft upper; ice the affected area; take pain relief; don't wear high-heeled or pointed-toed shoes in non-running life; some people find using a insole with a cut out under the big toe helpful to reduce pain; in extreme cases surgery may be necessary. Unfortunately bunion splints are a waste of time and money.
Achilles pain	The tendon that attaches your calf muscles to your heel bone becomes tight, stiff and too painful to run with.	Strengthening exercises are vital, especially around the calf. Using a shoe with a higher heel-to-toe drop or mid-sole rocker might help, as may increasing your cadence or slowing down your runs. Shockwave therapy also can be very helpful in reducing pain quickly.

INJURY	What is it/they?	Cure it
Ankle sprain	Sudden acute pain at the ankle after a trip, twist or fall (often when running without concentrating on your foot placement on easier ground – watch out!) with immediate swelling at the ankle. The most common cause is twisting the outside of the ankle. In severe cases you will be unable to put weight on the ankle.	We have moved on from the RICE principals (rest, ice, compression, elevation) – now it's PEACE and LOVE. The first few days after injury you need PEACE – protect, elevate, avoid anti-inflammatories, compress and educate yourself to understand the injury and healing process. Then move to LOVE – load, optimism, vascularisation and exercise. This means start using the ankle, stay positive, get the heart pumping and start doing exercises to strengthen the ankle back up.
Shin splints	Shin splints is an umbrella term for pain in the shins. The most common cause of shin splints is medial tibial stress syndrome (MTSS). There will be an ache in the lower third of the shin that's diffusely tender, then pain will build up during a run. However, you can run through it, it will not wake you at night and it will settle 24–48 hours after running. It can be linked to running too much/too far too soon, and there are some biomechanical elements that can increase your risk of getting MTSS. It is possible for MTSS to progress to a stress fracture, so if you get pinpoint tenderness and night pain and it's still hurting three days or more after a run, this could be caused by a stress fracture.	Load management is key. Reduce running to a comfortable level; cross-training and aqua-jogging can help here. Strengthen the calf and glute muscles (see p. 86). Some will benefit from an insole or adjustments to their gait (running style) and shockwave therapy can be helpful. However, this is not pleasant at all on the shin bone.
Knee pain	There are many reasons for knee pain, but the most common is pain behind the kneecap, especially running downhill – runner's knee (or patellofemoral pain syndrome, PFPS), which is closely linked to ITB pain (see p. 156). PFPS is an umbrella term for pain around the knee and means the knee has been irritated by an activity, for example a sudden increase in downhill running. If you are getting large amounts of swelling, and your knee is locking or giving way, this needs to be checked out, as there may be a ligament or meniscal injury, although with those injuries there is often a trauma, twist or fall.	Stretch and strengthen the glutes and hip flexors and build ankle and core strength (see p. 86). Have a gait analysis with a movement specialist to find out why the problem occurs and so you can strengthen any weaknesses found. Some runners find insoles helpful. Using a lower heel-to-toe drop shoe can be helpful as well, however this may increase the load in the Achilles and foot. Taping can also help.

TREATING COMMON INJURIES

INJURY	What is it/they?	Cure it
ITB pain	Illiotibial band (ITB) syndrome is very common. It is often confused with runner's knee (see p. 155), as it causes pain at the outside of the knee while running, especially downhill, disappearing when you stop. The pain comes from the friction between the knee joint with a tightened ITB which runs from the outside of your hip to the outside of your knee, due to overloading of the gluteus maximus (the largest bum muscle) and the tensor fascia latae (TFL) that hold it in place.	You cannot stretch or lengthen the ITB (it has the tensile strength of steel), so foam rolling it doesn't solve this. Instead the muscles that control it must be strengthened and stretched (see strength section starting p.86) to make sure it doesn't happen again. Have a gait analysis with a movement specialist to see why the problem occurs and so you can strengthen any weaknesses found – there could be a mechanical cause, so a change in running style may be helpful. The foot may be playing a part, so using an insole might also help. However, neither of these is a substitute for strength work. Taping can also help.
DOMS	A temporary injury that shows you're training hard, delayed onset muscle soreness (DOMS) occurs when muscles have been overloaded, causing micro-tears and pain. It's especially prevalent in the thighs of ultra runners after long and/or frequent downhills that the muscles are not used to. Pain peaks 24 hours after running, making getting downstairs particularly comical, but eases quickly after a couple of days.	There is no cure, but adequate training and ice-cold water during or straight after running can provide relief and ease symptoms. Easy activity like walking, swimming, gentle cycling, stretching and massage can help by increasing blood flow to the legs, which encourages repair.

MY STORY
RUNNING AS RECOVERY FROM CANCER

'**Aged 41,** I was diagnosed with breast cancer in 2020. Running got me through in so many ways. Most notably post-radiation treatments, which were daily for six weeks. If I didn't run, I would almost fall asleep on my drive home. If I did run right after, even 20 minutes, my energy level would stay good all day. Blew my mind. Running then became my go-to. I completed my first 30k and 50k in 2022 and my first 50 miler this year. It is the one place where everything feels right with the world. It forces me into the present moment and silences the worry and chatter of post-cancer life. Additionally, at the toughest points in my races, I am able to tap into the emotions and experiences from my treatment journey and dig deeper than I ever thought possible. I can tell myself that while my body may hurt, I have gotten through harder times. Running has been so healing and motivating. It has given me agency in my life at a time where everything has felt out of control.'
KATE BURCHELL, WYOMING

The best recovery mindset

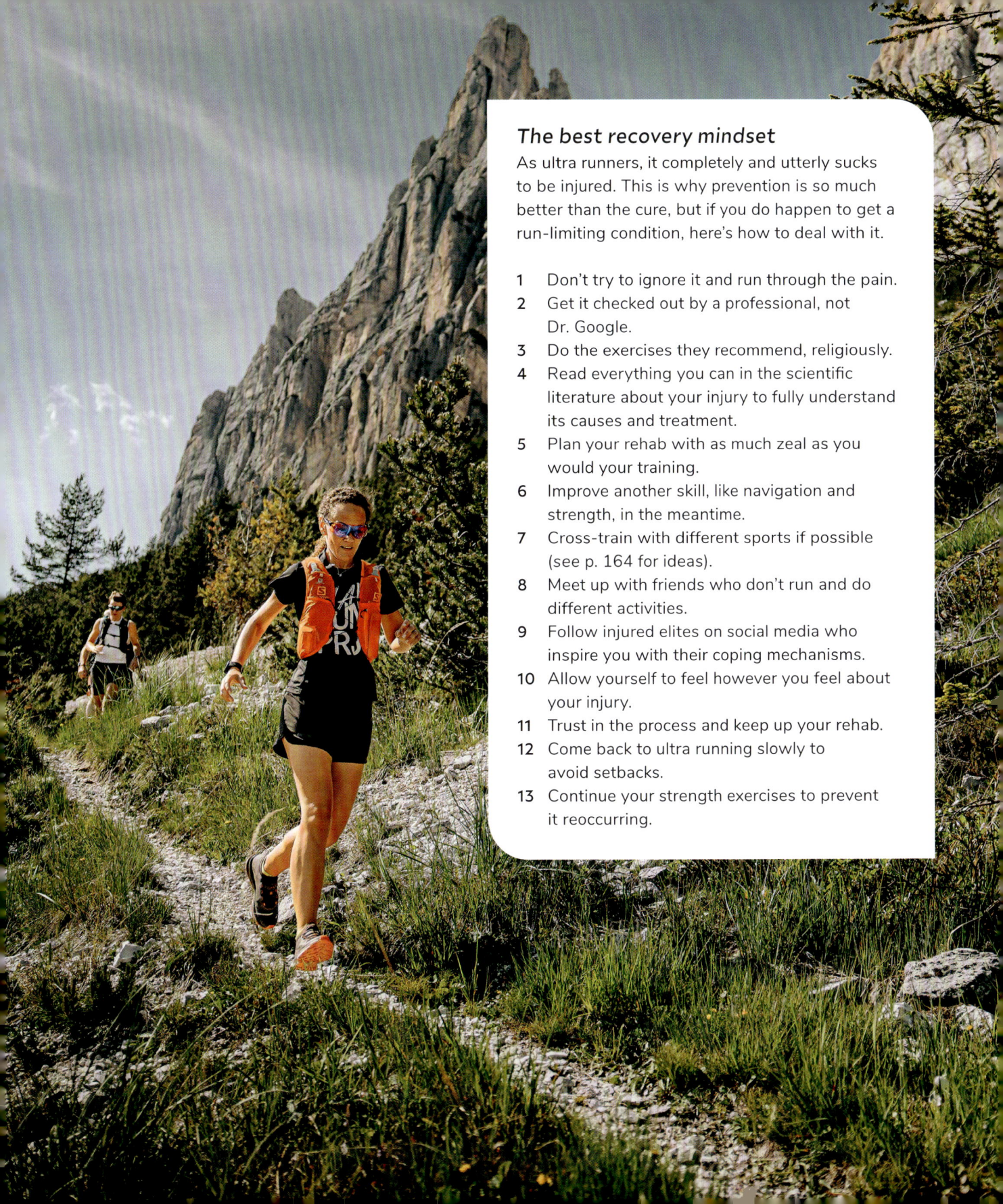

As ultra runners, it completely and utterly sucks to be injured. This is why prevention is so much better than the cure, but if you do happen to get a run-limiting condition, here's how to deal with it.

1. Don't try to ignore it and run through the pain.
2. Get it checked out by a professional, not Dr. Google.
3. Do the exercises they recommend, religiously.
4. Read everything you can in the scientific literature about your injury to fully understand its causes and treatment.
5. Plan your rehab with as much zeal as you would your training.
6. Improve another skill, like navigation and strength, in the meantime.
7. Cross-train with different sports if possible (see p. 164 for ideas).
8. Meet up with friends who don't run and do different activities.
9. Follow injured elites on social media who inspire you with their coping mechanisms.
10. Allow yourself to feel however you feel about your injury.
11. Trust in the process and keep up your rehab.
12. Come back to ultra running slowly to avoid setbacks.
13. Continue your strength exercises to prevent it reoccurring.

BLISTERS AND CHAFING

FOOTCARE PLAYS A MAJOR PART in ultra running success, as I found out to my dismay on the Cape Wrath Ultra in 2018. Blisters and chafing (anywhere on the body) can be so agonising as to prevent even walking, so prevention is always better than the cure. On long, wet races through mud, bogs and on gritty tracks, blisters might begin to rear their ugly heads even with the best-fitting shoes and clothing, so here's how to deal with them according to Ourea Events race medic, doctor and ultra runner, Dr. Nikki Sommers.

MEET THE EXPERT
DR. NIKKI SOMMERS

Dr. Nikki Sommers is a climber, turned Ironman triathlete, turned ultra runner, multi-day ultra event doctor for Ourea Events and a consultant in emergency medicine at Ysbyty Gwynedd hospital in Bangor, north Wales. Nikki completed the Cape Wrath Ultra in 2018, the brutal winter Spine Race in 2020 and the infamous Dragon's Back Race in 2022.

> *Learn how to look after your feet to get the most enjoyment and best performance out of your race. It's time well spent.*
>
> DR. NIKKI SOMMERS, @IRON_NIKKI

Before the race

- Thoroughly test all footwear, socks and clothing on your long runs and hikes in training – no new kit on race day.
- In stark contrast to all the 1990s advice to 'build up hard feet', the current school of thought is to have soft, supple foot skin through regular moisturising and exfoliation to prevent callouses contributing to friction and to reduce rubbing. This also reduces the risk of a hard patch of skin ripping off partly or entirely during a race, leaving a very vulnerable, painful area prone to infection underneath. Tape these areas instead, if they are hotspots. Using a urea-based moisturiser is the best way to soften tough skin.
- Keep toenails short and tidy, with no sharp edges to stab adjacent toes. Cut them four or five days prior to racing, so they're not too sharp on the day.
- Experiment with double-layered socks (the material rubs together instead of your feet) and toe socks (like gloves for feet) to see if these help.
- Try shoes a size larger or a dedicated wide-fit shoe like Altra or Topo.
- Experiment by taping known blister and chafing hotspots before you even start running. Physio K-tape is the best for your feet, while super-sticky Hypafix tape is really useful for any hotspots on your shoulders or spine from your running pack.

- Experiment by using sports lube or chafing cream (or butter as they're sometimes known) on hot spot areas beforehand. A cream like 'Trench' foot cream works really well on feet.
- Wear quick-draining, quick-drying footwear that doesn't hold water; this might be a shoe with more mesh in the upper and less robust materials. Make sure you also remember flip flops for your swollen feet after the race.
- Consider whether you might benefit from a waterproof sock. In cooler weather, calf- or knee-high waterproof socks can be a good way to keep your feet drier, but this works less so in the summer when your feet might get hot and sweaty inside them. You might also want to wear a thin liner sock inside your thicker waterproof socks, so you may also need to go up a shoe size.
- Experiment by using talc or a dedicated blister-stopping powder to dry out your feet.

On the run/race

1. Bring precut tape for your first aid kit for every day of a multi-day race, bagged and labelled day-by-day to save you time.
2. Tape any known problem areas before you set off.
3. Stop early on to readjust a wrinkled sock or re-lace/tighten/loosen your shoes.
4. Change to dry socks and/or dry shoes if possible from a drop bag.
5. Stop asap to address blister or chafing hotspots.
6. Clean and dry your feet as soon as you finish each day.
7. Massage the feet to encourage blood flow.
8. Wear open sandals to keep your feet dry.
9. Team up with other runners, tent-mates and team-mates to look after each other.

When to lube and with what?

First, our old friend the lip-salve champion Vaseline is not recommended – it's sticky, so attracts grit, and it goes hard in your socks and shoes. Use sports-recommended blister and chafing products. Learn where you chafe, pop the lube on shortly before the race (you see some runners doing this on the start line) and reapply the moment you feel any uncomfortable movement going on. Metanium (for nappy rash) is a barrier cream that 'soothes and protects', so this is also a good option for intimate areas like between bum-cheeks or in the groin area. It stains clothing but works better than Sudocrem.

ULTRA HACK

NIPPLE CHAFE

Pre-race, tape nipples with K-Tape, and round the corners of the tape, so it's less likely to come off (the tape, not the nipple, hopefully!).

Treat blisters right

Many smaller blisters can be self-treated using the following method:

1. Wash the whole foot to remove mud, debris and sweat, and dry it.
2. Clean your hands and the area around the blister with an antiseptic wipe and let it air-dry.
3. Let your feet air overnight if possible.
4. Cut your tape and padding to the required sizes, and round-off the corners of the tape so there are no corners to lift away from the skin.
5. Pad the blister with gauze or moleskin (but also be aware that moleskin is bulky and can cause more rubbing).
6. Rub the tape between your hands to heat-activate the glue, peel off the backing and tape the padding in place.

When to drain a blister?

The moment you make a hole in your skin to drain a blister, you increase the risk of infection, so only do this if the blister is too painful to run or walk on. Blood-blisters carry an even greater infection risk with the direct line to the blood, so drain these only if it's really necessary, and keep a close eye on them. You will need a sterile scalpel in your first aid kit; size 11 is the best.

HOW TO DRAIN

1. Wash the whole foot to remove mud, debris and sweat, and dry it.
2. Clean your hands and the area around the blister with an antiseptic wipe and let it air-dry (overnight if a multi-day race).
3. With a sterile scalpel blade, make multiple small slits to allow the blister to empty without refilling. Avoid removing the skin the blister formed under, as this is a useful natural protective layer.
4. Use a small amount of antiseptic cream, but not much, as you don't want the area to be wet.
5. For deeper blisters, apply zinc oxide cream to dry out.
6. Cut your tape and padding to the required sizes, and round-off the corners of the tape so there are no corners to lift away from the skin.
7. Pad the blister with gauze or moleskin (but also be aware that moleskin is bulky and can cause more rubbing).
8. Rub the tape between your hands to heat-activate the glue, peel off the backing and tape the padding in place.

No skin over the blister?

If the roof of a large blister has gone, revealing a sore, red patch underneath, possibly with slough (a wet, yellow/white by-product of wound inflammation) in it, there's a risk of infection. In this instance, place an Inadine dressing over the area to reduce the infection, before the padding and tape.

Compeed-style plasters?

These thick plasters are designed to be placed straight over the blister without padding and tape, sticking firmly to the blister as well as the skin around it. In a one-day event they can be the solution, but after this time (or earlier in hot weather), this type of plaster sticks to your sock as well, which can pull the whole thing off, making it difficult or impossible to change socks without ripping the plaster *and* blister away; and it can ruin your socks, leaving bits of hardened old plaster.

Avoid trench foot

Days of running with wet feet can result in macerated soles that are white, wrinkled and look like the start of trench foot. Use these tips to prevent this:

- Gently rubbing waterproof barrier creams such as 'Trench' foot cream on your feet prior to running can help protect them.
- In cooler weather, waterproof socks can help prevent all-day wet feet, as can quick-draining, fast-drying shoes.
- Waterproof running shoes are seldom recommended, as the water or sweat cannot get out once it has gotten in over the top.
- As soon as you finish each day, clean and dry your feet.
- Talc or specific blister powders can help keep feet drier.
- Massage the feet to encourage blood flow.
- Use comfy, open sandals around camp.
- Stick on moleskin padding to pad out painful areas on the sole.

ULTRA HACK

FOOTCARE IS TRAINING, TOO

Don't be a statistic. You might spend months and months training for a race and overlook footcare admin as a vital part of preparation, but preventing blisters (and any other chafing) on long runs and hikes is a training priority for ultras and multi-day races; it doesn't matter how fit you are if you can't move for infected, blistered feet that could have been prevented or treated effectively.

Toe nail gone?

Black toe nails and the eventual loss of toe nails (usually the big one) altogether are not ultra necessities. Prevent them by wearing shoes that are large enough for your feet and your sock of choice, and don't start races with manky toes and overgrown, sharp toenails – look after your feet as per the advice at the start of this section.

If you do start to lose a toenail, tape it back down from over the top to underneath, then back round again to hold it on. If it's gone altogether, tape the toe in the same way but without the nail.

Infection?

Prevent this at all costs by keeping everything as clean as possible. Use sterile dressings and scalpels, and use antiseptic on your hands and the affected area before you attend to blisters and open wounds. On multi-day races take the dressings off and clean everything each day or every 24 hours. Drink plenty of fluids and keep an eye on the area. See a medical professional for increased swelling, redness, pus and red lines tracking upwards, as this may mean you need antibiotics.

Race medics?

Many larger, longer, multi-day races have dedicated race medics to help runners with the worst blisters. However, the queues may be long, so it's best if you can be as self-reliant as you can, so that you can get more eating, kit-sorting and sleeping done.

When to stop?

Ultra runners have wildly differing pain thresholds, so it's up to you to decide when the enjoyment of the challenge is over, unless medical advice differs. If you have only a few miles or even one whole day of a multi-day race to go, it might make sense to put up with the short-term pain for the long-term glory. However, if you still have four days of foot-torture to endure, you might decide to gracefully bow out, promising yourself to prepare better next time. Treat a DNF due to blisters as a fantastic learning opportunity to improve your footcare regime to increase your chances of success at the next race.

MY STORY

BLISTERS ALMOST RUINED MY RACE

'**An airline lost my race kit** for the nine-day National Three Peaks Ultra. I decided to save money by buying cheap socks, but they stretched, allowing grit and sand through their fibres – cue multiple blisters 70 miles [112km] in. There were still 360 miles [380km] to go and the situation seemed bleak. I bought blister plasters and better socks from shops en route and fellow runners donated Vaseline and K-tape, such is the spirit of ultra events. I needed the blisters to heal whilst running... It would be hard enough normally just keeping them from getting worse. I had to pop them and think about the alignment of the tapes vs shearing forces. I also modified how I ran, paying constant attention to the underside of my toes and heel, which was tricky. But within two days the blister roofs had adhered to their bases and stopped hurting. After another three or so days I completed the race, with blisters from Loch Lomond to the finish in Llanberis. Not every run with blisters turns out bad.'

CHIN CHEAN YONG

BLISTERS AND CHAFING 163

CROSS-TRAINING

DOING TRAINING THAT ISN'T SOLELY running is a fantastic way to not only reduce your risk of succumbing to common running injuries, but also to make life more interesting. And if you do sustain an injury that stops you from running, these exciting alternative methods of getting your heart pumping can maintain your fitness and save you from going bananas.

> *Do whatever you can to bring joy to your life, outside of running. Try new things, meet new people, explore new places. Keep yourself afloat – the time will pass and you'll be back in no time.*
>
> FLORA BEVERLEY, YOUTUBER AT FOOD FITNESS FLORA, @FOODFITNESSFLORA

1 Strength sessions

Improving your overall strength is the single most important type of cross-training for ultra runners, especially as you get older and/or want to run longer distances. Strength sessions help you maintain efficient form and prevent injury over long distances when tired, and they help you recover more quickly from endurance events. Use any exercises given by your physio as your starting point, then use pp. 90–95 in this book as and when the exercises fit in with your rehab programme.

2 Road cycling

This is a fantastic way to build leg and lung strength without the impact of running. Runners often find that despite an injury that stops them running, they can often hop on the bike to maintain fitness, leg strength and sanity.

3 Mountain biking
Mountain biking's extra lumps and bumps compared to road cycling will give you an all-over body workout as you work hard to maintain your balance and co-ordination by using your arms and core.

4 Swimming
Great for the whole body, especially the breathing. Technique lessons will pay dividends for your running as you open up your lungs and learn to control your breath. A dip in a cold lake or river is also a fantastic way to soothe aching leg muscles after a long run.

5 Rowing
Rowing machines are commonly found in gyms and are reasonably inexpensive to buy, and rowing with good technique will give your whole body an incredible workout without the impact. It's also sociable, if you join a club.

6 Yoga/Pilates
Being more flexible and having good balance is always an advantage for running on twisting, quick-changing trails. Even just 10 minutes of regular yoga or Pilates in your morning or evening routine can improve your agility, balance and coordination.

7 Fitness classes
HIIT, boxing, body combat, spinning, martial arts – whatever is on offer at your local gym, have a go. Not only will these classes get you stronger and fitter, but there's also the social side – maybe convert a few people to ultra running and lend them this book…?

8 Hiking
Massively underrated, hill walking is one of the best things you can do to improve your trail running endurance, uphill abilities and footwork on uneven terrain. Get more bang for your buck by hiking high-altitude mountains with a heavy backpack. And practice your navigation while you're at it.

9 Scrambling and rock climbing
Another great activity for helping you pick a line through rocky sections, scrambling (easy rock climbing, often with no ropes), rock climbing and bouldering (climbing short routes on large boulders without ropes) are great for developing strength and flexibility, and pushing your comfort zone to improve your head for heights.

10 Cross-country skiing
Not available to everyone, of course, but ski-racing is the long-established winter sport of many European trail runners due to the fitness benefits and whole-body workout without the impact. Your next holiday perhaps?

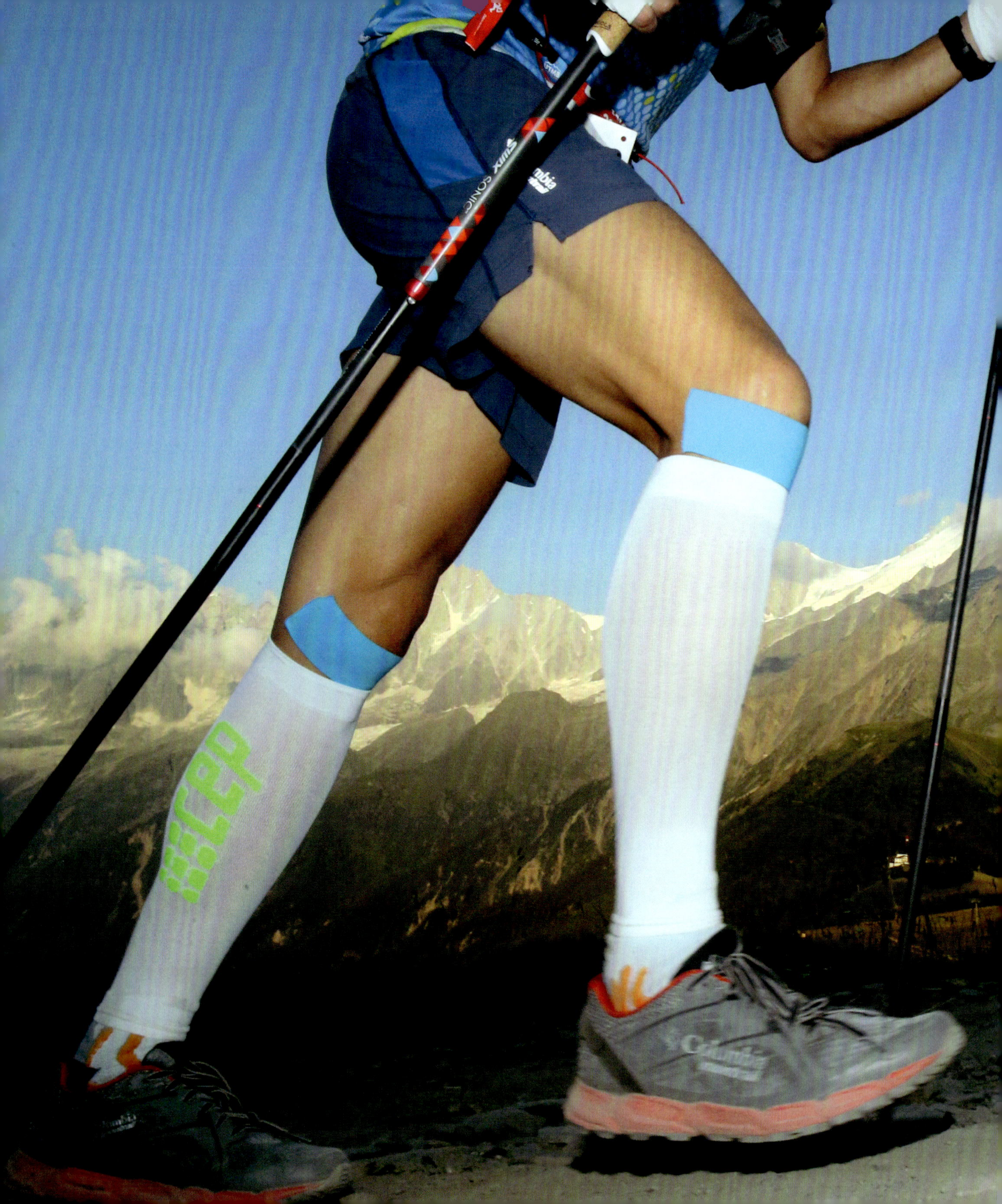
cep
Columbia

6
ULTRA GEAR

The best gear for ultra running is durable and well-designed, here's how to make sure you make the right choices the first time round.

ULTRA RUNNING SHOES

THIS IS A TRICKY ONE to address outright because ultras can be on any type of surface, so you need to use shoes appropriate to the terrain you're going to be training and racing on. While some ultras are held solely on Tarmac or round a track, the majority of ultra courses are a mix of footpaths, bridleways, towpaths and tracks, because trails are interesting and great fun, and there are fewer road crossings and traffic safety issues. So for many ultras you're going to be looking for trail shoes with varying levels of grip and cushioning depending on how muddy and rocky the paths are.

Fit

Fit is by far the most important feature of any running shoe, and it's even more so for ultra running shoes because of the long periods of time you'll be wearing them. If the shoes don't fit you right it doesn't matter how grippy or cushioned they are, or which pro runner swears by them, they could give you blisters, rub your heel raw or pinch your toes and end your race. That's why it's best to read as many reviews as you can to understand which foot shape the shoe seems to fit best, then to try them on with your usual running socks and jog around the house for a few days before deciding to keep them. Use an independent running shop, or buy a few pairs online so you can compare and keep the best-fitting ones.

- Check the drop
- Varied cushioning
- Varied level of grip
- Choice of lacing systems
- Do you need a wide fit?
- Breathable, quick-drying uppers
- Protective rubber rand

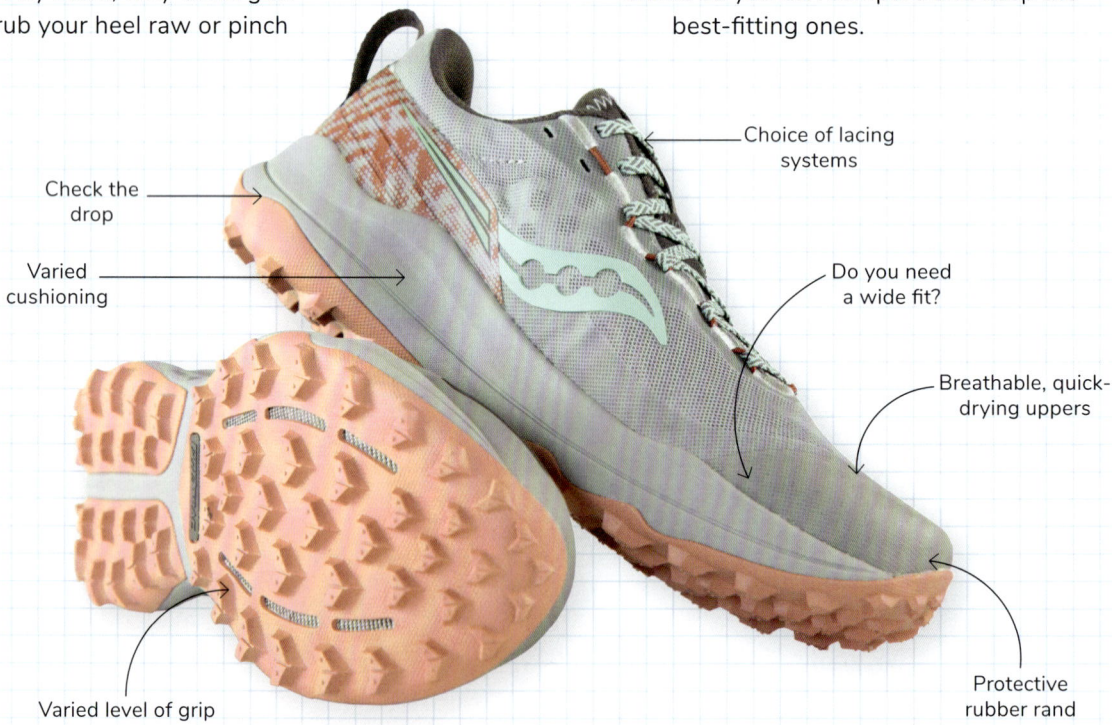

6. ULTRA GEAR

Drop

The drop is the height difference between the heel of the shoe and its toe and if you suddenly start using a shoe with a much lower drop (for example 12mm to 4mm) you risk straining and injuring your calf muscles and Achilles tendon. Trail shoes tend to be lower to the ground, sometimes with less cushioning to allow your foot to feel and respond quickly to uneven terrain, often with a 4–8mm drop. Zero-drop shoes for road or trail are considered a more natural option. However, if you're very used to having a higher stack under your heel, you must transition over a good few months to use these comfortably for long distances without strain or injury. Use them for a few miles once a week, upping the distance and frequency gradually.

Cushioning

For ultras on Tarmac and hard paths, you might want more cushioning to protect your feet from many miles of pounding, but if you're training and racing mainly on softer, lumpier ground, you might want less so your feet can feel the ground and respond faster. Much of this is down to personal preference, experience and heavier runners might enjoy a bit more cushioning than lighter ones.

> **ULTRA HACK**
>
> ### GO LARGE!
>
> When running a long way or doing multi-day races, your feet can swell a shoe size (sometimes even two sizes) due to fluid retention, swollen muscles and blood vessels. Training gradually, pacing your race sensibly and keeping your electrolytes topped up will help prevent this, and you could put a larger pair in your drop bag if you find this happening to you regularly on ultras.

Support

Many sports professionals don't believe overpronation exists or is a problem (see p. 170). Runners don't get injuries from wearing certain shoes, rather they need to strengthen up their feet, legs and whole body to run efficiently and injury free. If you're happy with your stability in your current road shoe, with no injuries, there's no reason to change it, but the vast majority of trail running shoes are neutral because you want a more flexible, less rigid shoe that lets the foot feel and respond faster to uneven ground. Strengthening up is the answer here (see p. 90).

Uppers

Uppers should be durable with strong stitching, with a reinforced or rubber rand at the front to guard against rocks. Some shoes have more mesh and are more breathable than others, but most are made from quick-drying fabrics that will drain water, and when combined with a good-quality sports sock, will dry off as you run.

Lacing

Most trail shoes have traditional, flattish, wide pull-through laces, but there are also other options like thin, wire-like pull-cords or a BOA turning-dial, which can be quicker and easier to use with cold hands. Personally I find traditional laces create the best fit, but there are many people who get a snug fit with the pull-cord and BOA dial lacing systems.

Wide-fit?

In ultra running especially, there's a call for a wider fit around the toes to accommodate foot swell over high mileages, so look to see if a shoe is available in a wider version if you feel your toes could do with more wriggle room. There are also dedicated wide-fit running shoe brands, such as Altra and Topo, which are worth considering if regular wide-fit shoes are still squashing your toes together.

Waterproof?

Most ultra runners need a shoe that drains water rather than a waterproof shoe, because water gets in at the ankle and can't get out again. However, they can be of use to keep your foot warmer in wind, snow, light rain, wet grass and small puddles on easy ground. The moment you head into any deep mud, bog and puddles however, water gets in over the top. It's for this reason that if you buy only one pair, non-waterproof is best.

Weight

Unless they're made of lead, most running shoes aren't too heavy to run in and so the weight of a shoe is far less important than the fit, the drop, the grip and the cushioning. If a pair weighs 100g (3 ½oz) more but they fit like a dream, those are the ones you should go for, especially for ultra running. Heavier shoes can also be more robust and last for a long time, which is another plus point for long distances, the environment and your wallet. Unless you're vying for a podium place or doing a short, fast race, buying a super-light shoe isn't necessarily that important.

EXPERT ADVICE
OVERPRONATION IS A MYTH

'The dreaded overpronation is actually a myth – a helpful marketing tool to sell insoles and trainers. It is actually very hard to find links to overpronation as the cause of injuries within the scientific literature. Pronation, aka the foot rolling inwards, is a natural and normal part of running, and if you didn't do it, you would be in big trouble. If you have an injury it can play a part in irritating the problem, but so can other aspects of the way you run. When we talk about overpronation, people often look at the position the foot ends in, they don't actually look at the journey the foot went on to get there and the starting position. Some of the greatest runners of all time have large amounts of overpronation and still can run sub 2-hour 15-minute marathons. So, pronation and the amount you do it is relevant for some people, but not all. Some people will feel more comfortable in a more supportive shoe or insoles and others will not. However, overpronation is not the route of all evil that it is made out to be and actually, if you have the strength to cope with the motion, then your body may cope just fine on its own.'

NICK KNIGHT, PODIATRIST AT NK ACTIVE, @NKACTIVECLINICS

ULTRA CLOTHING

HURRAH! CLOTHING FOR ULTRA RUNNING is much the same as for 'normal' running. You can spend a fortune on gear if you want the top-performance fabrics, the brand name and (hopefully) longer-lasting kit, but as long as you have a good sports bra if needed, your usual running clobber should be more than adequate. As long as it wicks sweat, dries quickly and fits comfily without chafing, it should go the distance.

Socks

Specific sports socks are a lot more expensive than those cute fashion ones with llamas on the sides, but they are very much worth it for their snug, elasticated fit that doesn't crumple up while you run and their quick-drying, breathable, anti-pong yarns that keep you comfy for mile upon mile. They come in different thicknesses with more or less padding under the heel and mid-foot, so it's good to have a range for cool or warm conditions, or for a better fit in shoes that come up slightly small or large. I prefer them to come up to the ankle to protect the skin at the heel and ankle bone. Double-layer socks, trotter socks (separate big toe pocket) and toe socks (like gloves for feet) can also help prevent blisters, and grippy silicone bands around the arch can prevent slippage within the shoe.

Insoles

Very much not essential, but I recently discovered that swapping the shoe's original insole for a specially designed running insole has some advantages when ultra running. First, if your shoes are a tad large (I have small volume feet) they can help to fill them slightly; you could also use just one if you have one foot smaller than the other. They provide more padding, support and stability for the foot over longer distances; they grip your sock and they don't slip down and ruckle up as some original insoles are prone to do.

Sports bra

Very important for women, especially those with larger boobs. You might need a tighter size to your non-running bra so try plenty of different designs and jump and jog around the shop or your house to check the bounce.

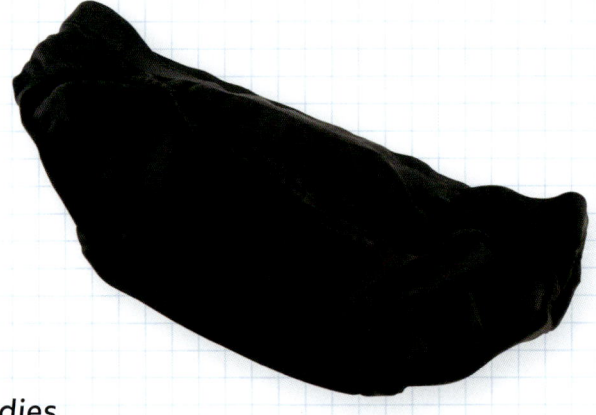

Undies

Often overlooked, but investing in a few pairs of sport-specific, quick-drying, seamless, chafe-free undies is totally worth it on long, wet or hot training runs and races.

Shorts and tights

For ultra running pay more attention to the seams, features and fit of your running shorts and leggings. Flatlocked seams are a must to prevent chafing, as are quick-drying, sweat-wicking materials. Make sure the pockets are big/small enough for what you want to put in them, zipped/elasticated and in a handy place. Look for a thick, comfy waistband with a drawstring so they don't keep slipping down. It's handy to have ankle zips on full-length leggings. And funky colours and patterns are fantastic at keeping you and others motivated as the miles creep up.

T-shirts and long-sleeved tops

Light-ish, quick-drying and moisture-wicking fabrics give the most comfort, and look for an antimicrobial treatment like Polygiene or natural yarns like Merino wool to protect from odours – especially useful on multi-day races. A collar is good for sun protection and shields the neck from running pack chafe. A zip at the neck is useful for more ventilation and getting the top on easily.

Compression clothing – useful for ultra runners?

Compression tights, calf guards and long socks are popular with some ultra runners while others aren't fussed or even find it detrimental to their comfort or performance. While there's no definitive answer, some aspects are backed up with more research than others. Here's the science:

POSSIBLY... IT BOOSTS PERFORMANCE DURING RUNNING

However, independent (i.e. not funded by compression clothing companies) scientific research has yet to verify this. On the other hand, there is definite scientifically proven value in the placebo effect, so if running in compression clothing makes you feel springy, supported and less wobbly then why not wear it? Compression wear is fine on any distance as long as it's not so tight it cuts off your circulation or stops evaporative cooling, leading to overheating and a reduction in performance.

DEFINITELY... IT HELPS WITH RECOVERY

Compression-wear is used medically in the treatment of circulatory diseases. Once you have the right size (a reputable brand will ask for your measurements) it works by placing pressure on blood vessels, which reduces their diameter and improves blood flow and valve function. This can increase lactate removal and nutrient delivery to the muscles, speeding up the repair process, and reduces swelling, inflammation and delayed onset muscle soreness (DOMS). This is especially useful if you have to sit for a long time after running a long way, for example driving home from an ultra.

Other useful running kit

ANTI-CHAFE CREAM
As you up the distance, you might find various parts of you begin to rub uncomfortably against each other, so a tube of sports lube and/or nipple tape for runners is essential in these situations.

SUNSCREEN
Especially for gingers like me! I use a transparent liquid spray that bonds to the skin like P20, which is waterproof, sweatproof and stays on all day after applying only once in the morning. Traditional creams can get grit stuck to them, make you sweatier, and need reapplying, which is a faff mid-ultra.

MIDGE HEAD NET AND INSECT REPELLENT
Essential for races in northern England and Scotland in breeze-free, warm weather from May to September, these little biting insects can be out in force, especially close to water and bogs. It's good to choose more eco-friendly versions if possible, and Avon Skin So Soft moisturiser works well as a repellent, too, but it isn't as effective as DEET, which is best if you need to protect from mosquitos to avoid malaria in other countries.

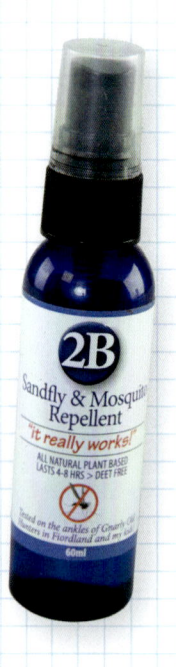

TRAIL HACK

WATERPROOF SOCKS
Waterproof socks can be a good shout for very muddy, wet trails. Combined with a non-waterproof shoe they keep your feet warmer in cold, wet and windy weather. However in warmer conditions they can lead to sweaty, rubbing feet, so they are best for winter running.

DRY BAGS
Keeping spare kit dry in winter is vital, so fold it and squash it into airtight, sealable sandwich bags or invest in some more robust, purpose-designed dry bags.

174   6. ULTRA GEAR

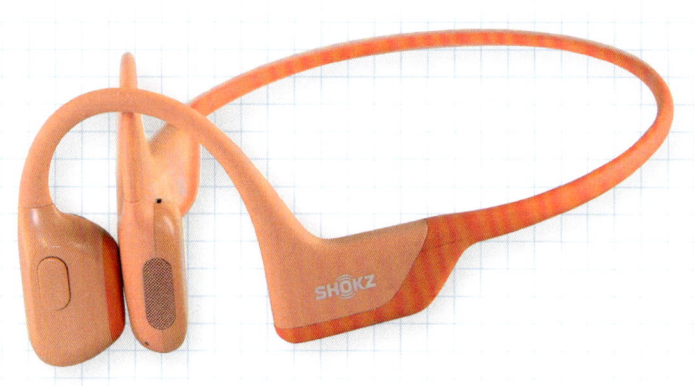

HEADPHONES

If you want to listen to music or podcasts (great motivation for longer runs), it's worth investing in some water-resistant, wireless, bone conduction headphones (or bonephones, as I call them). These are the best sort for running, as they send vibrations through your cheekbones straight into the inner ear without blocking your ear canal like earbuds, so you can hear traffic, birdsong, people and safety instructions from marshals.

COMPASS

If you want to start planning your own routes in the hills and mountains and doing events that require navigation, you can use a compass to orient the map correctly and take bearings, especially in misty weather. See Navigation and GPS on p. 68 for more.

ULTRA RUNNING JACKETS

THERE ARE A FEW DIFFERENT types of jacket to suit different situations. Here are all the options, and an explanation of taped seams, in case you were wondering...

Emergency waterproof jacket

This is the lightest taped-seam jacket that it's possible to make, around the 100g (3 ½oz) mark, often without pockets and no cuff, hem or hood adjustment, and sometimes in a smock version with a half or three-quarter length zip to save every gram and fold down as small as a tennis ball. They can feel quite thin and fragile, almost like (dare I say this?) a strong plastic bag. They are also generally very high in price. They are designed for situations where you are required or want to take a fully waterproof jacket on your race or run but don't think you will need to use it, so it's important for it to be very light and packable. If you're running in a remote location and/or heading out into a full day and maybe also a night and following day of rain it's wiser to take a more protective, slightly heavier jacket with more useful adjustment features to keep you warmer and drier.

Waterproof jacket

Running jackets are usually nice and light, around 200–300g (7–11oz). The heavier they are, the more features they usually have, although this isn't always the case in some of the more expensive jackets using the latest lightweight materials. Features that you want include a fully adjustable hood, zip pocket(s), adjustable drawcord hem, dropped tail, which is longer at the back to cover your bum, and Velcro-adjustable cuffs.

Jacket vents?

Some jackets have venting at the back that does become somewhat hampered by a running pack so is not recommended for ultra runners. Others have underarm holes for venting, which is fine for day-long, low level (as in altitude-wise) ultras, but for safety reasons in wild, remote, mountainous locations I prefer a waterproof jacket not to have any more holes than necessary (head, hands, hips) to reduce the potential for wind, rain and snow to get in. For venting, undo the main zip and cuffs, or take the jacket off and wear it back to front for a half-half effect.

Waterproof trousers

Not a jacket, obviously, but seeing as we're talking waterproofs, in trouser form you're looking for a relaxed rather than tight fit, stretchy fabric and articulated knees for complete freedom of movement. A zip or flare at the ankle is essential for getting them on quickly without taking your shoes off. It's great to pop a light pair (around 100–200g/3 ½–7oz) into your running pack for instant extra warmth in wind and/or rain. Always pack them with the ankles unzipped for minimal faff on the wet, cold and windy hillside.

Windproof jacket

Also known as wind-resistant or water-resistant jackets, these are more breathable than waterproof jackets, as they are often made from a single layer of fabric without a membrane, and they don't have taped seams. Often on a cold, dry or drizzly day, a t-shirt or long-sleeved top with a windproof jacket over the top is a warm enough combo, with a waterproof jacket carried in your pack just in case heavier rain occurs. The warmth of a windproof jacket in relation to its weight (the lightest are around 50g/1 ¾oz!) and pack size is brilliant. You can tie it round your waist or stuff it into your pack if you get hot, or pop your waterproof on top and treat it like a thin, insulating mid-layer when it rains.

ULTRA HACK

THE TRUTH ABOUT BREATHABILITY

A great many jackets are marketed as being highly 'breathable' with fabrics that let water vapour (hot sweat) escape without letting water droplets (rain) in. However, in my experience, apart from skin, there is no waterproof material breathable enough to let out all the sweat when you're running, unless it's so cold you're not making any. And, if it's not warm enough inside the jacket to turn all your sweat into vapour form, then it becomes water droplets of your own making, inside your waterproof jacket. Doh! You're better off learning by experience about when to put on, vent or take off your waterproof jacket depending on rainfall type, duration, temperature, wind chill and exertion level.

For example, if I was running through drizzling to light rain in July feeling warm, I wouldn't put on my waterproof unless I started getting colder from heavier rain or wind, or if I slowed down or stopped. That's why you wear quick-drying clothing. Keep your jacket handy (I thread it through my shoulder strap under my arm), so you can whip it on and off easily multiple times during a run. Wear it over your pack for less faff (buying a jacket one size larger helps with this), and you can also wear it back to front if the wind's coming towards you.

Down jacket

A bit like a half a sleeping bag but with arms, these down-filled jackets are toasty warm, but they're less useful than synthetic jackets while you're actually out running because you have to be so careful not to get them wet. Feathers provide less warmth when wet than synthetic fibres and although you can get waterproofed down jackets, these are much heavier, so keep them for indoor spaces, or store them in a small dry bag and save them for dry weather.

Synthetic jacket

These are lightweight, quick-drying jackets filled with insulating cotton-wool-looking fibres like PrimaLoft. They're like the outdoorsy version of a jumper/sweater and they're easy to pop into your pack. They're great if the weather turns cold or you need to slow down or stop to look at the views, take photos or spot wildlife; or for when the weather gets colder, you get slow from tiredness or injury or you need to stop at an aid station or to help another runner.

What are taped seams?

Taped seams means that where a waterproof jacket has been sewn together, the seams are covered in thin tape, usually on the inside. This is because the stitching process leaves small holes at the seams, which need to be secured so as not to allow rain in. 'Full body cover' with taped seams, which you may see on mandatory kit lists, refers to runners carrying both a hooded waterproof jacket and waterproof trousers with taped seams.

Save money – buy second hand!

All this essential kit can be pricey bought new, especially the lighter weight items, so before you fork out, ask friends if they have any old kit to sell (they might even donate it to you!), ask in a trail or ultra running Facebook group (if you're allowed under the group's rules), join a buy and sell Facebook group for outdoor or running gear, and check eBay and second hand sites online, try GumTree, Vinted, PreLoved Sports, and Facebook groups Running Gear Buy and Sell, and Outdoor Gear Exchange UK.

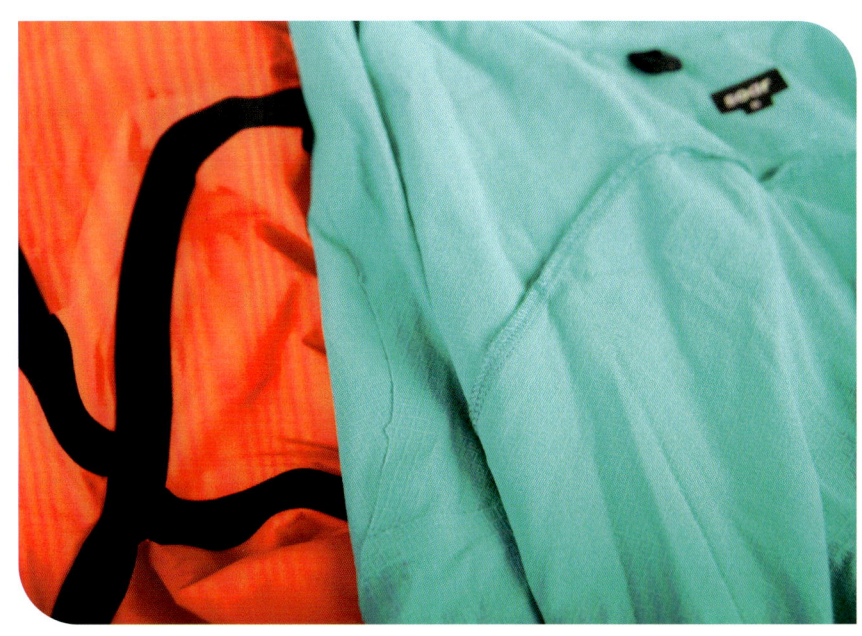

ULTRA HACK

BOOST WATERPROOF PERFORMANCE

Keep your waterproof jacket and trousers performing at their best by following their care instructions and washing them every few months in a dedicated, eco-friendly cleaning product like Nikwax or Granger's. Never wash them with ordinary detergent or fabric softener, as the chemicals can strip off the Durable Water Repellent (DWR) coating on your waterproof.

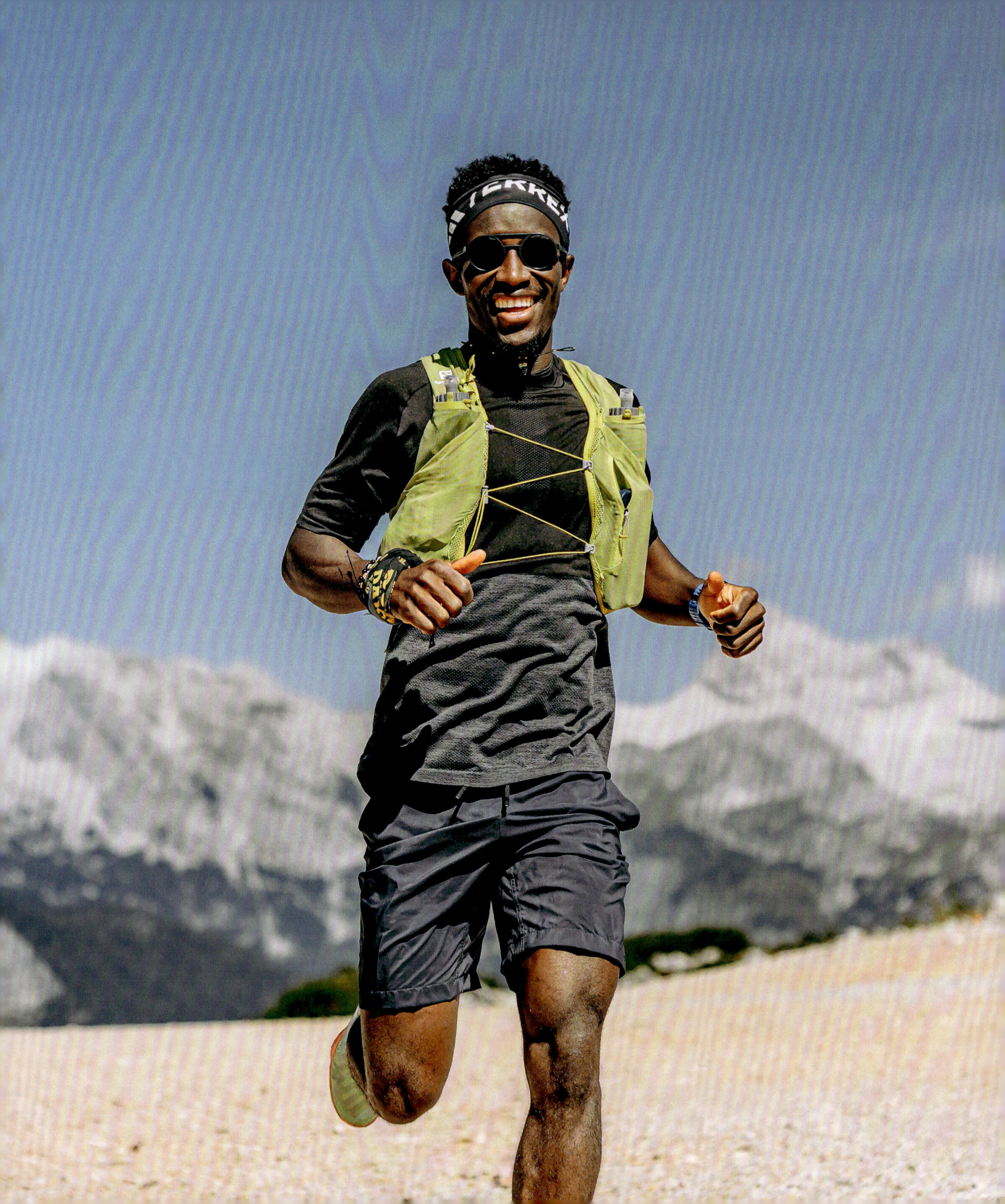

ULTRA RUNNING PACKS

IF YOU'RE OUT FOR A LONG TIME, potentially heading further into the unknown with less support, it stands to reason that you'll need to carry a few bits and pieces to survive along the way, like water, food, your phone, warm kit, waterproofs and a first aid kit. Here are the main features to look out for in an ultra running pack:

Capacity

The amount you need to carry to stay at the right temperature, get fed and keep safe while you're running depends on the distance, level of support, how remote the location is and the weather conditions. A 5-litre pack might be fine for a 50k ultra over rolling hills in the spring, a 10-litre capacity for a 100k in the summer and as much as 20 litres for an unsupported multi-dayer in remote, winter mountainside.

Fit

It's very important your running pack fits well without digging in or chafing because it's going to be hugging you round the shoulders and back for many, many miles. Any pack is comfy with nothing in it, so when choosing, fill the pack with all the kit you need for the race, in the pockets you think it should all be in (see if you can borrow and fill soft bottles so as not to open new ones) and jog round the shop or house in your usual running gear to check it's comfortable. Try the women's fit if you're a smaller man and vice versa; the fit is more important than the label.

Pockets

You're looking for a lot of easily accessible, stretchy pockets on the front of the shoulder straps and around the sides, so you can swig water effortlessly and grab a snack or a pair of gloves with ease. A couple with zips rather than all elasticated is a good idea to secure essentials like your phone, cards, money and car keys. Sometimes there's a handy zip pocket at the base of the main compartment that you can reach round and access without stopping to take the pack off too. Check you can reach and/or fit your hand in each pocket easily.

Main compartment

This is generally for things you don't need access to as often, like spare extra warm layers, your first aid kit, food and water for later on, if unsupported, a tracker if you're on a race that facilitates dot-watching for the folks at home (keep it near the top!) and waterproof trousers. If this compartment opens easily at the top via a horizontal zip or Velcro you can often reach to shove in your waterproof jacket on the move, too. If the zip runs downwards or there's a roll top with a clip, this is less easy.

ULTRA HACK

WEAR A BUMBAG TOO
Some ultra runners wear a 1–3-litre bumbag or waistbelt around their hips, under their running packs, to reduce the size and weight on the shoulders and back, and create even easier access to snacks, small, light bits of kit and running poles.

Bottles or bladder
Some running packs have a couple of different options for where you can store soft water bottles up front, either in a high pocket or lower down with long drinking tubes secured higher up with elastic. Some packs choose just one of these options, and most have a hook in the main compartment if you want to use a hydration bladder in the back. The advantage of bottles over bladders is that it's easier to get them out and quickly refill them at aid stations, and to gauge how much water you have left.

Design
The most efficient design for a running pack is a waistcoat with plenty of pockets. This is usually sized, for example S, M and L, to fit different body sizes; the other common design sees the side pockets replaced with compression straps so that one size fits all. I wouldn't recommend the latter, however, as you miss out on side pockets, which are super handy.

Weight
A good weight for a running pack including two 500ml (17fl oz) soft bottles is around 300–450g (11–14oz) depending on how large it is and how robust or lightweight the fabrics are. More importantly, consider if it is a comfy fit and has a big enough capacity, and whether you can access all the pockets easily.

Pole attachments
Some running packs, especially the larger ones, have elasticated pole attachments down the shoulder straps, across the chest or across the back, or you can attach a quiver-style bag. Test these with your poles before you buy to make sure they're easy to access on the move and don't bounce about or get in the way.

Save money – make a Frankenpack
Sometimes we can get a running pack (or any running gear, really) that's almost perfect, but wouldn't it be nice if there was an extra pocket there or a zip here, or if the poles attached here instead of there? No problem, within reason; you can add or detract what you need. Simply get your scissors, needle and thread and set to work – or get someone else with better skills to do this.

ULTRA RUNNING WATCHES

A LONG BATTERY LIFE and navigation capabilities are very useful when choosing a GPS watch to track your ultra running training and the race itself. You can measure an overwhelming number of metrics from your wrist these days, so here are the main features you will most often need for ultras.

Data screens

You can often adjust and scroll through several different data screens on a watch to display anything from one to even eight separate metrics, like time, distance, heart rate, time elapsed and pace. You can also scroll to a navigation screen to follow your GPX track or the gradient profile of the route, downloaded from your computer or smartphone.

GPX tracks and navigation

These are files containing route data that you can either create yourself using mapping software or download from another person, race organiser or brand. Follow your specific watch's instructions for the precise steps to upload GPX files, as it's a little different for each. The result is a thin line on the screen with a direction arrow to indicate the way, and the top models will show helpful map features on-screen, too, like contour lines, buildings, forests, rivers and lakes. Take a back-up paper map in case your watch runs out of juice or breaks, and keep aware of your surroundings, especially near to cliff edges and bodies of water, as the accuracy of the track depends on how accurately the route file was created.

Altitude

This is a very useful navigation aid, especially in mountainous areas and fog, as you can get a reliable reading for how high you are above sea level, which will help you confirm where you are using the contour lines on the map (see p. 68).

Battery life

Many GPS watches will last 6–10 hours on their default settings, but that won't be long enough for some ultra runners. Each watch varies, so look at the manual for extras, but here are a few things you can do to extend battery life:

1. First, check to see if you can charge your watch while in use on your wrist as it's not always possible with the position of the charging connection. This isn't ideal and blocks out any wrist /heart rate (HR) measurements, but it can save you from buying a more expensive watch.
2. Turn off extra features and connectivity like automatic backlight, Bluetooth and Wi-Fi that drain a small but noticeable amount over longer distances.
3. Change the frequency of the GPS fix. It's usually set on fixing every second, so a change to every five seconds, or even every 60 seconds will extend battery life considerably, but this obviously results in less accurate data.
4. Switch to GPS only mode rather than the speedier GPS + GLONASS (an additional global navigation satellite system using 24 Russian satellites), which is often a default setting. The latter system uses more battery life to track two satellites for better accuracy in built up areas or forests, which isn't always essential. Sync your watch via Wi-Fi to its connecting app every few weeks on its GPS-only setting to make sure it's fully updated to predict and find the satellites efficiently.
5. Switch off the map display when you're not using the navigation function and turn the navigation off altogether if you don't need it for a while on certain parts of the run or race.

Time

Sometimes this basic measurement is overlooked, and it's pretty important, especially when keeping aware of ultra cut-off timings, so you might have to adjust the data screens if you don't want to have to keep pressing buttons and scrolling to find out the time during your run.

Heart rate

HR can be a useful measure of effort, and some runners will be training to specific HR zones. Most GPS watches now have the HR sensor in the wrist and while not quite as quick to respond or accurate as the chest strap, they're easier and less faff if you don't need pinpoint accuracy and can combine your HR reading with perceived effort from experience, especially if you're juggling a bra strap, too. However, you can get bras with built in monitor pads in the bra chest strap, so that's an option if you want to improve accuracy.

Speed and pace

This is one of the most basic functions of the runner's watch and it's useful to have an indication of how fast you're going, your pace in minute miles or kilometres, your mile or kilometre splits and your average speed over the whole route. They might also have a race time predictor at your current pace, but with such varied hills, tough terrain and navigation possibly to contend with on your ultra, this is not always a super-useful feature.

Intervals

This is a super-useful feature for sessions when you want to work at a certain pace or effort level for a certain amount of time, and then set a rest/recovery time before you repeat this. You can choose the interval length, the recovery time and the number of repeats you wish to do, and the watch will beep at you when each interval is up so you don't have to keep looking down at it.

Multi-sport options

If you're keen on not just running, look for a watch that offers a change of activity profile for sports such as cycling, swimming, strength work and yoga, so you can keep track of all your workouts.

Syncing

Check how your watch syncs up to a program where you can see and analyse your data. Most upload to their own app, but these can vary in their user-friendliness and usefulness. So many runners set their watch app to automatically upload each training session to Strava (aka Facebook for sporty people) and analyse it there using the maps, training and gear diary function, pace and heart rate graphs.

Other useful features

CADENCE AND STRIDE LENGTH

This helps you get a feel for whether you are taking the recommended 180 steps per minute, not overstriding and minimising your ground-contact time. However, for off-road ultras, your steps might vary a lot with the terrain and gradient so there's no need to obsess about this.

VIRTUAL COACH AND WORKOUTS

This can be useful as a guide and give you suggestions for training sessions to follow or remind you to either run harder or not overdo it based on previous runs, but it doesn't necessarily know what other activities you've been doing without wearing it. A human coach is a much better option to get the most from your performance.

SMART NOTIFICATIONS

If you like to stay in touch rather than escape life while you run, look for watches that sync up with your smartphone to continuously ping you messages, emails and calendar notifications on the move. Er, great..!

MUSIC AND PAYMENTS

Many watches now integrate with your smartphone and wireless headphones so you can control music and podcasts on the go and pay for things in shops. It looks whizzy, but if you always carry your phone with you anyway it's not essential, and takes up more battery life.

RUNNING POLES

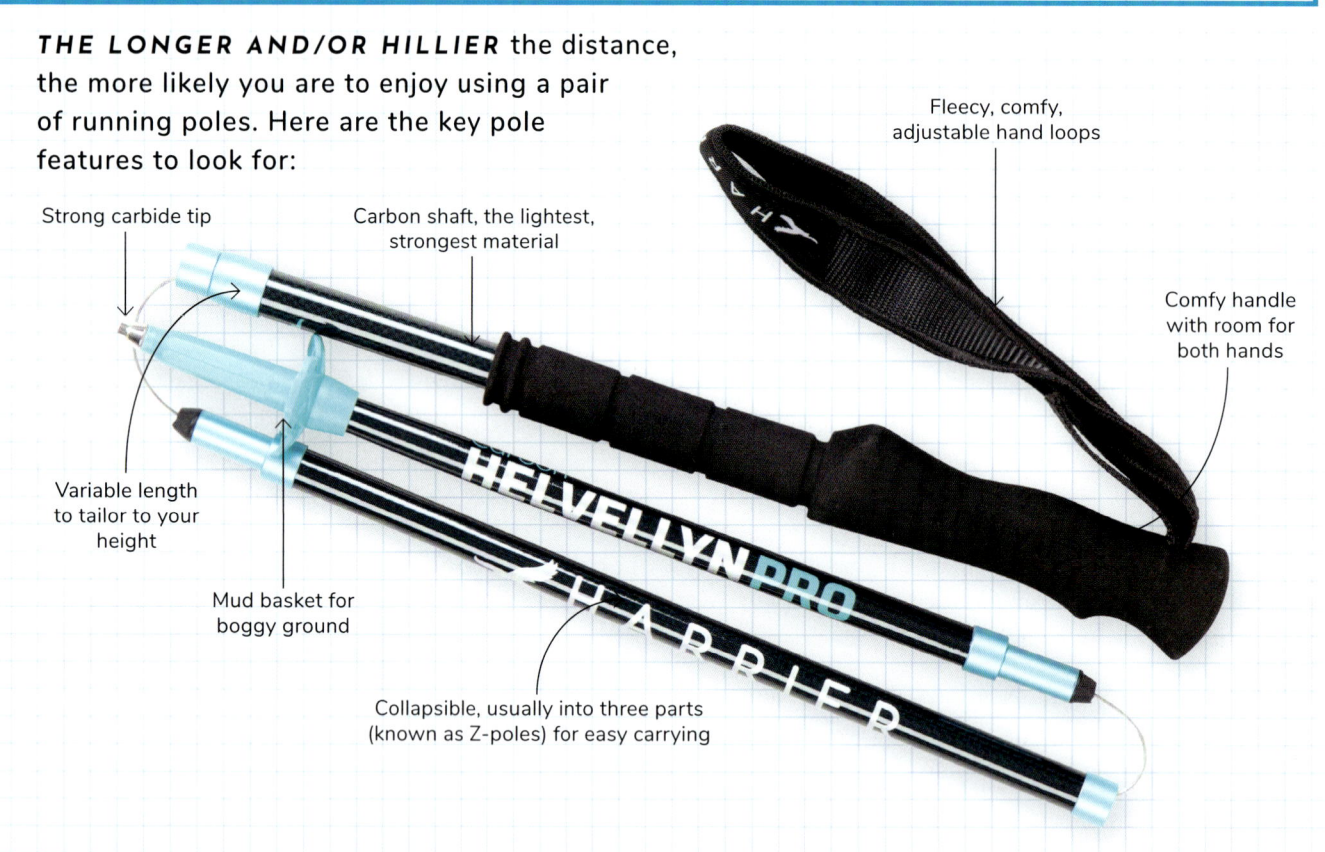

THE LONGER AND/OR HILLIER the distance, the more likely you are to enjoy using a pair of running poles. Here are the key pole features to look for:

- Strong carbide tip
- Carbon shaft, the lightest, strongest material
- Fleecy, comfy, adjustable hand loops
- Comfy handle with room for both hands
- Variable length to tailor to your height
- Mud basket for boggy ground
- Collapsible, usually into three parts (known as Z-poles) for easy carrying

Material

The lightest material for its strength is carbon (around 130–200g/5–7oz per pole), which suits most ultra runners, but it doesn't bend, so snapping is a possibility under extreme stress like a fall or placing heavy bags on top of it. Wind 50cm (20 in) of Gaffa tape around the top of one pole for a DIY repair to get you through the race. An aluminium pole is a heavier but cheaper, more robust, slightly bendable option, if you need it.

Type

Poles come in a few styles. Adjustable-length collapsible, fixed-length collapsible and fixed-length not-collapsible are the main options for ultra runners. Poles that collapse into three are often called Z-poles to represent the way they fold. For your first pair, go for adjustable-length collapsible poles that give you the option to change the height of the poles via a quick-release lock; these usually fold down into three sections for easy stowing in your running pack. Once you know what length of pole you will most often use, you can save weight by upgrading to a fixed-length collapsible pole. To save even more weight, if you know you will be using your poles the entire time, go for fixed-length not-collapsible poles, like ski poles.

Handles

The pole handle material should feel comfy on bare skin; it might be cork or a plastic-based foam. Ribbing on the handle looks good for grip, but it can become abrasive on a long race, so a smooth surface contoured to a hand-shape is optimal. It's quite good if the handle material is long enough to fit both hands on in case you just want to grip one pole with both hands to help you balance across a river or snow patch, or you can hold the pole lower down when climbing very steep ground.

Hand-loops

Some poles have an adjustable, fleece-lined strap in a loop from the top of the handle to slide your hand through and help you hold the pole with ease. Others have a glove-style attachment that clips into the top of each pole. The advantage of being constantly attached to your pole like this is that you don't have to grip the handle, so your hand gets a rest on each swing. The disadvantages are slightly more difficulty unclipping in a fall, but the quick-release button should give it up under unusual force; you mustn't lose the gloves, and it's a bit more faff to take off normal gloves from under them once you warm up.

Mud basket and carbide tip

Mud baskets vary in size and stop the pole sinking too far into muddy ground. The larger the basket, the muddier surface they can cope with. Look for a strong tip made of carbide for durability and grip, and if you're going to be using the poles a long way on roads it's useful to have a pair of rubber tip-covers for grip and to stop that annoying tip tap noise mile after mile!

RUNNING POLES 187

MANDATORY RACE KIT

FOR YOUR OWN SAFETY, ultra races have a list of mandatory kit that every runner must take. It's usually on the race website and it's wise to check it well before the start, so you have enough time to borrow or buy anything you don't have. If you have queries, ask in the race Facebook group or email the race organiser (RO) before they get too busy before the race.

You risk not starting (DNS), a time penalty or a disqualification (DQ) if you lack an item. It's a tough job organising an ultra and everyone's safety is paramount; it's only with that in mind that ROs create these lists, so we must respect them, even if we disagree – it's their race and their word is final.

Full-body waterproof cover
A waterproof jacket with a hood and waterproof trousers, both with taped seams (see p. 179) to keep you warm and dry in wind and rain. The kit list may also specify how waterproof they must be with a hydrostatic head (HH) rating; the more waterproof 15,000 HH is a good start; 30,000 is the common upper rating.

> **EXPERT ADVICE**
> **DON'T BE THAT RUNNER!**
>
> History shows that most deaths at ultras involve hypothermia and a mandatory kit list and check by the race organisers is vital in keeping runners safe. Everything you bring must be fit for purpose and that means it must fit you.
>
> SHANE OHLY, AN OMM (ORIGINAL MOUNTAIN MARATHON) ELITE CATEGORY WINNER AND EVENT DIRECTOR FOR OUREA EVENTS

Water
Races sometimes stipulate a minimum amount of water or water-carrying capacity to get you safely between aid stations, especially in hot climates or summer races. It's often 500ml–1 litre (17–34fl oz).

Head torches
If there's a chance you might finish in the dark on the shorter ultras, the RO may require everyone to carry a light head torch and they may specify the brightness – for example, minimum 200 lumens. If you are definitely running before sunrise, after sunset or through the night, they will ask you to carry either spare batteries and/or a spare head torch. A spare head torch is best, as it's easier and quicker to swap than faffing to change batteries in the dark, but make sure it's at least 200 lumens or there's no point having one; the brightness will be so low that you can't see clearly enough to run.

Survival bag
A superhero cape-style survival blanket won't retain as much heat as a survival bag that you can get one or two people inside. This is more like a very thin, foil sleeping bag and most ultras will ask you to carry one of these in a certain size, to be sure you can fit a whole human being inside it.

Whistle
A lot of running packs have these on the chest strap clip or dangling from a shoulder strap, but if not, these are easily purchased from outdoor shops.

Waterproof trousers

Buff

Hat

Full length thermal leggings

Waterproof jacket

Extra-long sleeved layer

Insulating layer

Head torch(es)

Whistle

ID

Mobile phone and charger

Emergency food

Reusable cup

Water

Survival bag (not blanket)

First aid kit

Gloves

MANDATORY RACE KIT 189

Emergency food
Some races require you to finish with a certain number of calories stowed away as emergency food. On the stricter races you might face disqualification if you fail to produce this at a random spot check. Light but high-calorie energy bars or gels are ideal for this.

Mobile phone and charger
You might be carrying your smartphone anyway, but if you want to save weight, consider a tiny, old-school, 40g (1 ½oz) phone that does only phoning and texting (remember those days?). Either way, make sure it is fully charged, or take a charger and portable battery if you plan use it much or be out for a long time.

First aid kit
The RO may specify what should go in a first aid kit, including blister treatment (see p. 192 for what I usually carry).

Full-length leggings
Thermals to keep you warm should the weather turn cold.

Extra layer
Usually a long-sleeved base layer made of technical, quick-drying material.

Insulating layer
A lightweight synthetic or down jacket for very cold conditions. Keep this in a dry bag so it doesn't get wet from your sweat or rain.

Hat, headband or BUFF®
Pay close attention to what the RO allows here as there is often a great debate over whether a BUFF®-style tubular headband can also be called a hat, since although you can fold it into a lightweight hat, this is not considered warm enough by some ROs.

Gloves
The RO might suggest lightweight or waterproof gloves, or a certain number of pairs. If you suffer with cold hands or Raynaud's syndrome (hands that get cold easily and are difficult to re-warm, becoming pale and numb), take warmer or more pairs of gloves than the mandatory kit list requires.

Reusable cup
Many races are becoming more sustainable by requesting runners carry their own reusable cups for water station drinks, hot and cold. A lot of brands sell squashy, semi-rigid plastic cups that easily clip to your running pack and don't clang about, but some races require a hard plastic or metal cup that won't bend and scold you or the marshals as the hot water is poured into it.

ID and medical details
In case of an emergency (in training and racing), carry your driving licence or a photocopy of your passport ID page during a race, along with any other medical details responders should be aware of, especially if you are racing abroad. Some races will ask for this; others may not.

What's in a first aid kit?
You never know when you might need to help someone on the trail or to patch yourself up. This is why it's a good idea to take a small first aid kit with you on every run, if you're already carrying a pack, as well as cash for a taxi or snacks just in case. A bit of extra weight is great training, after all. The first aid kit list from the mandatory kit section of a race website is a good place to start; here's what I have in mine for different levels of run.

ULTRA HACK

SAVE A LIFE!
If someone collapses with a heart problem, time is of the essence; a shock from an AED (automated external defibrillator), followed by chest compressions until further help arrives, can increase chances of survival. 'Defibs', as they are commonly known, are available at many locations and can be accessed by calling 999 and asking for the release code. They come with simple instructions for use, so don't worry if you're not familiar with them. Find your nearest one using the Save a Life app.

Why not do…
A basic first aid course? They're fantastic for giving you the skills and confidence to cope with potentially life-threatening situations. Would you know how to save someone's life on an ultra?

In an emergency
In an emergency situation, call 999 and ask for the service you require, or Mountain Rescue if you're in the hills. Keep calm, stay as warm as you can, give them all the details and follow their instructions. To indicate you need help in a mountainous location, use the international distress signal: six whistle blows or torch flashes, wait one minute, repeat. If waiting for a Search and Rescue helicopter, flash the light on the ground, not up at the pilots, as this affects their night vision. A rescue team will flash three times at you in response.

BASIC FIRST AID KIT: FOR SHORTER, LOW-LEVEL RUNNING CLOSE TO CIVILISATION

- K-tape in precut strips
- Energy gel
- Small bandage
- Plasters
- Electrolytes
- Safety pins (to hold a bandage in place)
- Tampons (handy if you or a friend unexpectedly gets their period)
- Whistle
- Smartphone (fully charged)
- Antiseptic wipes
- Small dressing (or a sanitary towel works too, as a wound dressing)

192   6. ULTRA GEAR

FULL FIRST AID KIT: FOR LONGER AND/OR REMOTE, HILLY OR MOUNTAINOUS RUNNING

- Sterile cotton swabs (about 5x5cm)
- K-tape in precut strips
- Hydrocolloid blister plasters (only for blisters where the skin has been removed)
- Spare head torch (minimum 200 lumens)
- Anti-chafe cream
- Sugary snacks (plural!)
- Tampons (handy if you or a friend unexpectedly gets their period)
- Electrolyte tablets
- Regular plasters
- Safety pins (to hold bandage in place)
- Whistle
- Sterile scalpel blades (size #11) (to lance and drain blisters)
- Antiseptic wipes
- Smartphone (fully charged)
- Phone charger cable and portable battery
- Small sterile dressings (about 6x7cm)
- Small scissors
- Survival bag
- Small bandages

MANDATORY RACE KIT 193

DROP BAGS AND SUPPORT CREW KIT

MANY ULTRAS ALLOW YOU to leave a drop bag at the start to access quickly at the finish, or they may transport it to the finish if the start was elsewhere. Some super-long races, for example 100-milers, allow you to access a pre-packed drop bag around the halfway point. You might also be allowed a support crew who can meet you at various points along the course to resupply, re-energise and patch you up. Multi-day races very often transport a larger kit bag for you so that you can run with just a day pack.

Top drop bag tips
- Use a sturdy, waterproof bag to guarantee dry kit.
- Adhere to any size, weight and weatherproofing rules set by the race organiser.
- Think about what time(s) of day and distance(s) you will likely reach your drop bag/crew.
- Pack items in clearly labelled, transparent, plastic sandwich bags, so you can quickly find what you need even while tired, hungry and hurting.
- Try not to pack the kitchen sink, as someone has to haul your stuff (and everyone else's!) into a vehicle and out again, but if in doubt (within the weight limit), pack it – you will hone your kit list down with experience.
- Avoid packing anything valuable, irreplaceable or that you absolutely need during the race (like essential medication or allergy-free fuel), just in case there's a problem with lost (or sadly stolen) drop bags.
- Post-race, note what didn't get used and consider if you need it next time.

Start/finish drop bags
- Recovery fuel – maybe a heavy luxury item like a cold can of pop, chocolate milk and a tasty meal that doesn't need immediate refrigerating like pesto pasta or a cheese sandwich (depending on the temperature of your race of course – I'm thinking UK weather here!)
- Warm layers – for example, down jacket, synthetic insulating layer, hoodie or jumper, tracksuit trousers or thermal leggings

MY STORY
TOO MUCH KIT = TOO MUCH FAFF

'On a 100-mile [160km] race I write my drop bag kit list down as part of my race planning and I actually write at the top of it "Beware, too much kit = too much faff", so I don't pack too much! In my drop bag I also have a list for what I need to do as soon as I get to the drop bag point. First thing is to take shoes and socks off, wipe clean with baby wipes and dry if needed and leave to air out for a short while before re-applying trench cream and putting on clean socks, then recharging stuff after that. I only changed my knickers on my last 100 as my first pair were covered in salt and were causing a bit of chafing. Sometimes I barely use any of my drop bag kit, but I always make sure I top up my nutrition, energy drink powder and electrolytes; and brushing my teeth is essential.'

CAROLINE CAREN, ISLE OF MAN

- Spare, comfy bra top – a clammy, sweaty bra makes me feel super cold after racing, so a comfy bra or crop top is a must
- Wet wipes and a travel towel for cleaning or a possible shower
- Fresh socks – in case your feet are begging for comfort
- Flip flops – in case your feet are begging to be un-shod
- Portable charger and cable for your phone – let the sharing of your amazing achievement begin!

Mid-ultra drop bags

- Spare head torch/batteries
- Portable battery for charging phone/GPS/headphones
- Fresh t-shirt/undies that smell nice!
- New socks to wake up tired feet
- Change of shoes – slightly larger, if your feet are prone to swelling, or with different cushioning or grip for different terrain
- Spare hot/cold/waterproof kit
- Running poles – you might need them for certain sections or towards the end
- Wet wipes and a travel towel for cleaning
- Anti-chafe cream, blister kit and K-tape
- Medication/contact lenses/period stuff/sunscreen
- More fuel and hydration this could include a caffeine pick-me-up or heavier luxury item like chocolate milk
- Toothpaste and toothbrush to freshen up your mouth after eating sweets and gels
- Cards, motivational pictures, photos or messages from loved ones
- Water treatment, depending on aid station availability
- Plastic bag to put wet/dirty items in

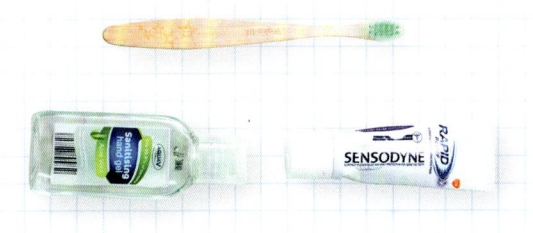

Multi-day race drop bags

- Multiple changes of clothes
- Spare hot/cold/waterproof kit
- Anti-chafe cream, blister kit and K-Tape
- Sunscreen and insect repellent
- Portable battery for charging phone/GPS/head torch/headphones
- Flip flops or comfy shoes for walking around camp
- Bowl, mug and cutlery
- Luxury fuel items
- Sleeping bag, pillow and mat
- Washbag and travel towel

- Medication/contact lenses/period stuff
- Ear plugs for snorers in the tent next door!
- Cards, motivational pictures, photos or messages from loved ones
- Running poles – especially for the later stages of the race
- Plastic bag to put wet/dirty items in

Support crew kit

As well as all the items in the mid-ultra drop bag list above, having a crew makes a little more mid-ultra magic possible. Very importantly, make sure your crew know all the race rules for where, when and with what they can meet you, so you they don't accidentally incur you a DNF. Spend time planning this and delegating different responsibilities to your team. A spreadsheet is a wonderful way to organise this. Here are some common items you might need:

- **Picnic table and chairs** – but beware the chair, as you might not get up again! A small table is ideal for setting out a wide variety of food to quickly munch down and/or pocket and go
- **Large water carrier with tap head** – make one person in charge of filling water bottles
- **Plates, bowls and cutlery** for proper hot meals – with the food ideally ready and at eating-temperature on arrival
- **Gas stove** for cooking bacon butties and making cups of tea with extra sugar – go on, spoil that runner!
- Wide variety of **extra food and drink,** including heavier, bulkier luxury food items – maybe a whole cake? Or a huge pizza? Keep dreaming
- **Towel, warm water and soap** for a quick face, or even body, wash – possibly before a night section, or in the morning, to wake you up
- **Sleeping area** for a quick power nap in comfort – get them to set it up ready at the pre-arranged time/distance
- **Solar panels** for charging electronics – make one person in charge of powering up gadgets, replacing batteries or swapping in fully-charged gadgets and making sure nothing vital is left behind
- **More substantial first aid,** blister and chafe kit (including period stuff) – and ideally a crew member who knows how to use it properly
- **Bin bags** and plastic bags to put wet/dirty items in

HEAD TORCH

ULTRA RACES CAN SOMETIMES have you ending in the dark at 2a.m. or starting at 6p.m. on a Friday night (we know how to party!) and running through one or two nights for a 100-miler, or even more nights on a non-stop multi-day race.

The brighter the head torch, the easier it is to run (or stumble) along at a fair lick, and the easier it is to navigate, especially when you're tired, if you're less experienced or have eyesight problems. However, of course, brighter for longer means a heavier battery, so it's a case of finding that sweet spot for your race and training needs. For a summer ultra, waymarked on easy trails or roads, and ending just after dusk, you won't need as bright a light as a remote, self-navigated winter race through multiple nights, so I cover all extremes here.

EXPERT ADVICE
WATCH OUT!

Be wary of low-cost head torches promising 1000+ lumens and long burn times. They may be a) lying; b) quoting the burn time for their highest light setting confusingly near the highest battery length value; c) not using the best beam pattern. Read the small print, and better still, buy from a reputable outdoor brand with all the right safety and brightness test data clearly available.

Brightness

Lumens is the measure of head torch brightness. Go for at least 200 for easy trails and roads. I find 400 lumens is better for rougher paths and straightforward navigation at a steady pace, and if you really want to feel confident navigating in the dark, a maximum output of 1000 lumens is really useful for scanning ahead to find that stile or feature.

Beam pattern

Some head torches allow you to switch between a bright, narrow spotlight beam that allows you to look into the distance, and a wider flood beam, so you can see the whole path using your peripheral vision without having to keep turning your head to keep lighting up different parts of the trail. Some head torches have both spotlight and flood features built into their one main beam, so there's no need to switch from type to type.

Batteries

The lower-light head torches might take AAA or AA batteries, or their own unique rechargeable lithium ion batteries, and some will allow you to use both, which is handy for long-distance or multi-day trail races. These smaller, lighter (around 100g/3 1/2oz) head torches will often have the batteries on the front of the head behind the lamp.

Brighter head torches need bigger batteries, especially if they are to last throughout the night, so these are located on the back of the head, or come with a cable extension so you can pop the battery in your running pack or pocket. They are rechargeable and unique to each, so you can buy extra and swap in new batteries from your drop bag or running pack.

Burn time

Check the technical specs to see how long your headlamp burns for at certain levels of brightness; usually they will have two or three. The brighter the light setting (the higher the lumens), the more battery power it eats, and vice versa, so check if it will last the time you need it too, and always take spare batteries (and/or a second head torch) just in case.

Settings

Too many light settings can be confusing, so the best torches have a simple click-by-click succession of low, medium, high, possibly flashing options, and sometimes a boost button for a few seconds of super-bright light. You might also consider a red light option for night vision. You might want one with the option of a rear red flashing light for road safety.

Buttons

Look for large buttons that can be used easily with gloves on, but not so easily pressed that they switch on in your bag. Travelling with the battery disconnected or the wrong way round is a good way to prevent this happening, but remember to reconnect before you start.

Customisation

Some torches come with an app for customising the light settings. For some, this adds extra faff, but for others, it's a welcome upgrade. Check what settings you can only change via the app and make sure they're set correctly before you set off, so you don't have to stop and get your phone out mid-run, especially on a wet, cold hillside.

MY STORY

TAKE A SPARE HEAD TORCH

'**It always baffles me** why people don't carry two equally good head torches with spare batteries for both. The second torch is in case the first fails, so it needs to be as good. It matters not that you saved a bit of weight if you can't see where you're going! I'm very particular about it when I do the kit check. And a power pack is as much use as a chocolate fireguard if your other torch has failed, unless you have time to sit and wait for it to charge! Two torches with new batteries in and spare for both.'

JANE STEPHENS

Reactive lighting

This is when the head torch adjusts it's brightness level to what it thinks you need depending on the surrounding light. Some runners really like this for handsfree, faff-free running and extending battery life, while others prefer to be in full control of their light level and don't appreciate it dimming or brightening unexpectedly when not needed, such as when running with others wearing bright headlamps, when getting reflections off signs, when running in fog and as car headlights blind you.

High-vis running gear

When running on pavements and roads, it's wise to wear bright, lumo and reflective items like the following to make yourself as visible as possible to pedestrians, cyclists and vehicles. If you run with a dog, deck them out like a moving Christmas tree to protect them, too.

CLOTHING

Choose a light-coloured, neon or specifically high-vis T-shirt or jacket with plenty of reflective strips. The more reflective strips you have on your shorts and leggings, the better, too.

REFLECTIVE LED VEST

Look for a bright, luminous harness or mesh vest with reflective strips and flashing LED lights on the front and back.

ARM AND ANKLE BANDS

Movement attracts the most attention, so having luminous, reflective LED bands on your swinging arms and striding ankles makes you highly visible.

DOG STUFF

You can get fantastically bright, collars and coats with lights on for your pooch to keep them safe too. And on the plus side, you can see where they are if they run off in a dark field after a rabbit.

COLD-WEATHER RUNNING

YOU CAN EXPERIENCE A WHOLE RANGE of weather conditions on long training runs and ultras that go through the night, even in summer, so extra insulating gear and safety kit (see p. 171) is a must. Packing using your own common sense based on your experience level and the predicted weather conditions is much more important than getting your pack weight down and going for the bare minimum race requirements.

The clever and experienced ultra runner will put extra layers on before they get too cold, and if things get really gnarly they understand there's no shame in staying at lower altitudes, turning back on a training run or DNF-ing a race. Here's the kit you need:

Thermals
Windproof, fleece-lined leggings and super-warm long-sleeved tops, layered over sweat-wicking vests or T-shirts, are the order of the day for runs in very cold weather or climates.

Waterproof jacket
It's always a good idea to run with a light waterproof jacket in case conditions change, but in winter you might want to wear a slightly thicker, heavier weight waterproof jacket with more features, so you can properly batten down those hatches to protect you from cold, wind, rain, sleet and snow.

Insulating jacket
Packing a super-lightweight, synthetic (man-made fibres) insulating jacket is prudent on very cold days in case you have to stop or slow down. Keep it in a waterproof bag so it doesn't get wet.

Gloves

These range from slim liner gloves to medium to full-on mountaineering mitts. I've been known to take all three types on one freezing, snowy run – you never know how cold your hands might get and working digits are vital for feeding yourself and operating the zips and Velcro needed to keep the rest of you warm. Functioning hands are your priority.

Hat

Always take a light, fleecy, windproof hat to keep the chill off. A bobble-free beanie is lighter and easier to pack.

Buff®

A fantastically versatile tube of quick-wicking fabric that you can make into lots of different headwear, including a headband, neck warmer, balaclava and hat. I use this most often in headband mode to keep my ears warm.

Waterproof socks

These are great for keeping the feet warm while you thrash through freezing bogs and puddles. The higher up the ankle they go, the more protection they give.

EXPERT ADVICE
IS IT HYPOTHERMIA?

Being alert to the early signs of mild hypothermia is the best way to prevent it. These include:

- shivering;
- cold, pale skin;
- confusion;
- tiredness;
- slurred speech or mumbling;
- fast breathing.

TAKE ACTION FAST

Get the person warm and dry, try to persuade them to eat a sugary snack and sip a warm non-alcoholic drink if possible, put them into a survival bag if they're immobile, with another person for body heat if space allows, or add layers and keep moving to a place of warmth and safety (usually downhill). If a person stops shivering or passes out, urgent medical help is needed – call 999 and ask for Mountain Rescue.

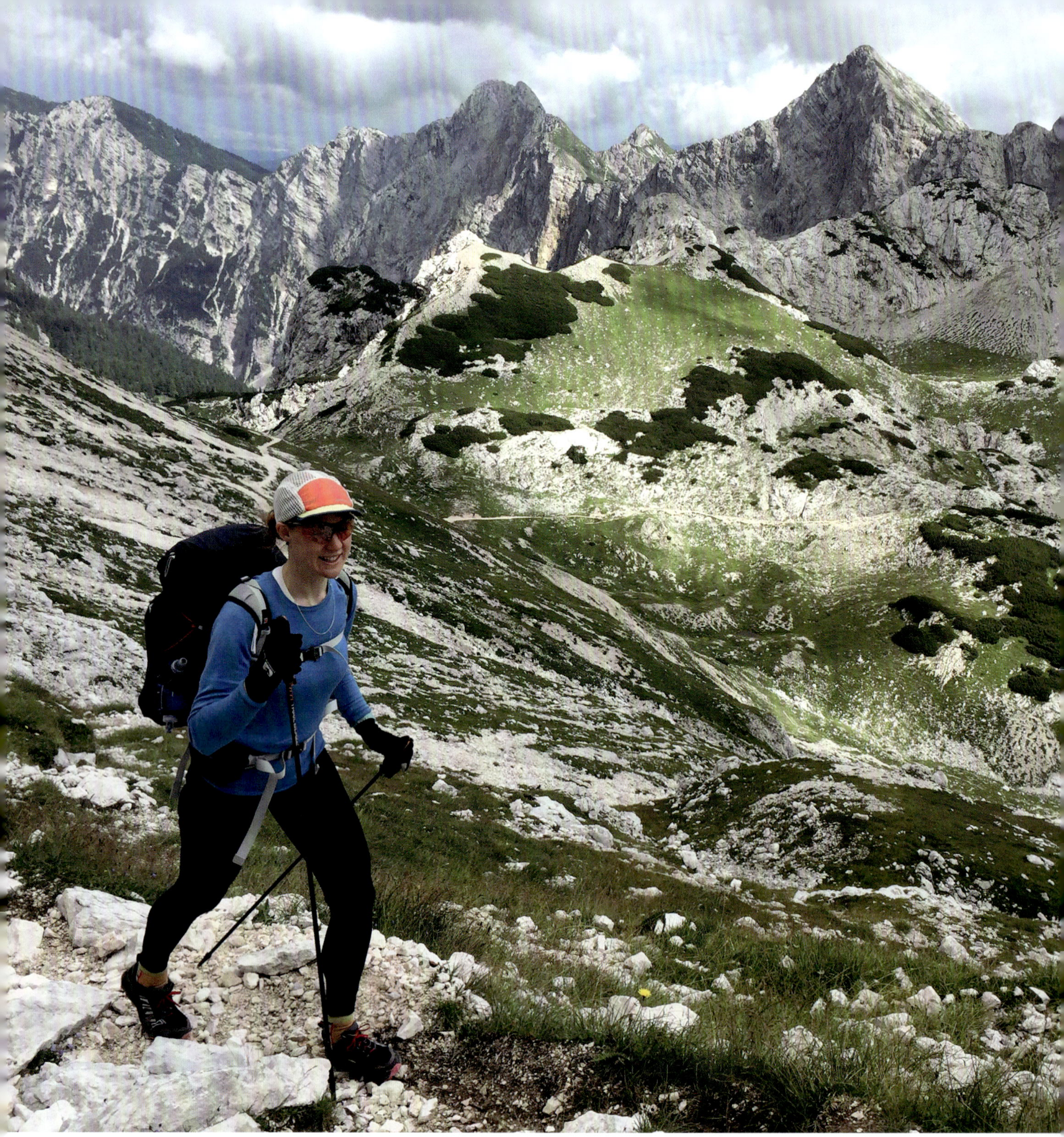

Running crampons or ice spikes

When tackling higher hill or mountain trails in icy conditions, you need these spikes over your trail shoes to dig into ice or hard-packed snow. The moment you feel out of your depth, however, do stay low level or turn back – respect snowy mountain trails and only run them if you are experienced.

Ice grippers

Great for icy pavements, these nifty over-shoe grippers will save you from slipping on low-level icy trails, such as canal towpaths, country parks and easy forest trails.

Hand warmers

If you know you get cold hands easily, particularly those with Raynaud's syndrome whose blood does not circulate effectively in cold weather, take a pair of hand warmers to pop inside your gloves.

ULTRA HACK

WARMER FINGERS

To warm up cold fingers quicker, ease them out of the glove fingers so you can curl your hand into a fist inside the palm of the glove. Windmill your arms and keep squeezing and wriggling your fingers in this position to warm them faster. Add a hand warmer for an extra boost.

TOP TIPS FOR RUNNING IN COLD WEATHER/CLIMATES

- Warm up for five minutes inside before venturing out.
- Keep your head and hands warm with gloves and a hat.
- Wear a technical, quick-wicking thermal base layer.
- Layer up your clothing so you can peel layers off as you warm up.
- Avoid stopping for too long and cooling down.
- Keep drinking – you breathe out moisture with every exhale.
- Start your run into the wind and finish with a tailwind.
- Make sure you're fully warm before doing any speedwork.
- Get dry and warm quickly after running – this is where that big down jacket comes in!

HOT-WEATHER RUNNING

RUNNING AN ULTRA in hot weather can be even more challenging than in the cold – it's far easier to warm up while running than it is to cool down! One of the world's most famous ultras, the Marathon des Sables (Marathon of the Sands) takes place over six days in the Sahara desert each year and even in the UK temperatures have been known to hit 42°C (108°F) of late. So here's the kit and advice to make hot-weather running easier and safer.

Lightweight vest and shorts
Save your lightest-weight vest or T-shirt and shorts for hot weather. A T-shirt can be more comfy under a running pack than a vest, and helps prevent sunburn.

Headband
You can get specially designed SPF 50 headbands (like a BUFF®) for sun protection. Dip them into a stream and wear them as a hat or headband to keep yourself cool.

Cap or visor
A vital part of everyone's summer kit to help guard against sunstroke. Often, if it's not too sunny, you can get away without sunglasses under the peak of the cap.

Sunglasses
The best sunglasses wrap all the way around the eyes and have rubber nose grips and arms to stop them slipping off your sweaty, sunscreened nose and face. Cat 3 is a good level of lens protection, or photochromic lenses that change with the sunlight levels, and I like to have a rosy tint to my lenses to make sunsets look even better. Watch out for polarised lenses as these make it very hard to read phone, watch and gadget screens.

Sunscreen
I use spray-on P20 oil, which ranges from factor 15–50+ rather than a cream. You apply it once in the morning and it bonds with the skin to give sweat-resistant and waterproof UVA and UVB sun protection all day. Try not to get it on your clothes – it stains.

Debris gaiters
Very useful in hot places, these light, breathable (and often brightly-patterned) fabric gaiters hook on to your shoes to provide a protective barrier against debris like grit, stones and sand.

EXPERT ADVICE
HEAT EXHAUSTION OR HEATSTROKE?

Heat exhaustion isn't usually serious if you can cool down within 30 minutes. Signs include:

- headache;
- dizziness and confusion;
- thirst;
- loss of appetite;
- nausea;
- excessive sweating;
- pale, clammy skin;
- arm, leg and stomach cramps;
- fast breathing or pulse;
- a temperature of 38°C (100.4°F) or more.

TAKE ACTION FAST

Move the person to a cool place, lie them down with feet raised, persuade them to drink plenty of water or electrolyte drink, cool their skin with water and fan them. Call 999 and ask for Mountain Rescue if they move into heatstroke – this would be if they are no better after 30 minutes, feel hot and dry, are not sweating, have a temperature of more than 40°C (104°F), have rapid breath or shortness of breath, are still confused, have a fit, lose consciousness or become unresponsive.

Top tips for running in hot weather/climates

- Have a cool shower and wet your hair before you run.
- Avoid running at the hottest times of the day.
- Run slower – don't expect to be able to run as fast.
- Drink regular sips of water mixed with electrolytes (salts).
- Wear breathable clothing – light-coloured, loose fabrics.
- Wear a cap and sunglasses to create your own shade.
- Dip your cap into streams or water at aid stations as you pass.
- Spray yourself with water or crocodile roll in streams.
- Wrap a BUFF® round your wrist and keep wetting it.
- Familiarise yourself with the first signs of heat exhaustion, and stop and get into the shade if you experience them.

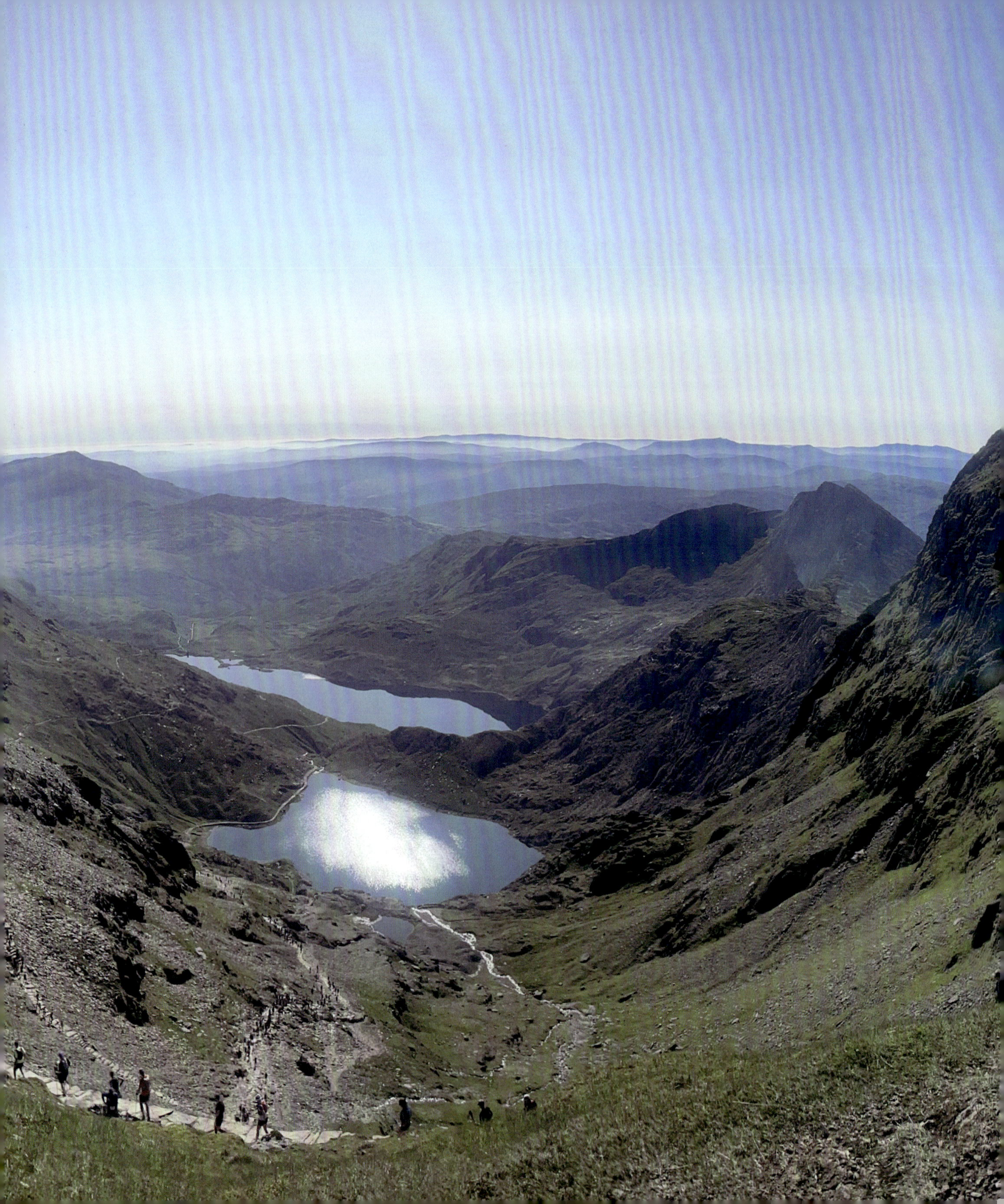

7 EVENTS

Whether you call them races, events or long-distance hikes, exploring new routes and revisiting old classics are exciting ways to explore the world within the relative safety of an organised environment, chat to likeminded people, test your limits and/or eat a lot of cake.

YOUR FIRST ULTRA?

DEPENDING ON YOUR OUTDOOR SKILLS, experience, fitness level and appetite for challenge, you might want to pick an 'easier' first ultra. By this I mean shorter in distance and with generous cut-off times. You might also want to look for less hilly, less ankle-biting terrain and straightforward navigation or more waymarking. However, strangely, as a former hill walker, in my opinion these seemingly 'easier' factors can actually make ultra running harder because on flatter courses with smoother paths you'll be able to actually run more rather than hike! So do bear that in mind, especially depending on whether you're coming at your first ultra from a road running or hiking background.

Top five first ultras

Whatever your fitness level and outdoor experience, the 50km (30-mile) distance is a great starter for your ultra, and these events all have generous cut-off times for a less pressured challenge.

1 LAKELAND TRAILS 55K, NORTH WEST ENGLAND

My first ever trail races were around 15km (9 miles) in the then much smaller Lakeland Trails series, starting from various stunning locations in the Lake District on waymarked trails. It's fantastic to see they have many more races now, including a 55k and 100k ultra, both of which make fantastic first events at that distance, with fully-waymarked courses and multiple aid stations.

2 MAVERICK X-SERIES, SOUTH (ISH) ENGLAND

These multi-distance events each include an ultra option around the 50km (30-mile) mark in the Peak District, Exmoor, North and South Downs, and Suffolk. They make for very welcoming beginner trail ultras on waymarked courses.

3 ENDURANCE LIFE ULTRAS, UK AND EUROPE

Endurance Life run 10k to 50k (ish) ultra distance, fully waymarked and well-supported races at various, usually coastal, locations all over the UK and further afield, including the Giant's Causeway in Northern Ireland, Northumberland, Pembrokeshire and Dorset.

4 RACE TO THE KING/STONES 50K, SOUTH ENGLAND

These are two of the UK's biggest ultramarathons with a real inclusivity drive towards encouraging diversity and an equal male:female participation. There are 50k and 100k one-day and two-day races with camping options, and the very generous cut-off times welcome walkers as well as runners on these fully waymarked, linear courses along ancient National Trails.

5 CENTURION HUNDRED HILLS 50K, SOUTH EAST ENGLAND

Fantastically well-organised and well-established long-distance events, this is one of the shorter races from Centurion Running which is well known for its 50- and 100-miler in the south east of England. This rolling, fully waymarked and supported route through the Chiltern Hills is a great stepping stone to their longer events.

YOUR FIRST ULTRA? 209

MY STORY
RUNNING AFTER LIFE-CHANGING EVENTS

'**When faced with the prospect** of surgery in late 2022, I believed my running days were over. My dreams of conquering 100-mile [160km] races seemed shattered, as the operation was to remove my entire colon, leaving me with a permanent ileostomy (stoma) due to severe ulcerative colitis. I couldn't find anyone running such distances with a stoma, but in the hospital, post op and feeling better than expected, I registered for my first 50-mile [80km] race in the Arctic Circle, just seven months away. I tackled 43 gruelling miles [69km] and 3000m [9842ft] of climbing, narrowly missing the time cut off due to brutal weather. I want my journey to inspire others facing health battles, proving that even amid adversity, epic achievements remain within reach!'

ROB BEAVEN, CHIROPRACTOR AT THE DYER ST CLINIC, @ROBTHECHIRO

My fave 50 milers

You don't have to go longer each time, but once you have enjoyed a few 50k races, you might like to try bobbing along for longer by signing up to a 50-mile (80km) event. Unless this is your first ultra (in which case, woah there, read the first ultra info above) it's harder to create a generic list, as fitness, experience and outdoor skill level varies wildly from person to person, so you might not need a generous cut-off time nor want a flat, easily navigable course. Instead, here I have listed some of my own favourites with fantastic views, great organisation and super camaraderie.

My top five 50-milers

1 MONTANE LAKELAND 50, LAKE DISTRICT
The Lakeland 50 is a wonderful first 50-miler (the second half of the infamous Lakeland 100), with incredible pre-race training and info via a newsletter, a lively Facebook group, plentiful aid station support and easy navigation via GPX, map and route book. Combine this with a cracking linear route with 3000m (9842ft) of ascent through the beautiful Lake District in July and you have the makings of the perfect beginner race for this distance.

2 ROUND THE ROCK, 48 MILES/77KM, JERSEY
What a fabulous Strava route map this easily navigable, circular course along the entire Jersey island coastline gives you! OK, it's not quite 50 miles (80km), but the rough terrain, sharp cliff-top to beach ascents totalling 1500m (4921ft), tough 12-hour cut-off time and hot August weather make up for the 2-mile (3km) deficit. Marathon and half marathon distances are also available.

3 HARDMOORS 55 MILES/88KM, NORTH YORK MOORS
Hardmoors runs a stepping-stone series of longer and longer events from 15 miles (24km) all the way to 200 miles (322km), and the 55-mile (88km) course along the Cleveland Hills is not to be underestimated, with 2000m (6562ft) ascent and a late March date when snow or a heat wave could abound.

4 ARC OF ATTRITION 50 MILES/80KM, CORNWALL
If you're experienced, fit and used to self-navigating and supporting yourself over challenging, coastal terrain in the darkness of winter, the second half of the infamous Arc 100 linear route along the Cornish coast might appeal at the end of January.

5 MANX MOUNTAIN MARATHON, 50K/31 MILES, ISLE OF MAN
Ok so I'm going off brief here with this 50k race, but the steep nature of this rough, relentless route through the Isle of Man mountains with sharp cut-off times makes it harder than the Lakeland 50! You need to be able to navigate and look after yourself on the hills to survive this iconic island race held annually on the Easter Bank Holiday weekend. There's also an (equally steep!) half marathon route from just over the half way point.

Your first 100 miler

Apart from picking one that truly inspired me, in choosing my first 100 miler, I made a spreadsheet of 25 events to compare the actual distance (often more than 100 miles/160km!), time of year, ascent, terrain type, course cut-off time and start time (this influences the number of nights you might run through); whether the course was linear, circular or laps; the number of aid stations and level of support; and the cost of entry – because these beasts can be mighty pricey. I highly recommend doing this so you can hone in on the one that plays best to your strengths and excites you the most – this is very important with training motivation.

ULTRA HACK

AN 'EASY' 100 MILER
While obviously there is no such thing as an 'easy' 100 miler, it's a bit of a paradox that selecting a super flat one might turn out to be harder than one with rolling hills because there will be more (or faster) running involved and less 'breaks' for hiking with poles up and down the hills. Most importantly, use your other ultra event experience to consider what kind of 100 miler might suit your skills and personal preferences best.

100 MILES IS NOT MANDATORY

There's no law of ultra running that says, 'You must be working towards a 100-miler to be considered worthy,' or any kind of ever-lengthening distance. That's because the hills, weather, terrain and sometimes navigation all play a part in how difficult that distance really is. If you enjoy a scenic, all-day 50k the most, then that's fantastic, so crack on! This book isn't about getting everyone to run 100+ miles (160km); it's about enjoying the preparation, training and event day for whatever distance you choose.

Top five first 100-milers

1 ENDURE 24
Lapped ultras are becoming more and more popular as a brilliant way to test out what you're capable of without finding yourself 50–100 miles (80–160km) away from the start line. Endure 24 in Reading or Leeds offers runners (and teams) the chance to run as many laps of their undulating 8k loop within 24 hours, with a chance to see your supporters and drop bag each lap.

2 GRIM REAPER 100, LINCOLNSHIRE
This May-time event comprises up to 10-mile (16km) loops over easy ground around Grimsthorpe Castle Estate. With an ascent of only 1700m (5577ft), it's very scenic and very runnable with a shortish 26-hour course limit, which may suit ultra runners who like to, er, actually run...

3 LDWA ANNUAL 100-MILER, VARIES ANNUALLY WITHIN UK
The Long Distance Walkers Association (LDWA) organises long hikes throughout the year via its local groups, to which runners are also welcome. Groups take it in turns to host a 100-miler with a very generous 48-hour, walker-friendly cut off. You must complete one of their UK-wide 50-mile (80km) qualifying events in the lead up and be on the ball with navigation, but these are the lowest-priced long-distance events (not races), with further discounts for members.

4 CENTURION RUNNERS 100-MILERS, SOUTH-EAST ENGLAND
The level of checkpoint support, reasonable cut-off times, waymarked trail courses, rolling hills and mainly good underfoot conditions on the Centurion 100-milers makes them firm favourites for first 100-milers. Their Thames Path, South Downs Way, North Downs Way and Autumn 100-mile (160km) races are a great shout for your inaugural attempt.

5 CHESTER ULTRA 100
Organised by GB Ultras, April's Chester Ultra is the 'easiest' one of the four 100-milers they offer throughout the UK. You get 32 hours to complete the waymarked course with 1500m (4921ft) elevation on easy trails with plenty of aid-stations en route.

Your first multi-dayer

I recommend a three-day stage race rather than a non-stop one for your first, simply so you can get the hang of the multi-day aspect without also coping with intense sleep deprivation. I do find it slightly strange that all the multi-day races in the UK seem to be ultras each day in themselves, many just peaking over the marathon distance each day, if not more. You don't see many half marathon to marathon distance multi-dayers, which would be fabulous for beginners, and hopefully someone reading this book will cover this gap in the market!

Top three first multi-dayers

1 DRUID'S CHALLENGE
A fantastic triple dayer from family-run event team XNRG (Extreme Energy) every November, each day nudging just over the marathon distance along the Ridgeway National Trail, with two nights sleeping in school halls. This was my first multi-dayer and I found it super friendly and welcoming to beginner multi-day runners, with easy nav, great checkpoints and delicious food, morning and evening.

2 VOTWO COAST CHALLENGES
Two coastal trail races in Dorset and Cornwall in March and October, respectively – approximately three well-organised marathons in three days, with plenty of ascent along the beautiful, rolling South West Coast Path (hard to get lost!). Catering is also available, as is transport to and from event HQ to the start and finish each day.

3 GREAT LAKES 3-DAY
A three-day mountain navigation journey in the Lake District with two overnight camps, kit transportation between each and a variety of courses to choose from.

Create your own!

Many multi-day races have high daily mileage and take place on challenging terrain, so don't be afraid of creating your own challenge catering to your preferred daily distance and ascent. Take National Trails at your own pace and circumnavigate islands with coastal paths with time to breathe in the views. There's a bit more organisation involved, but many popular routes have bag-drop companies you can hire and lots of accommodation options along the way. My favourite has been the 100-mile (160km) Raad ny Foillan (Way of the Gull) coast path around the whole of the Isle of Man, which I completed over six days in 2019 with local runners and friends.

ULTRA HACK

RACE MEMORABILIA
If you're wondering what to do with the many medals and race T-shirts you've accumulated, how about these ideas? Hang the medals on a display hanger or make coasters out of your favourites by surrounding them in plaster in a square container. Or sew patchwork quilts or a beanbag cover from your T-shirts.

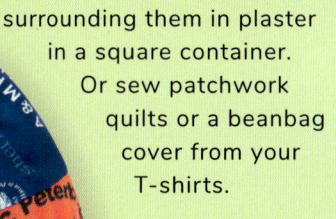

DREAM RACES

ULTRAS AND MULTI-DAY RACES are an utterly incredible way to see the world, and there are some awesome events promising unforgettable memories whether you complete them or not. Here are a few that may or may not be on my bucket list...

Seven Sisters Skyline, Ireland
55KM/34 MILES, 14 HOURS
The toughest mountain running event in Ireland, with 4000m (13,123ft) total ascent along the beautiful Donegal coastline over the steep Derryveagh Mountains.

Lakes Traverse, England
100KM (62 MILES), 30 HOURS
A mountainous, west-to-east traverse of the entire Lake District, with 3500m (11,483ft) ascent from St. Bees to Shap; it's also the little sister of the 300km (186-mile), five-day Northern Traverse, which continues east to finish at Robin Hood's Bay.

Dynafit Hardangerjokulen Ultra, Norway

Comrades Marathon, South Africa

Comrades Marathon, South Africa
88KM (55 MILES), 12 HOURS
One of the world's most famous road ultras, held in KwaZulu-Natal province and changing direction each year for alternate 'Down' and 'Up' runs with differing total ascents.

Ultra Tour Monte Rosa, Switzerland
105 MILES (170KM), 60 HOURS - 4 DAYS
Race the whole thing in one go or enjoy it as a four-day stage race with 11,600m (38,058ft) ascent. This gorgeous, steep Alpine adventure circles the 4634m peak of Monte Rosa from Grächen.

Spine Challenger South, England
108 MILES (174KM), 60 HOURS
This notorious winter 'fun run' along the Pennine Way is the little brother of the original, infamous 268-mile (431km) Spine Race along the whole trail from Edale to Kirk Yetholm.

Western States, USA
100 MILES (160KM), 30 HOURS
The world's oldest 100-mile trail race and 5500m (18,045ft) climbing, from Olympic Valley to Auburn, California, through high canyons and sun-bleached wilderness, with only a limited number of places and a lottery race entry.

Hardrock, USA
102 MILES (164KM), 48 HOURS
The hardest, hilliest, high-altitude 100-miler in the USA, with over 10,000m (32,808ft) total ascent, crossing 13 major passes in southern Colorado's San Juan Range, ending with a kiss of a ram's head.

Tor des Geants, Italy
330KM (205 MILES), 150 HOURS
A stunning, gruelling race from Courmayeur, with an incredible 24,000m (78,740ft) ascent as it dives and rolls around the highest 4000m (13,123ft) peak in the Alps, plus Gran Paradiso Natural Park and Mont Avic Regional Park.

Spartathlon, Greece
245KM (152 MILES), 36 HOURS
The most historic road ultra following the footsteps of ancient Athenian runner Pheidippides who ran from Athens to Sparta to seek help before the battle of Marathon.

Marathon des Sables
250KM (155 MILES), 5 DAYS
The original multi-day, self-sufficient expedition race in the hot, hot, hot Moroccan Sahara, first run in 1986 and featuring 50 nationalities, 30 per cent of whom walk the course within the generous cut-off times.

Fire + Ice, Iceland
250KM (155 MILES), 6 DAYS
A wild, remote footrace from central Iceland towards the coast and artic circle in the north, with stunning glacial views, lava and volcanic ash fields and bubbling mud pools.

ULTRA HACK

BEAT POST-RACE BLUES
When you've been focusing on preparing for a big trail race, once it's over it's not unusual to feel lost and depressed with all the excitement suddenly gone. Beat these post-race blues by reviewing training, nutrition and kit that worked well or didn't, and picking another goal to get excited about. It might be a longer or shorter ultra or your own running challenge, but the goal doesn't have to even be running related. Maybe it's a family holiday or a skills course, or making a patchwork quilt out of your old race T-shirts (see p. 213). Whatever it is, choose something that excites and re-energises you and your support team.

Marathon des Sables

Dragon's Back Race, Wales
200 MILES (322KM), 6 DAYS
Ankle-twisting terrain, sky-scraping scramble-ridges and incredible mountain views await any who are brave enough to take on this dragon of a race from north to south Wales.

Cape Wrath Ultra, Scotland
250 MILES (402KM), 8 DAYS
You'll need top tip fitness and plenty of bog-hopping and mountain skills for this awesome, remote race northwards from Fort William in the Scottish Highlands all the way to Cape Wrath lighthouse on the far north-western tip of Scotland.

FURTHER READING

Now you've devoured this book, it's time to find out more:

The Ultimate Trail Running Handbook: Get Fit, Confident and Skilled-up
 to Go from 5k to 50k, by Claire Maxted
Training Food: Get the Fuel You Need to Achieve Your Goals Before,
 During and After Exercise, by Renee McGregor
Barefoot Britain: A Running Adventure Like No Other, by Anna McNuff
We Can't Run Away from This: Racing to Improve Running's Footprint
 in Our Climate Emergency, by Damian Hall
Roar (female physiology) and Next Level (through and beyond menopause),
 by Dr. Stacy Sims
Period Power and Perimenopause Power, by Maisie Hill

ACKNOWLEDGEMENTS

Thanks to Jasmin Paris and Sabrina Pace-Humphreys for the awesome forewords.

Thanks so much for all the experts who read whole chapters of this book and added their hard-won knowledge – Tim Pigott, Nick Knight, Dr. Howard Hurst, Carl Morris and Rob Beaven.

Thank you so much to my awesome Wild Ginger Running YouTube channel Patreons Jeff Graham, Johnny Doyle and Andrew Knox for reading the first manuscript and sharing their valuable thoughts.

Many thanks to all the runners who shared their incredible stories of resilience, pain and achievement against all odds. I wish I could write a separate book with all your inspirational words.

Thank you to all the athletes and experts who provided inspirational quotes and advice throughout.

Thanks to my amazing sister for all her proofreading and support.

Many thanks to my fantastic parents for looking after Finley during the day for a whole week close to the book deadline, so I could get my head stuck into it properly.

Thanks to my ever-lovely and patient husband Steve for sticking with me through thick and thin.

PICTURE CREDITS

Jake Baggley pp. 2, 20, 25, 27, 31, 36, 63, 65, 104, 136, 152–153, 157, 180, 212, 220; **Konrad Rawlik** p. 8; **Innov-8** p.9; **Getty** 6–7, 24, 61, 80–81, 84–85, 88, 97, 122, 123, 127, 139, 140, 141, 142, 143, 144, 146, 151, 164–165, 166-167, 169, 183, 185, 199, 205, 206-207, 214, 215, 216-217; **Author's own** 5, 10, 11, 12-13, 15, 18, 22-3, 30, 33, 34, 40–41, 43, 45, 50, 53, 54–55, 57, 58, 59, 71, 72, 73, 75, 79, 89, 106, 107, 120–121, 126, 138, 148-149, 155, 161, 163, 171, 174-175, 190, 196, 201, 202, 203, 206–207, 209, 211, 213, 218, 219; **Thom Starnes** p.16; **Studio shots Daral Brennan** pp. 28-9, 30, 38, 46, 49, 51, 52, 56, 58, 62, 67-68, 70, 76, 77, 82-83, 86-87, 90-97, 98-103, 106, 107, 124, 131, 132, 134, 135, 137, 159, 160, 162, 168, 172-173, 174-175, 176-177, 178-179, 181, 182, 184, 186-187, 189, 192–193, 195, 197, 200, 204, 213; **Tazneem Anwar** p. 129; **Andrew Yang** p. 210

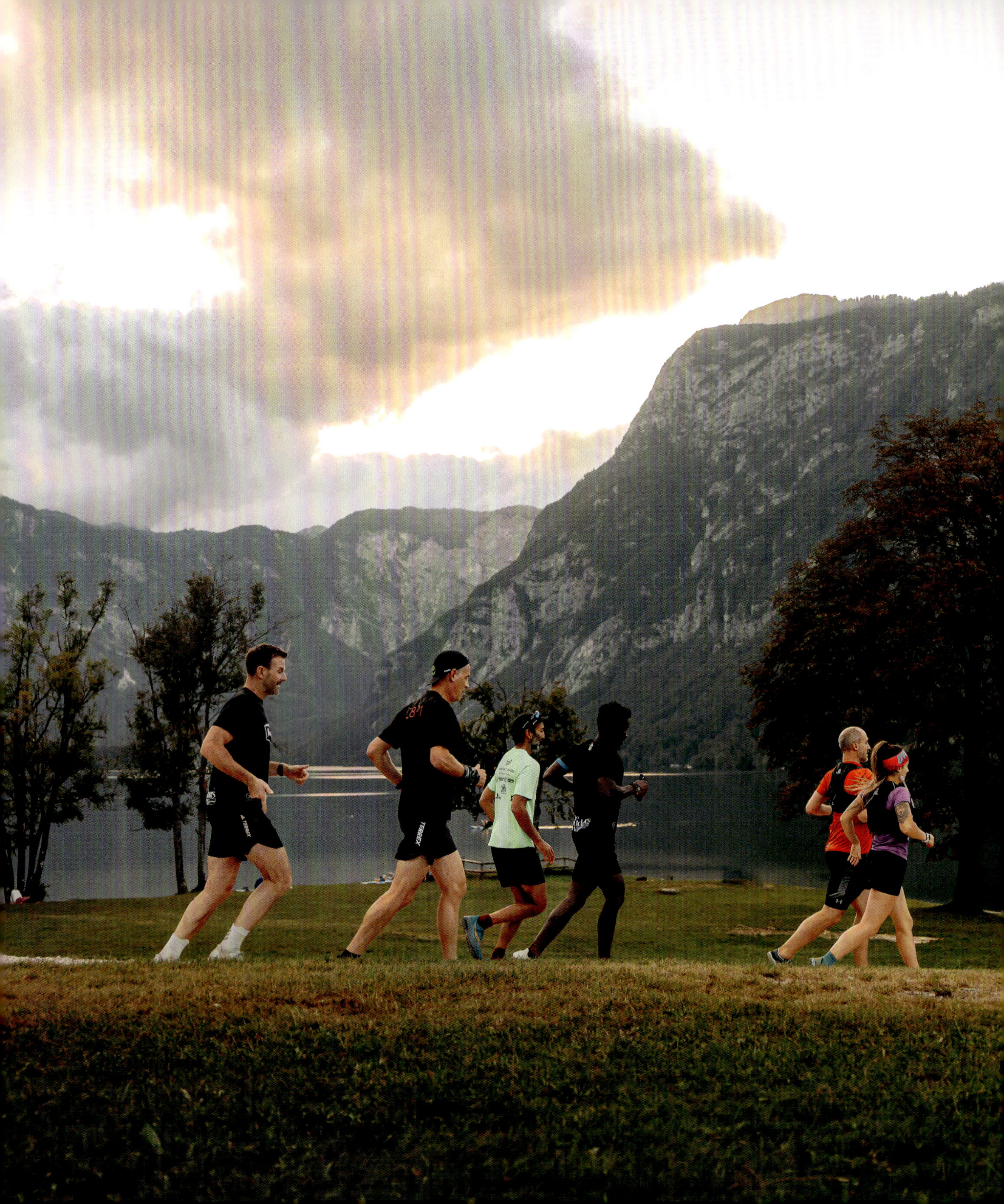

INDEX

50 milers 112–15, 210–11
100 milers 116–19, 211–13

A
age and ultra running 72–4
aid stations 16, 17, 43, 49, 63, 147

B
black toenails 17, 24, 162
blisters and chafing 17, 32, 158–63
bowel problems 145
bumbags 182

C
caffeine 62, 64, 127
cancer recovery 156
caps and visors 204
chafing creams and lubes 159, 160
checklist, pre-race 46
checkpoints 27, 44, 55
children, training with 35
circular races 14
clothing 17, 28, 30, 32, 39, 49, 58, 66–7, 71, 158, 168–73, 176–7
   for cold-weather running 200–1
   for hot-weather running 204
   mandatory race 188, 190–1
cold-weather running 200–1, 203
comparisons, unhelpful performance 45, 62, 67
compasses 17, 70, 175
compression clothing 173
conservation and volunteering 38
cramp 130
crampons, running 203
cross-training 151, 164–5
cut-off times, race 27, 44
cycling/mountain biking 164–5

D
defibrillators 191
diabetes, Type 1 130
diversity 24
DIY races 39, 213
DNFs (did not finish) 44, 45, 56, 163
dot-watching 17–18
drinks see hydration
drop bags 67, 194–5
dry bags 174

E
eco-ideas/sustainability 18, 37–9, 147, 191
electrolyte tablets 137
emergency services 191, 201
emotional responses 18
energy/protein bars and chews 136–7

F
Facebook 47
family and friends 57, 67, 196
   see also people, running with
first aid kits 190, 191–3
first races, top five 208
fitness classes 165
food/nutrition 17, 25, 32, 38, 39, 43, 49, 51, 54, 61, 62, 66, 122
   caffeine 62, 64, 127
   carb-loading 129–30
   carbohydrates 123
   cold weather nutrition hack 137
   dietary supplements 124, 125, 127
   electrolyte tablets 137
   emergency supplies 190
   energy gels and fuel pouches 135–6, 137
   fad diets 128–9
   fats 125
   iron 151
   protein 123–4, 136–7
   during Ramadan 128
   recipes
      dinners 143–5
      ultra breakfasts 139–40
      ultra lunches 141–3
   recovery snacks 133
   salt and cramp 130
   snacks 124, 125, 134
   sports nutrition products 135–7, 145
   superfoods 127
   tooth care 123
   Type 1 diabetes 130
   ultra fuelling timeline 146–7
   veggie and vegan diets 124, 129
   see also hydration
footcare 17, 25, 32, 66, 67, 158–63

G
gaiters, debris 204
gels, sport nutrition 135–6
global/dream events 216

GPS (global positioning system) 17, 30, 49, 71
GPX tracks and navigation 183–4
Green Runners organisation 39

H

hallucinations, sleep deprivation and 61
hats and gloves 190–1, 201
head torches 30, 32, 58, 59, 62, 188, 197–9
headphones 175
health, physical 21, 25, 32, 130, 156, 210
heatstroke 205
high-vis running gear 199
hiking/walking 14, 24, 80, 165
hills 14, 33, 50, 69
hot weather running 204–5
hydration 62, 162
    alcohol 132
    avoiding dehydration 131
    avoiding overhydration 131–2
    salt supplementation 132
    sports drinks and drink powders 135, 137
    water supplies 131–2, 133, 188
hypothermia 201

I

ice spikes and grippers 203
ID, personal 191
ill health and ultra running 21, 130, 152, 153, 156, 210
injuries
    Achilles pain 154
    ankle sprain 155
    bunions 154
    DOMS 156
    feet and toes 17, 25, 32, 66, 67, 154, 158–63
    getting medical advice 151–2, 163
    illiotibial band (ITB) syndrome 156
    joint damage 25
    knee pain 155
    painkillers 152
    plantar fasciitis 154
    shin splints/medial tibial stress syndrome (MTSS) 155
insect repellent 174
intermittent fasting (IF) 128–9

J

jackets, running 176, 177
'jog-hiking,' ultra 14

K

K-tape 158, 160, 161, 162
kit 17, 25, 28, 30, 32, 47, 52–3, 58, 59, 62, 71, 174–5, 181–7, 194–5, 197–8, 203
    mandatory race kit 188–93
    repairing and second hand 37, 38, 39, 179
    support crew 196
    see also clothing; head torches; running packs; running poles; running shoes

L

lapped races 16
Long Distance Walkers Association (LDWA) 26
low carb high fat (LCHF) diets 128
low points, dealing with race 54–7, 67
lubes and barrier creams 160, 162, 174

M

mantras, motivational 61
mapping race plans 42, 69
maps and compasses 17, 68–70, 71, 175
meat-free days 38
medals 38, 56, 57, 213
medics, race 163
menstruation 75–7
mental health 21, 22, 216
mindset, the right 33, 47, 48, 54–7
mistakes, planning for and learning from 44, 45, 56, 163
motivation 33, 35, 57, 59, 61, 67
multi-day races 66–7, 105
    author's top three 213
    clothing 66–7
    DIY challenges 67
    food and drink 66, 67
    footcare 66, 67
    motivation 67
    navigation 67
    non-stop races 17, 65
    overtraining 66
    pace 66
    sleeping 67
    stage races 16–17, 65, 67
    staying motivated 67

N

National Trails 14, 15
nature, being out in 21, 22, 23
navigation 14, 17, 32, 33, 49, 67
    courses 71
    escape routes 71
    GPS watches 17, 30, 49, 50, 183–5
    map orientation 68
    map scale and distance 70
    memorising a route 70–1
    at night 71
    recce-ing/researching courses 45, 71
    thumbing the map 69

tick off route features/catching points 69, 70
understanding contour lines 69
nerves, race day 46
night running 32, 49, 58–62
   dealing with fear/apprehension 58
   food/fuel 61, 62
   head torches and kit 30, 32, 58, 59, 62, 71
   motivation 59, 61
   navigation 71
   pace 59
   sleep and sleep deprivation 58, 61–2
   training practice 58, 59, 61
   water splashing 62
nipple chafe 160

O

offsetting carbon 37
out and back races 15
overpronation 170
overtraining 66, 77, 150–1

P

pace 49–51, 66
   'chatting' pace 50, 51, 66
   estimating 43
   GPS watches 50
   hills 50
   night running 59
   race of perceived exertion (RPE) 51
   resting and naps 51
   starting speed 49, 50, 66
   time food/fuel 51
packs, running see running packs
painkillers 152
pantyliners/sanitary products 64, 76–7
peeing and pooping 63–4
people, running with other 49, 55, 59, 67
periods, losing your 77
pets, training with 35, 59, 199
plans, race 42–9, 57
   aid stations 43, 49
   back-up 42, 44, 56
   checkpoint cut offs 44
   food and drinks 43, 49
   learning from mistakes 44
   mapping 42
   pack weight 47
   plans for when sh*t happens 44
   race day preparation 46
   recce-ing and researching the course 45, 48
   replicating terrain in training 47
   section timing and pace 43, 49
   weather and weather forecasts 44
plasters, Compeed-style 161
plyometrics 93
point to point races 15
poles, running see running poles
positivity 48, 54–7
post-birth performance 45
post-race blues 216
'power hiking' 14
price of races 26

R

race t-shirts 38, 213
races, choosing 26, 39, 44, 62
races per year guidance 152–3
Ramadan 128
rate of perceived exertion (RPE) 51
recovery, race 48, 153, 157
RED-S 77, 126
researching/recce-ing courses 45, 71
rest see sleeping/power naps
rivers and puddles, shallow 53
road racing 14, 16
rock climbing 165
rowing 165
running packs 28, 47, 158, 181–2
running poles 17, 30, 33, 52–3, 182, 186–7
running shoes 17, 28, 32, 39, 66, 158, 159, 160, 162, 168–70
running technique 99

S

safety 17, 33, 71, 188, 190, 191
salt tablets 130, 132
sanitary products/pantyliners 64, 76–7
screen detox 35
second hand kit 37
section timing and pace 43
SheRaces 78
Shewees 64
shoes, running see running shoes
skiing, cross-country 165
sleep deprivation 58, 61–2
sleep hygiene 150
sleeping/power naps 14, 16, 17, 32, 51, 55, 61, 62, 67, 150, 153
socks 28, 158, 159, 160, 162, 171, 174, 201
speed of races 27
sports bras 28, 172
sports drinks 135, 137
strength/resistance training 35, 74, 151, 164
   10-30 minute routine for speed 93–5
   20-30 minute routine to beat injury 90–2
   benefits 86, 88, 92
   essential moves 86–7
   plyometrics 93
   warm up and cool down 96–7

INDEX 223

weight and number of repetitions 88
yoga and Pilates 98–100
stretching routine, ultra 101–3
sunglasses 204
sunscreen 174, 204
support crew 196
survival bags 188
swimming 165

T
tape, physio K- 158, 160, 161, 162
technique, running 99
toenails 17, 24, 158, 162
toileting 49, 63–4
tops, shorts and trousers 28, 38, 172–3, 200, 204, 213
torches, head 30, 32, 58, 59, 62
trackers 17
tracks, race 16
trail running 11, 14
training 150
  children and pets 35
  commuting and short journeys 34, 35
  cross-training 164–5
  fitting it in 34, 107
  fuelling long runs 51
  ill health 152
  motivation 35
  navigation courses 71
  night running 58
  overtraining 66, 77, 150
  plans 27, 42, 105–7
    30 mile/50K plans 108–11
    50 mile/100K plans 112–15
    100 mile plans 116–19
    first timers 108–9, 112–13, 116–17
  with poles 33
  replicating race terrain 47
  strength/resistance 35, 74, 86–95
  time 24, 27, 34
  warm up and cool down 97–8
  wearing your backpack 47
  for your age 72–4
  see also strength/resistance training
travel, greener 37
trench foot 161
Type 1 diabetes 130

U
ultra running/ultramarathons
  overview 14–17
  100-milers 211–13
  author's favourite 50-milers 210–11
  day-in-the life of an ultra racer 19
  global/dream events 214–16
  myth busting 24–5
  picking the right ultra 26, 208–13
  races per year 152–3
  reasons to choose ultra running 21
  top five first ultras 208
  top three first multi-dayers 213
underwear 28, 172

W
watches, GPS 17, 30, 49, 50, 183–5
water supplies 131–2, 133, 182, 188, 191
waterproof clothing 17, 28, 49, 58, 66–7, 170, 176–7, 179, 188, 200, 201
weather/weather forecasts 44, 66–7, 71
  cold-weather running 200–1, 203
  hot-weather running 204–5
weight loss 32, 126
whistles 188
women and ultra running
  abortion 78
  approach to multi-day races 66
  birth control 77–8
  fertility and infertility 78
  menopause and peri-menopause 82
  menstruation 64, 75–7
  miscarriage 80, 81
  pelvic floor exercises 82–3
  pregnancy and postpartum 78, 80–1
  RED-S 77, 126
  safety 33
  sanitary products/pantyliners 64, 76–7

Y
yoga and Pilates 98–100, 165